Everything You Need
to Know About

Birding

and

Backyard
Bird Attraction

Everything You Need
to Know About

Birding

and

Backyard
Bird Attraction

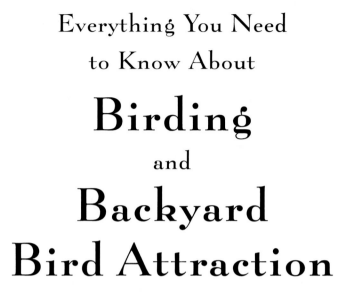

Alan Pistorius

Houghton Mifflin Company

BOSTON NEW YORK 1998

For information about permission to reproduce selections from this
book, write to Permissions, Houghton Mifflin Company,
215 Park Avenue South, NewYork, New York 10003.

Library of Congress Cataloging-in-Publication Data

Pistorius, Alan.

Everything you need to know about birding and backyard attraction / Alan Pistorius.

p.   cm.

Rev. ed. of: The country journal book of birding and backyard attraction. 1st ed. 1981.

ISBN 0-395-89274-0

1. Bird watching. 2. Bird attracting. I. Pistorius, Alan.

Country journal book of birding and backyard attraction. II. Title.

QL677.5.P57   1998

598'.07'234 — dc21   98-17820

Originally published as *The Country Journal Book of Birding and Bird Attraction*
Reprinted by arrangement with Cowles Enthusiast Media, Inc.

Parts of Chapters 2, 3, and 6 originally appearerd, in
somewhat different form, in Blair & Ketchum's Country Journal.

The list of nesting materials on page 196 is reprinted from *The New Handbook of
Attracting Birds,* Second Edition, Revised and Enlarged, by Thomas P. McElroy Jr.
© 1960 by Random House, Inc. Reproduced by permission of Random House, Inc.

The four lines on page 43 from "Shapes of Things to Eat" are reprinted from *The Sesame
Street Storybook* by Albert G. Miller. © 1971 by The Children's Television Workshop.
Reproduced by permission of The Children's Television Workshop.

Illustrations on pages 168 and 172 by Vince Babak.

Book design by Susan McClellan

Printed in the United States of America

WCT 10 9 8 7 6 5 4 3 2 1

Photo Credits

Contents

Introduction

THIS BOOK SETS OUT TO CHRONICLE AND EXAMINE the major birding activities through a year in the life of a "working" birder. As such, it is a "home and away" book, the "home" chapters adding up to a basic bird-attraction manual, the "away" chapters illuminating from an inside vantage point the major field birding events of the year. I have, in its writing, rejected the tempting shotgun approach, whereby every subject from the self-evident (How to Bird-Watch) to the peripheral (How to Photograph Birds) to the impossible (How to Treat Sick and Injured Birds*) is given a chapter, with the result that, while much is *introduced*, nothing is *treated*.

The only generally valid rule for lay people with regard to treating a sick or injured bird is — don't. Take it to a clinic with experience in treating wild birds, or, failing that, to a veterinarian. Unhappily, even professional care often proves inadequate to what is usually a difficult and exacting task.

The aim of the attraction chapters has been to discuss, against the appropriate background of bird biology and behavior, the basic issues involved — especially feeding, housing, and planting. I have assumed an intelligent general audience, one willing (dare I hope eager?) to see these subjects approached more substantially and less piously than has usually been the case, and without the conventional overlay of trivial anecdote. (Adventure and anecdote find better scope, and are more illuminative, in the field chapters.)

Interwoven with the attracting chapters, after the dictates of a seasonal schema, are field or "event" chapters, by turns narrative and discursive in form. The complex and fascinating subject of bird migration is examined — mostly from the points of view of the birds, but also from that of the migration watcher — in the light of contemporary research. We look at the celebratory (some would say "insane") spring Big Day, at the burgeoning Christmas Count phenomenon and at the Atlas, a mammothly ambitious breeding-bird census program ongoing in North America. It is hoped the field ornithologist and veteran birder will find these chapters authentic as well as entertaining, while the neophyte learns — sometimes, no doubt, to his amazement — something about what these people do, and something about birds along the way.

It proves more difficult than usual to assign this book an appropriate geographical area. The "event" chapters have a generally North American range, although the migration and Atlas chapters necessarily treat European ideas and experience, and Middle America (Central America plus Mexico) is important to the Christmas Count chapter. The bird-attracting chapters are inevitably more restrictive, their arena of primary relevance being what I have called, for want of a better term, the "extended Northeast." The extended Northeast (or Northeast, for short) refers, in this book, to the inverted bell-shaped region enclosed by a line extending from Newfoundland down the Atlantic Coast to North Carolina, then west (dipping south with the Appalachian chain into Georgia) to the Kansas/Oklahoma border, hence northwest through the Plains states and Saskatchewan, and finally back east across Hudson Bay to the Atlantic. (It may well surprise the residents of Nashville, Tennessee, Topeka, Kansas, and Regina, Saskatchewan, to learn that they live, even peripherally, in the Northeast, but so, for our purposes, they do.)

This huge region, encompassing over half the territory of Canada and over half the population of the United States, contains habitat as diverse as the spruce-fir forests of Quebec and the grass communities of the prairie states. But it is also a region whose overall identity in terms of climate reflects itself in terms of plant and animal life. It includes, for example, the whole natural range of such trees as the eastern white pine, the black (as well as the mountain and striped) maple, the American basswood, the black ash, the butternut, and the yellow birch. If Peterson and McKenny or Newcomb is among your local wildflower guides; if staghorn sumac, fox grape, or lowbush blueberry is indigenous to your area; if the woodchuck, eastern chipmunk, and short-tailed shrew are among your mammal neighbors; if your typical summer birdlife includes such things as black duck, broad-winged hawk, barred owl, ruby-throated hummingbird, eastern phoebe, blue jay, brown thrasher, common grackle, Baltimore oriole, rose-breasted grosbeak, indigo bunting, and white-throated sparrow; and if, among your breeding birds, there is a possibility of black-billed cuckoo or least flycatcher or any of a variety of warblers (Cape May, black-throated green or blue, blackburnian, chestnut-sided, blue-winged, ovenbird, mourning, Canada) — then you live in the (extended) Northeast.

The attraction chapters can, of course, be used in the Deep South as well, although many of the species here treated as breeders, for example, will be known there rather as migrants and/or wintering birds, and I have not attempted to discuss the birdlife unique to that region. Similarly, much of the information in these chapters will be helpful in the West, though substitutions will sometimes have to be made (violet-green for tree swallow, western for eastern bluebird, and so on), and, again, exclusively western jays and thrashers and flycatchers have been ignored in favor of their eastern counterparts.

The traditional focus for bird-attraction books has been the suburban backyard and garden. This decision is not, on the face of it, unreasonable; but the resulting tameness is constantly apparent in the reading experience. The focus for this book, through attraction as well as "event" chapters, is neither virgin wildland (there is precious little of that left in the East) nor the urban-suburban complex, but rather the rural landscape in between — the world of field and river, woodlot and marsh, cropland and lake, town and village. It is this world that provides the various habitats in which the majority of our birds breed and winter, and it is here, perforce, where the bulk of field birding goes forward. To those readers accustomed to the backyard and garden books, this one may well seem extravagant; but extravagance — the Latin words *extra vagans* mean "wandering beyond (bounds, fences)" — is a relative term, depending, as Thoreau pointed out, on how you're yarded.

BIRDERS LEARN, OF COURSE, IN THE COMPANY OF BETTER BIRDERS, and I am happy to acknowledge the comradeship and expertise of birding friends both East and West, without, however, subjecting most of them to public identification. (Some who recognize their exploits in these pages may well be thankful for the anonymity.) This book is most heavily indebted to two sources. First, to the mostly technical journals and books reporting hard-core ornithological research from both field and laboratory, a rich source of information tapped by few. And second, to personal observation in the field, regarding which one can do no better than to repeat Gilbert White's comments, relative to his monograph on the European house martin, penned over two centuries ago: "My remarks are the result of many years' observation; and are, I trust, true on the whole: though I do not pretend to say that they are perfectly void of mistake, or that a more nice observer might not make many additions, since subjects of this kind are inexhaustible."

My thanks, finally, to all those at Houghton Mifflin who assisted with this project, and especially to editor Barry Estabrook, who shepherded it through the customary labyrinthine course to publication.

CHAPTER I

Winter Feeding:

CALORIES AND CAVEATS

Cold and raw the north wind doth blow,
Bleak in the morning early;
All the hills are covered with snow,
And winter's now come fairly.
— "WINTER," *from* **Mother Goose Rhymes**

WE MODERNS TEND TO VISUALIZE WINTER in terms of scenery (moonlight through sifting snow), sport (rosy-cheeked ice skaters), and celebration (mistletoe and carol singing); in those terms, that is, enshrined in calendar and Christmas-card conventions. If we think about it, of course, we realize that these conventions are cultural fallout, the accidental by-products of tight houses and affordable heat; but mostly we don't think about it. It is a useful antidote, in either case, to read the folk songs and folk verse of earlier ages — the European medieval lyric tradition is a good place to start — for an entirely different attitude toward winter, which, in the northern latitudes, was a season anticipated with fear and dread, a season man and beast alike sought merely to survive.

Something of the foreboding associated with winter survives even in the light verse of the Mother Goose collection, and we are asked, in "The Robin," to consider the plight of the birds:

The north wind doth blow,
And we shall have snow,
And what will poor robin do then,
*   Poor thing?*
What will poor robin do then?

A GOOD QUESTION, AND ONE TO BE ASKED WITH MORE URGENCY about our own robin; for the "robin redbreast" of the verse has only the temperate English winter to face, while our own dooryard bird winters as far north as New Brunswick and Saskatchewan without benefit of house or heating oil. As far as the birds are concerned, it is still the Middle Ages. How do they make it through the rigors of a northern winter?

Of course, the majority of northern breeding species don't face the problem. They migrate south; a neat evasion, though also, as we shall see, a hazardous one. But our winter residents have to gut it out, with little in the way of special defenses. Mammals are much better at wintering. They grow fur, put on fat, store food, den up; some avoid the whole problem by sleeping through the winter. With a few exceptions, birds don't store food. Neither do they den up, although woodpeckers will excavate winter roost holes, and several other species will roost in hollow trees, woodpecker holes, birdhouses, or roosting boxes. (It's curious that birds, the master nest builders, don't make winter nests, while many mammals do; indeed, some small mammals simply roof over a last summer's bird nest for cozy winter quarters.) Putting on fat isn't much of an option, either; birds, like other flying machines, cannot tolerate excess weight. Besides, an adult chickadee weighs less than an ounce. How much fat can it be expected to put on?

Several western North American birds handle inclement weather with a strategy

A puffed-up dark-eyed junco (page 13) and a
northern cardinal (page 12) cope with the vagaries of winter.

"remembered" from their reptilian past. Ornithologists were astonished when, in 1947, a poor-will (a relative of our eastern whip-poor-will and nighthawk) was discovered holed up in a crevice in California's Colorado Desert in a trancelike state. The bird seemed perfectly healthy, but did not respond to handling, noise, or light. It has since been learned that the poor-will (like certain swifts, which also feed exclusively on flying insects) can survive extended foodless periods by falling into a torpid state, during which body temperature falls by half and bodily processes all but cease. (Some species of hummingbirds employ the same strategy briefly, during cold nights, but they must revive and feed every day.) The early notion that birds hibernate, so roundly discredited by scientists for so long, has turned out to be not quite so absurd after all. Yet this trick of reversion to coldbloodedness is apparently available to very few species, and probably only in regions where food-threatening weather is likely to be relatively short-lived. A bird falling into torpor at the onset of winter in Pennsylvania or Manitoba would obviously never wake up.

Most of our wintering birds have few options when it comes to coping with winter weather. The concluding stanza of "The Robin" points out two of them:

He'll sit in a barn,
And keep himself warm,
And hide his head under his wing,
     Poor thing!

MOST BIRDS WON'T UTILIZE BARNS even if available, but they do take advantage of protective cover, especially for roosting purposes. And those bird species living year-round in regions with seasonable climate extremes have more feathers in winter than in summer, feathers they will fluff out in extreme cold to maximize their insulation value. Further, they protect unfeathered body parts to reduce heat loss. Every feeder watcher is familiar with a bird's cold-weather habit of drawing the legs up alternately into the body plumage; and it is the extra measure of brain-protecting heat in its head that the bird conserves at rest and in sleep by tucking its head "under its wing" (into back feathers, actually).

What these few anatomical and behavioral strategies aim at is the conservation of heat, heat that originates as a waste product of metabolism. Birds — especially small birds — metabolize more rapidly than we do, in order to maintain geared-up life-support systems. Birds' respiratory and heart rates, for example, are higher than ours. (A starling's heart beats 600 or 700 times a minute *at rest*.) Birds maintain a higher internal body temperature (about 106° F.) than we do. Small wonder that, in order to support this high metabolic rate, birds have large hearts; small wonder, too, that birds require prodigious amounts of food. For it is food that fuels the metabolism that produces the heat that keeps the bird alive. So that food, in a word, is the answer to the question of how birds make it through a hostile northern winter.

All birds must eat regularly, but during cold weather small birds must eat frequently. Large birds have the advantage simply because the surface-to-bulk ratio decreases as body size increases, just as fat people have less heat-losing surface per pound than do skinny people.* The result of this simple equation is that, while a healthy hawk or wild turkey can fast for a week or more even in bitter weather, a small songbird under similar conditions must feed every day or it will not survive the following night. These statements are not based on guesswork. In experiments for which one hopes the scientists involved had little enthusiasm, birds of various sizes have been caged and starved to death at constant temperatures. White-crowned sparrows, for example, typically survive thirty-seven hours (while losing 20 percent of their body weight) without food at 45° F. Even at this moderate temperature, then, this typical small passerine could be expected to survive fasting but one day (and the night before and after); if it did not eat the second day, it would not survive the following night. The northern winter simply leaves songbirds no cushion, no margin for error.

Birds are in something of a bind, then. In the winter, when their need for food is most critical, it is often least available. Indeed, during stormy winter weather birds typically cease to forage altogether, presumably because, under the difficult circumstances, they would be unlikely to be able to replace even the energy con-

---

A resting northern flicker conserves heat and warms its bare face parts by tucking its bill into back feathers.

---

* *This is part of the reason that fingers and toes — with little bulk and lots of surface — are especially vulnerable to frostbite. This principle suggests that large body size ought to be an advantage in the far North, and in fact Bergmann's Rule declares that individuals of northern populations of a given species tend to be larger than individuals of more southerly populations of the same species. And arctic birds have larger hearts, relative to body size, than do tropical species. It is also interesting to note that the larger males of some species of birds (dark-eyed junco is one) winter farther north than do the smaller females.*

sumed by the foraging activity itself. Another Mother Goose rhyme, "When the Snow is on the Ground," recognizes the problem and suggests an obvious solution:

The little robin grieves
When the snow is on the ground,
For the trees have no leaves,
And no berries can be found.

The air is cold, the worms are hid;
For robin here what can be done?
Let's strow around some crumbs of bread,
And then he'll live till snow is gone.

I F WHAT WINTERING BIRDS NEED TO STAY ALIVE is food, the logic of bird feeding seems inescapable, and indeed since mid-century the casual hobby of "strowing" bread crumbs has mushroomed into big business. Surveys suggest that over 20 percent of American households regularly feed birds, spending more than $300 million per year on the pastime.

There may have been minor problems with this system (mostly having to do with less than ideal ingredients in commercial seed mixes), but basically things were going swimmingly — the birds were delighted with the food, the feeder watchers were delighted with the birds, and the handful of large corporations selling most of the food were delighted with the business. Then, as we moved into the 1980s, doubts about the whole enterprise began to surface. The popular press, ever eager to report the charge that apple pie and Chevrolet are in fact *un*-American, picked up the question, and poor feeder watchers, who had thought they had been having some innocent fun while doing the birds a favor, were told that their magnanimity was misguided, that they were harming birds and people alike. We used to start with the question of *what* to feed; now we must ask *whether* to feed.

The arguments against feeding birds seem to be four in number:

(1) "You may get a bad batch of seed, and kill your birds outright through aflatoxin poisoning." Aflatoxins are fungal metabolites, by-products of the molds *Aspergillus flavus* and *Aspergillus parasiticus*. These molds infect foodstuffs — especially grains and nuts — exposed to varying temperatures, and may be expected to occur in wild and domestic bird feed when old or carelessly stored ingredients are used. The

aflatoxins are highly toxic liver poisons ("weight for weight . . . second only to plutonium as a carcinogen," the National Audubon Society writes me), and have completely destroyed poultry flocks ingesting contaminated feed. While there is little doubt that aflatoxin poisoning is a potentially serious threat to wild birds, it should also be pointed out that there is a notable lack of records of such poisoning. The answer to the problem is simple — wild birdseed should be tested for aflatoxin. At this writing, about half the major suppliers do test for contamination; let us hope all will shortly do so. If you have doubts about your bird foods, ask your sources if their products are tested for aflatoxin contamination.

(2) "Your feeder birds are sitting ducks for predators; what the cats don't get, the hawks will clean up." It is true, of course, that any reliable food source will attract appropriate consumers; peregrines came to city skyscrapers for pigeons, and kingfishers gather at uncovered fish hatcheries like Friday shoppers at the supermarket. It figures that if you attract fifty or 500 birds to your feeders every day, they will sooner or later attract predators. The most likely candidate, city or country, is our friend the domestic cat, about which I have nothing to suggest beyond the obvious: bell your own, or keep it indoors; live-trap problem strays for delivery to the nearest SPCA; for untrappable, unshakable problem strays, chase and endure, or ease a .22 out the window, depending on your attitude toward domestic predators.*

People's attitudes toward wild predators differ also. Most birders are delighted when a merlin, sharp-shin, or northern shrike shows up to ogle the feeder birds simply because they are — as predators must be — relatively scarce. A few people become enraged at the very thought of predation, depending on the intended victim.

---

* One occasionally sees the notion expressed that dogs and cats are perfectly natural predators, operating like any bobcat or broad-winged hawk. They are not, any more than man's cattle and sheep are natural operatives in a grazing ecology. Natural predators have, perforce, to live with their resource; they cannot afford to exterminate it. They tend to range widely, exploiting one or more ecological niches, cropping individuals of abundant prey species. The domestic dog and cat (especially the former) have become politicized by long association with man. The instinct to kill and the territorial imperative, though largely irrelevant, have been retained and confused. Consequently, predatory pets tend to hunt the limited territory described on their owners' deeds; and the results, if the pet is a skilled killer, can be disastrous for the area's wildlife. Obviously cat and dog breeds, and individuals within breeds, are very different, and the above by no means describes all pets.

(The robin is a ruthless and effective predator on worms, but one seldom hears it berated on those grounds.) Occasionally a deer hunter maintains in print that it is vicious and cowardly in a wolf or coyote to attack a deer; and a couple of years ago I ran into a state park manager who was livid over the attempts of a pair of red-tailed hawks to capture park chipmunks. He meant, he said, to kill the hawks in order to teach them a lesson, a position which seemed to me philosophically (not to mention educationally) unsound. We need not, I think, resurrect the old arguments about natural predation. The prejudice that once resulted in the widespread shooting of hawks and owls has steadily eroded, and probably those who still hold it are unconvincible. Suffice it to add that all North American birds usually referred to as predators — the eagles, accipiters, buteos, falcons, osprey, harrier, kites, owls, and shrikes — are fully protected by federal law.

However you feel about predation in the abstract, you needn't worry that your feeders are merely fattening juncos and grosbeaks for slaughter. The notion that hawks are chillingly efficient killers is one widely held by people who have never seen them at work. The battle between the outsized, hook-billed, cruelly taloned Cooper's hawk and the tiny, defenseless chickadee ("monster and morsel," a naturalist called them a century ago) is grossly unfair — and the chickadee wins nearly every time. Feeder watchers learn to look for a hawk or shrike when a preternatural quiet prevails about the feeders, for at the appearance of a predator feeder birds will typically dive for cover and sit tight. Hawks do not normally carry the fight into cover, which means that there *is* no fight.* The sharp-shinned hawk or northern shrike sits glumly on its perch until it gets bored, then leaves to pursue the hunt elsewhere. Our native birds handle avian (and other) predators pretty adeptly, and the notion that stocked feeders somehow make the clientele complacent is absurd. Our own feeders, in the rural Northeast, have been constantly watched for the past twenty-five winters; during that period we have seen (or found direct evidence of) perhaps a half-dozen kills, including a blue jay (predator unknown), an unidentified sparrow (taken by a northern shrike), a mourning dove (caught by a sharp-shin), and an evening grosbeak (surprised by a short-tailed weasel). It may be worthwhile to point out what should be obvious, that our songbirds and gamebirds are always and everywhere

---

* The subject of avian predator hunting tactics and small-bird response is developed further in the discussion of protective cover in Chapter 4.

vulnerable to predation. Feeders get bad press because the occasional kills in front of people's picture windows are likely to be witnessed. Who's to report the winter kills from your north forty or back in the neighbor's woodlot?

(3) "Even if your feeder birds escape poisoning and predation, your artificial, out-of-season food sources will foul up their migratory instincts." A recent magazine article raises this fear, and points to the unprecedented numbers of far-northerly-wintering cardinals, mockingbirds, and tufted titmice as evidence. The problem with the evidence cited is that the indicated species don't happen to be migratory! Cardinal, mockingbird, and tufted titmouse are among a number of species that have dramatically enlarged their ranges northward during the last four decades, presumably taking advantage of a warming climate cycle. Probably access to winter feeders has helped these species consolidate their advances, so it may be fair to say that, while widespread winter feeding did not bring them northward, it plays an important part in maintaining northern populations. We have plenty of opportunity for outrage when, through human agency, species' ranges are constricted or fragmented; it is unclear to me why we cannot take satisfaction when, through human agency, a few species are helped to secure range expansions.

But what about migrants? Will not the easy pickings at your feeders "trap" passing migrants into a wintering situation they probably can't survive? Oddly enough, bird-attracting manuals sometimes argue that waylaying migrants is part of the point of putting out food. One such book says: "A successful winter feeding program must begin early in fall — even late summer is not too soon. As the birds migrate to the south, they will come to your feeders for food, and if the other facilities are also satisfactory, they may stay over the winter. . . . Local birds will be the first to become familiar with the facilities and frequent your premises. They will attract migrating birds who will also feed. Gradually the newcomers will become acquainted with the surroundings and adapt themselves to the conditions they find. Then, as the colder weather comes, they will be ready for it."

This passage apparently begat the following, in a recently reprinted book: "There are advantages in starting the winter feeding program early. During the early fall months many birds are migrating; some will be content to stop and make their winter home at a feeding station already supplied with food. They will have ample opportunity to adapt themselves to the surrounding environment before the more critical months."

We could afford to ignore this curious scenario were it not for the fact that the

**A tufted titmouse checks for potential danger before
hammering open a sunflower seed.**

same argument is now being used to condemn bird feeding. Notice the misguided assumptions underlying these passages — i.e., that migrants *decide* where to winter, the migratory urge and winter-site fidelity presumably evaporating at the first stop featuring attractive "facilities"; and that birds normally wintering in the South can, in the space of a couple of months, "adapt themselves" *(how?)* to a northern winter.

As we shall see in Chapter 9, "calendar" migrants move irrespective of food supplies; they leave the nesting territories to the north when food is still abundant, and certainly won't be "tempted" by your offerings, whatever the facilities. "Weather" migrants are more responsive to food supplies and weather, and some individuals among them will remain north of normal wintering range. If you feed birds, you will occasionally play host to one of these "half-hardies"; more rarely, a sick, injured, or lost (misprogrammed?) calendar migrant also appears at a northern feeder. The point is that most of these birds are stuck in the North for reasons having nothing to do with feeding programs — they would likely be just where they are had bird feeding never been invented. If these out-of-range birds find feeders, they naturally take advantage of them, leading people to conclude that they are there *because* of them.* Remember, too, that even if I were quite wrong about this, it would do little good to shut down the entire backyard bird-feeding industry. To put an end to artificial feeding, we would also have to close down every working farm in the North, for every working farm is a giant bird feeder.†

The arguments holding that winter bird feeding is bad for birds seem, then, to have little merit. The problems they point up are either avoidable (in the case of aflatoxin poisoning) or non-problems, based on faulty assumptions about bird behavior. This brings us to the final argument:

(4) "Bird feeding is bad for people; it constitutes a tremendous waste of food and energy in a world increasingly short of both." This is a more serious charge, one well worth consideration. It has been pointed out, in defense of bird feeding, that much of what ends up as birdseed is culled from elevator grains as inappropriate, for one reason or another, for human consumption. I know of no information indicating what percentage of birdseed could have been used for human food. There is no doubt that energy is expended getting birdseed grown, harvested, mixed, and trucked around the continent. Is bird feeding, then, an "energy-intensive" sport, as critics have claimed — rather like snowmobiling, only quieter? I know of no data to

---

* *This is not to rule out the possibility that extensive supplemental feeding in the North may one day indirectly alter the migratory habits of some bird populations. For if feeders enable enough "strays" to survive overwintering, those that stayed for "inheritable" reasons (as opposed, for example, to injured or weather-trapped birds) will tend to produce offspring showing a similar propensity to winter in the North, leading, theoretically, to the building of nonmigratory populations. It has been argued that this is already happening for a variety of species; to my mind, the evidence is unconvincing. A possible exception is the Baltimore oriole. A field guide published in 1977 says this familiar bird winters "from southern Mexico southward," but orioles in some numbers now stay in the Northeast year-round. This may be an indirect response to winter bird feeding, as described above; many variables have to be considered when analyzing animal range changes, however, and it would be difficult to prove that this is, in fact, the case.*

† *I'm not referring just to the feed grains about silos, the ear corn in cribs, or the waste cereal left in fields, though these are important foods for wildlife. Consider manure. Ted Walski, state Fish and Game biologist in charge of New Hampshire's wild turkey restoration program, believes that turkeys can survive in his state as far north as there are dairy farms, for evidence suggests that the most important winter food source for the birds is cow manure. The farmers spread it on snow-covered fields, and the turkeys compete with crows, pheasants, snow buntings, horned larks, and other species for the undigested corn, weed seeds, and grain waste found therein.*

help us determine this issue. Doing cost/benefit analysis to settle a resource-allocation question of this sort is extremely difficult even when all the costs involved are known (which they aren't in this case), because people value the various potential benefits very differently. Which is more venal — supporting the wild birdseed industry or the pet-food industry? Can you object to wasting protein by feeding edible grain to meat animals and still feed cereal grains to birds? Can you drive a car and still object to feeding birds? The question of whether bird feeding is a defensible form of resource consumption must, perforce, be left to the reader's determination.

I F YOU DECIDE TO FEED BIRDS, the next important question is *what* to feed them. Most people don't ask the question at all. They simply drop by the local supermarket or hardware store and pick up a bag of wild birdseed mix, assuming the compounders and retailers know what's best for the birds. But the compounders and retailers probably don't have exactly that goal in mind. From a market standpoint, it is more important that their product be attractive to the people who buy it than to the birds that may or may not consume it. And what people apparently fancy in the way of birdseed is something cheap, pretty, and "clean." The resulting commercial seed mixtures are less than ideal from the point of view of the birds.

A typical commercial mix contains, in order of decreasing amounts, red millet, white millet, milo, sunflower, and wheat. A four-year study — run in the late 1960s by the Pennyfeather Corporation in Delaware — sought to determine what seeds birds actually prefer by feeding unlimited supplies of fifteen varieties of commonly and uncommonly fed seeds. Feeding a typical variety of middle-latitude eastern birds (mourning dove, downy and red-bellied woodpeckers, mockingbird, Carolina chickadee, tufted titmouse, white-breasted nuthatch, blue jay, starling, common grackle, red-winged blackbird, cardinal, evening grosbeak, and several other finches), the Pennyfeather people found that five kinds of seed constituted more than 80 percent of all seed taken. In decreasing order of preference, they were sunflower, peanut hearts, cracked corn, white millet, and canary seed. Red millet, milo, and wheat, which make up about 60 percent of the typical commercial mix, amounted to less than 2 percent of the birds' diet at those feeding stations. Other dead losses which show up in commercial mixes were oat groats, white rice, hemp, and buckwheat.

It should be pointed out that this study does not prove that birds *won't* eat the ignored foods, but rather that they *don't* eat them if preferred foods are available. If you put out nothing but red millet, milo, and wheat, you'll find that a variety of ground-feeding birds will sample them. The problem with the typical commercial mix is that the birds eat all the token sunflower and some of the white millet and ignore everything else, or kick it on the ground. Then they await the next feeding and do it all over again. It is probably fair to say that, in practice, half the annual multi-million-dollar birdseed pie ends up as waste.

The National Audubon Society inaugurated its own birdseed sales program in 1978 with a full-page ad in *Audubon* magazine. The headline read: AUDUBON'S VERY OWN WILD BIRD FOOD FORMULATION IS FINALLY AVAILABLE. The results of the Delaware study (and several others) had long been available, and I was surprised at Audubon's formulation: white millet, sunflower, wheat, sterile hemp, milo, hulled oats, cracked corn, and peanut hearts. An inquiry elicited this information: Audubon had adopted its ingredients list from the writings of John H. Baker, who was president of the organization in the 1940s and 1950s; Audubon discovered, "after a year of testing" on the market, that birds didn't care for half those ingredients; Audubon has dropped wheat, hemp, milo, and oats from its mixes.

Alternatives are now available to the typical commercial mix I've been describing. Most major suppliers now offer one or more "premium mixes" as alternatives for those who have seen through the false economy of the "wild birdseed mix." The typical premium mix drops the milo, oats, wheat, and the red millet, leaving white millet and/or cracked corn as the cereal base. Although many ground feeders prefer white millet, corn has important advantages. It is cheap, readily available, and attractive to a variety of birds. Its only significant disadvantage is that it requires some storage care; it must be kept cool and dry to avoid moths and mold.* Probably the main disadvantage from the retailer's point of view is appearance — cracked corn isn't nearly as pretty as those shiny, colorful, interestingly shaped small grains which people love to sift through their fingers at feed-store and garden-center bins. In addition, cracked corn leaves a dust on your hands and probably reminds lots of folks of keeping chickens. If you can forgive the dust and forget the chickens, cracked corn

---

* *Unbroken grains and seeds are less susceptible to spoilage, but all birdseed should be kept cool and dry. Secure storage can be a problem — mice will eat into bags of feed, and squirrels will chew their way into plastic cans. A midwestern correspondent suggests two sources of good (and probably free) containers: seventeen-gallon air-raid-shelter drums, which have been declared surplus by the Civil Defense; and the heavy paperboard fifty-gallon drums in which some bakeries receive their flour.*

may be your choice for the main cereal grain in your feeding program. But it should be *yellow* corn, relatively *fine*-cracked. Fine-cracked is more palatable to the smaller birds (some mills overdo it — you don't want corn flour); and yellow corn, unlike white, is a good source of vitamin A. If you like variety, by all means add other small grains; again, white millet and canary seed will probably be most readily accepted. If you insist on buying a mix, and want to feed your specialty seed separately, try chick feed — a cracked-corn and wheat mix. It will cost less and produce less waste than the typical wild birdseed mix.

Though rich in carbohydrates, and therefore good energy suppliers, the cereal grains are less good sources of protein, fat, and some vitamins and minerals. Probably the best sources of protein for birds are sunflower seed and peanuts, the latter usually fed in the form of peanut hearts or peanut butter. Sunflower and peanuts are so popular with so many birds (and other animals) that they have been called the candy of bird foods. Nutritionally they are anything but candy. Peanuts and sunflower, compared pound for pound with hamburger, provide an equal amount of protein, more than twice as much fat (the other energy producer), and a fair amount of carbohydrates (hamburger has none). A pound of either provides twice the calories available in a pound of hamburger. The reputation of sunflower as the preeminent food for wild birds is well deserved. It is more widely popular than peanuts among birds; and though very similar to peanuts nutritionally, it gets the nod for providing three times as much iron, twice as much calcium and phosphorus, half again more potassium, and a better vitamin complement. Every bird feeder will want to provide sunflower; many will feed some form of peanuts as well.

The other high-fat, high-protein seed popular among feeder watchers in the North is niger, often called "thistle." (Some people are frightened off by that nickname, fearing the niger will germinate and produce a thistle garden. Niger is not a thistle, the sale of whose seed is illegal. Niger may occasionally germinate in the southern half of the Northeast, but the plant looks more like a Jerusalem artichoke than a thistle; and unlike the pest thistles, niger is an annual, and hence easy to eradicate.) Niger has largely replaced hemp as a wild birdseed. Hemp was highly touted in a more innocent age, but people then began to grow it for something other than birdseed — marijuana, to be specific — and the government stepped in to require that all hemp seed be sterilized before marketing. Unhappily, birds don't seem to care for sterilized hemp any more than pot smokers do.

Niger has long been fed to cage birds, and has in recent years exploded on the wild-bird-food market, having proved a favorite of such popular birds as American goldfinch, pine siskin, and common redpoll. Most ground feeders, from doves to juncos, relish it also. If you have any doubts about the legitimacy of feeding birds, you probably won't want to buy niger. Most of the world's supply is grown in Ethiopia and India, where it is cultivated for oil for human consumption. The Ethiopian export supply dried up some years ago with the onset of war in that area, and India placed a restrictive embargo on niger export in the late 1970s, arguing that the American appetite for birdseed was pricing poor Indians out of the protein market. Not everyone believes the Indian government was being candid, but whatever the point of the niger embargo, the North American supply was for a time uncertain and expensive as a result of it. But the popular seed many call "black gold" is once again readily available at moderate prices.

In addition to various seeds and nuts, beef suet has long been a standard feeder item. Suet is pure fat; as such it is extremely high in calories. A winter insect substitute, it is the feeder staple for the woodpecker tribe; chickadees, nuthatches, titmice, creepers, mimics, and other species may also be attracted.

MUST WE PROVIDE WATER AND GRIT in addition to food? Some birdfeeding manuals stress the importance of a year-round water supply, implying that we ought not feed if we don't mean to water as well. Birds will, indeed, use water both for drinking and bathing in a northern winter; and birdbaths can be kept open in subfreezing weather by using submersible heating units or by hauling boiling water. A few commercial feeders even come equipped with a pre-wired sunken bathing pan. But one might well question any such expenditure of power; and no antifreeze preparation is safe to use. On the other hand, wood-stove owners have a free source of heat energy at hand. Heat four bricks on the stove, and your birdbath can be kept open by rotating them two at a time. The birds will get by, in any case, without artificial sources of water. They derive more water from their food than you might imagine (corn is 12 percent water; niger, 6 percent; sunflower, 5 percent), and they will supplement that source, if necessary, by eating snow.

Birds do need grit all year long, and grit, like food, is less generally available in the winter. It is not really necessary to provide it, however. Plowed roads are a rich (albeit sometimes dangerous) source of sand and other hard materials, and birds are often seen foraging winter road shoulders for grit and salt. Road cuts, gravel banks, and backyard sandboxes are other available sources. If you want to provide grit,

consider ashes, ground eggshell, and ground oyster or clam shells, which supply minerals as well as grinding material.

We have, now, the basic ingredients for a northern bird-feeding program: cracked corn and/or white millet (plus other cereal grains if you like), sunflower (plus peanuts if you can afford them), niger (if you feel comfortable about using it), and suet; water and grit optional. Where does one obtain the food items, and how much do they cost? The rule is simple: get each item as near its source as possible. If you have time and some spare land, and desire a labor-intensive product, you can grow your grain and sunflower. Or — what requires much less labor but is no more energy-expensive — glean them. Many farmers will give you permission to pick over a cornfield after harvesting, and a morning spent gleaning will provide all your winter's corn. Take it home and dry it thoroughly (whether on the ear or shelled) before storing. Grind it as you use it, and feed some on the cob.

If you live in sunflower-growing country, it will pay you handsomely to glean your sunflower (which is more expensive than corn to buy, and you don't have to grind it). A correspondent from the fertile Red River Valley of western Minnesota writes that he fills his two-wheel trailer in a freshly combined sunflower field in a couple of hours. "Be sure to take along a good knife or pruning snippers. The heads will be attached to five-foot stalks that are tough as nails." Get your sunflower heads dry, and keep them that way in storage.*

If growing and gleaning are impractical, buy your grain and seed in bulk from farm elevators, mills, feed stores, or garden centers. Investigate cooperative buying

---

Some feeder owners appreciate the blue jay's handsome plumage, while others resent the bird's brassy personality.

---

* *Ear corn is relatively easy to dry. As soon as you collect it, spread the ears out on something (wire screening is ideal) which will allow air to circulate around them. Air them for ten dry days or so before storing in open baskets or whatever for the winter. Sunflower heads are a stickier problem. In the humid Northeast it is not a good idea to line the heads up along your walls; they will ooze an insidious moisture, leaving appalling spots on the floor. Stringing them on wires is a good bet, except that, wherever you hang those wires, mice are virtually certain to figure a way to get at the heads. They then proceed to eat a few seeds and hide the rest; so you must be prepared to find in-hull sunflower seed all over the place, secreted in hiking boots, woodpiles, dresser drawers, and the like. There seems to be no easy answer to this problem, which is probably why few people grow sunflower for winter feeding.*

programs sponsored by local conservation organizations. If you buy in bulk, expect to pay $7 or $8 for fifty pounds of cracked corn, and $10 or $12 per fifty-pound bag of in-hull sunflower (which, amazingly enough, is exactly what sunflower was selling for a half century ago.) (Don't, incidentally, agonize over the choice between gray-striped and black oil sunflower varieties. There is little difference between them. Buy whichever is less expensive.) Ask about niger and peanut hearts wherever sunflower is sold; and don't be surprised if they want $1.25 (or more) a pound for the former, two-thirds that for the latter. Premium mixes cost $10 to $15 per fifty-pound bag; the cheaper ones — minus the safflower — are fine. Likely you will save little buying niger or peanuts in bulk (but ask); if you buy corn or sunflower in those three- and five-pound grocery-store bags, however, you will pay twice or even three times the figures quoted above. Suet used to be free for the asking, and some butchers still give it away. But suet is cheap enough even at 89 cents a pound at the supermarket, for a little goes a long way, especially if you don't have starlings. The ingredients, then, for a modest bird-feeding program — featuring a sunflower feeder, a thistle feeder, a suet basket, and a mix for ground feeders — needn't be terribly expensive: $50 or $75 should take you through the winter except for northern-finch invasion years, when your niger bill will skyrocket.

THE FOODS DISCUSSED ABOVE will set up your feeding program quite nicely, though of course there are a number of possible substitutions and virtually no end to the list of available additions. If you have access to a feed mill, for example, you may be able to substitute "screenings" for your cereal grain. Screenings are the miscellany left after various grains are "cleaned" before processing — mostly undersized or deformed grain kernels, grit, weed seeds, chaff, and the like. Screenings will be much appreciated by your ground feeders, and can be had, if available, for next to nothing. Uneaten weed seeds may germinate, of course, so don't use screenings if you're finicky about your lawn. Most authorities recommend beef suet as the best fat for birds; but some people substitute bacon grease or hang up a ham skin, and the birds will utilize those as well. And I recall someone pointing out in print that the cheapest way to get peanuts is to collect broken jars of peanut butter at the grocery store. If that word ever gets out, America's grocers will be puzzling over the rash of accidents along the jam and peanut butter aisle. . . .

How about additional foods? Some people gather nuts and berries during autumn outings to store for winter feeding. Cracked walnuts and butternuts are good feeder items; ground dried melon seeds are another. Try crumbled dog biscuit or cornbread; in more temperate regions, raisins for mimics (mockingbird, catbird, brown thrasher) and thrushes (robin, bluebird, hermit thrush). Virtually any bird-attracting book or article will suggest other offerings purportedly attractive to one species or another, the items ranging from the mundane to the exotic. The Carolina wren, it is claimed, relishes American cheese, while blue jays appreciate an occasional hard-boiled egg. The Baltimore oriole dotes on oranges and grape jelly (whose sole virtue is that it absolutely refuses to freeze), while a catbird likes a bit of fried fish with sour cream on the side. Your typical mockingbird enjoys halved pear, and, if you really want to know, nothing pleases crows and starlings more than fresh grapefruit.

If people are willing to buy eggs and fish for jays and catbirds, you can imagine what happens when something rare turns up at a feeder. I like the story of the wayward yellow-breasted chat that passed up a conventional winter in the tropics for one in Rye, New Hampshire, where chats don't belong at any time of the year. Did this erratic warbler succumb to the rigors of a northern New England winter? It did not. It overwintered quite handsomely, taking its meals — doughnuts and bananas mostly — at a protected breezeway feeder under the comforting rays of an infrared lamp.

CHAPTER II

Feeders

FROM THE GROUND UP

*After 15 years of research [our company] has developed the
world's most effective feeder for attracting wild birds. . . .
Wherever you live, we guarantee you will attract more species
with our feeder than with any you may be using now.*
— from a recent advertisement for a new feeder

FOR THOSE WHO DECIDE TO FEED BIRDS, *what* to feed is only half the battle. The where, how, and when must also be considered. Let's postpone the when for a moment and consider the where and how together. When the ad featuring the bold claim quoted above arrived in the mail recently, I opened it expecting to find a revolutionary and complicated new device, something replete with moving parts and looking like an integral component of a spaceship. Inside the flyer I found a photograph of — a tray. An unadorned 12 x 36-inch polystyrene *tray*, looking like something you'd pass the cheese dip on, only bigger. What was going on here?

A capsule history of bird-feeder development passed before my eyes. The tray — usually called a feeding shelf — is what we started with. But that design exposed the food to the weather; so the shelf developed a roof (and subsequently food hoppers and fancy weather vanes), and we had the feeding station. This design had problems (which we'll get into in a moment), and advanced plastics technology gave us tube and bubble specialty feeders. And now someone resurrects the old shelf feeder, done up in plastic, and expects us to believe it's both new and better? What do they take us for? Are they serious about that guarantee? I settled down and read the ad through. No secrets, no tricks, no joke. And the sole guaranteed claim — that the feeder would attract a greater variety of species than any other — was, I saw upon consideration, perfectly reasonable.

The objection to the old-fashioned feeding shelf had not been that it attracted too few birds, but that it attracted too much weather. The food you put on it either blew away or got wet and turned to glop. The feeding station was a great improvement — both food and birds were somewhat weather-protected, and gravity-feed hoppers could supply fresh food over a period of time. The feeding station was thought to be convenient for birds, too; with seed in the hoppers, suet feeders on each end, and perhaps a water dish inside, the birds could satisfy all basic consumer needs in one place. (The analogy of the feeding station, you see, is to the gas station; indeed, one company still calls its station feeder the Bird's Filling Station.) The problem with the feeding station is not with attracting birds, but with accommodating them. By putting everything under one roof, the feeding station tends in practice to deny most birds access to anything. A couple of blue jays or squirrels munch away all day while the other birds look on forlornly from surrounding trees and bushes; so there is an ironic appropriateness about the misplaced apostrophe in the just-mentioned feeder name.

The whole point of bird-feeder design development in recent years has been to deal with this problem; to find, that is, a way to attract not *more* birds, but *fewer.* The goal has been to build feeders which would dispense that expensive sunflower and niger selectively. So the feeding-tray company's claim that your newfangled specialty feeders aren't attracting as many kinds of birds as they might is really admitting, in a backhanded way, that those feeders are fulfilling their intended purpose. When

A chickadee and a titmouse (page 32) sample suet.
American goldfinches and pine siskins (page 33) relish niger.

you can find a way to hold a competing product's success against it, you've got a clever piece of advertising going!

So what *is* the best way to feed? Let's take the four basic foods one at a time, starting with cereal grain. Where and how can corn, millet, canary seed, screenings, or whatever be best dispensed? Our friend the feeding tray (polystyrene or not) would be perfectly appropriate, but I prefer to take the tray one step further, to utilize its prototype — the ground. You're paying rent or taxes on it anyway, and it has important advantages over the tray: it's bigger, you can't misplace it or break it, and seed won't blow off it. Your cereal grain is put out for ground feeders (the native sparrows, doves, cardinals, and so on), and, as dictated by their basic winter weed-seed diet, the ground is where they are accustomed to feed. Choose protected areas near cover along the south wall of your house, along a tree line or fencerow, and simply scatter your cereal grain, along with some niger if you choose to use it. Feeding on the ground requires some clearing work after snowstorms — look for wind-scoured areas, and feed in the driveway, which you have to plow anyway — but it is a practical, flexible, and effective way to feed small grains.

The use this scratch feed will get depends on several factors, not all of which are under your control. Some years ago I published an article on winter bird feeding in *Country Journal* magazine. The next spring a letter was forwarded to me from a disgruntled reader. The gist was this: "I followed your suggestion and bought fifty pounds of cracked corn. Problem was the birds didn't eat it. How would you like to buy forty-five pounds of cracked corn, cheap?" That feeder watcher's problem had been twofold. First, it had been a bad winter for ground feeders in her part of the country — there had been very few tree sparrows or juncos around to feed. Second, she had fed her corn out of a hanging feeder, whence she had previously fed a mix. The chickadees and nuthatches and purple finches that had been editing the goodies out of the mix were no longer interested, and the confirmed ground feeders, which had never flocked to that hanging feeder, weren't about to start now. It is *much* better to feed small grain in a low, open situation — off a low shelf, under a picnic table, on the ground.* Remember, too, that corn represents the food of first

---

* *Don't, in particular, try to feed corn from a lantern-type feeder, which is essentially a hopper sitting on a small tray. When the corn in the tray gets wet, the moisture travels well up into the hopper. When everything dries out, you're left with a feeder full of yellow concrete, which will have to be broken out with hammer and chisel.*

**Many ground feeders, such as this northern cardinal,
will use old-fashioned shelf or station feeders.**

choice for very few species; as long as most seed eaters have access to either sun-flower or niger, the other small grain will get little use. But give it a chance: corn is a second choice for lots of species, and a recent bird-foods study in Virginia found that it received twice as many visits per penny of cost as any other seed or grain food.

If you are lucky enough to live on land supporting gamebirds, you can set up a special ground feeder for them. Traditionally this has been a rustic lean-to structure, built with poles, corn shocks, brush, or whatever, its back to the predominant winds (and drifting snow) and completely open in front. It should be built adjacent to good cover — ideally along a heavy fencerow or where a grain field abuts a woods. Pheasant, quail, grouse, turkey, prairie chicken — all will appreciate small grains (cracked corn, buckwheat, millet, barley, scratch feed), which are most easily fed in poultry-type ground hoppers. Whole ear corn can also be fed in your gamebird feeding shelter, either in wire baskets or on a spike feeder. The latter is the most sim-ply constructed feeder I know of. You take any length of board and drive a couple of large spikes through it, on which you impale ears of corn. One or more of these belongs in a backyard feeding program also, where they will help occupy your squirrels and jays. (Any spike feeders placed around houses should be fastened well up somewhere; you don't want anyone's children walking or falling on them.) You will want professional advice before starting an ambitious gamebird feeding program; for that, contact your local Fish and Game officer.

WHY CANNOT ONE FEED *everything* on the ground and save buying or building feeders altogether? Why not scatter the sunflower and peanuts and niger as well as the corn? You can, and the birds will be perfectly delighted to have you do so. This contradicts the notion, still popular in the birding literature, that different species have different "preferred feeding levels"; that some birds like to feed on the ground, some at five feet, some at fifteen feet, and so on. This is not implausible; if we admit that ground feeders prefer to feed on the ground, why is it not reasonable to assume that birds accustomed to taking seeds or insects from trees would prefer to feed from an elevated feeder? My guess is that the answer is simple. Birds that feed exclusively on the seeds of low forbs and grasses will never find their food up in trees; they have no experience seeking food anywhere but on the ground. The grosbeaks and northern finches, on the other hand, eat their maple and birch and cone seeds on the trees as long as they hang there, and on the ground after they fall. Similarly, the insect pupae and egg-sac winter foragers — the woodpeckers, chickadees, nuthatches, and so on — seek their prey from treetop to trunk bottom, as well as on bushes, piles of fence rails, and the like. Both groups of tree feeders, then, are also accustomed to foraging on (or very near) the ground; so it shouldn't be more than mildly surprising to learn that every one of the hundred-plus species of birds that visit winter feeders in the Northeast, even the brown creeper, will accept your offerings on *terra firma,* and most will do so readily. A document I have before me claims that evening grosbeaks "prefer to feed four or five feet — or more — above the ground," but a food-preference chart on the adjacent page indicates that grosbeaks prefer to feed on the ground! Both, of course, are right. Where grosbeaks prefer to feed is at the exact level of the local sunflower supply — whether on the ground, five feet up in a feeder, or thirty-five feet up on the top of a telephone pole.

As far as the birds are concerned, then, you should feel free to throw your sunflower and peanuts and niger right on the ground. Everything from pine siskins and goldfinches to nuthatches and blackbirds to chickadees and titmice to cardinals and towhees to purple finches and sparrows will be delighted with the arrangement; and your woodpeckers will soon be hopping about on the ground like so many ant-hunting flickers. There is, alas, a serious hitch in this arrangement. The hitch is blue jays and squirrels, which will hit your property the moment the seed and nuts hit the ground. All but the raw uninitiate are familiar with the ensuing scenario. The jays choke down thirty-seven sunflower seeds each and fly off to mysterious destinations, returning five minutes later for another round. Gray (and other) squirrels haven't even the decency to interrupt their pillage. They work sunflower mostly with the nose, which does the detection; the front feet grab the seed and pass it to the mouth, and the squirrel eats, paws poised before nose, the body at something less than half-mast (not in the upright, full-alert position illustrators prefer). A sunflower seed is the work of two seconds, and the nose is back to rooting. So that, between the jays and the squirrels, $5 worth of sunflower and peanuts — neither will bother the niger — lasts about five minutes. After a couple of days of *that* routine, most people are ready to talk specialty feeders.

The point of specialty feeders is to make sunflower, peanut hearts, or whatever, available to the smaller birds, while preventing squirrels and the larger birds from exhausting the supply. There are three basic approaches. The "fence" feeder is simply a box feeder whose open sides have been screened with wire grids, the apertures sized to exclude (usually) anything grosbeak-sized or larger. These feeders, posted or hung, will work fine (especially when they can be placed out of wind and weather), though cleaning the tray through the "fence" poses a problem. (All feeder surfaces subject to fecal buildup should be scrubbed down occasionally.) Then there is the "gadget" specialty feeder. Most work with counterweighted perches, which drop under the weight of a squirrel or large bird, simultaneously blocking access to the food. One such feeder requires a *partially* depressed perch before the feeding hole is uncovered, the point being to exclude large *and* small birds. This snobbish feeder is advertised, in fact, to exclude everything but cardinals! Obviously this is the ideal gift for the gadget-loving birder, who can spend the winter fine-tuning his cardinal feeder against the similarly weighted starling, not to mention combinations of small birds: *viz.,* two purple finches, or one nuthatch and two chickadees, or four goldfinches, or . . . .

The third specialty feeder has, I think it is fair to say, revolutionized sunflower

A downy woodpecker checks out a wire mesh tube feeder designed to dispense peanut meats.

feeding. This is the clear plastic tube (and its spherical relative, the bubble) feeder, de-signed to dispense seed through feeding ports or simply through small holes stamped out of the plastic. The genius in this design is that consumer and food are rigor-ously segregated: the birds stay outside the feeder (where they are happiest, because safest) while the food is on the inside, protected from both weather and bird drop-pings. In addition, these feeders lack a horizontal feeding surface, thus automati-cally accommodating the smaller clinging birds while discouraging the larger, less agile birds. Most bubble feeders are small (these are porch feeders, really) and lack perches altogether. The tube feeders come with perches and feature an optional seed-catching tray. With perches and tray in place, the feeder will accommodate most of the larger perching birds; pulling the perches and omitting the tray make the feeder more restrictive. Tube feeders with stamped-out holes are much cheaper than those with metal ports, and work just as well — with one proviso. They must be carefully protected from squirrels, which will enlarge those feeding holes in short order, ruin-ing the feeder.

Another member of this family of feeders is the "dome" feeder, which is essentially a bubble feeder cut in half and modified, so that you end up with a small bowl sus-pended under a large inverted bowl; or, alternatively, a round tray under the dome. The trick here is that the rim of the dome is very little above the rim of the bowl or tray, making it difficult for a jay or a grackle to fly into the feed container. (Several models enable one to raise or lower the dome, so that you can choose the size of your clientele.) Both tube and dome feeders hold more seed than the bubble feeder.* Which is better? The tube feeder has three major advantages, the dome feeder two. The tube feeder presents much less wind-resistant surface, and hence whips about less in stormy weather. And you will find, watching birds feed day after day at the two feeders, that they tolerate much more feeding company on a vertical plane than they will on a horizontal plane. This means in practice that a six-port tube feeder will ac-

---

**Sunflower feeders may attract rose-breasted grosbeaks
and other migratory species in spring and fall.**

---

* *I have seen standard-sized dome feeders only, while tube feeders come in several sizes. Space-age plastic and metal feeders are fairly expensive (though not as expensive as the gadget feeders), and obviously cannot be copied in the home workshop. Workable facsimiles of the tube feeders have, however, been constructed, using everything from stovepipe to plastic mailing tubes to plastic drainpipe.*

commodate six birds at the same time, while a dome feeder with identical seed capacity will accommodate but two or three. Finally, the tube feeder is "self-cleaning," while hulls and feces build up in the dome feeder's bowl or tray. A disadvantage of the tube feeder represents a dome feeder's advantage by default. If you feed sunflower in the hull, some of your birds will soon find that a certain percentage of those seeds *are* hulled, and will then sit at a port and toss the seeds out one at a time until a kernel turns up. Some spillage is inevitable with a tube feeder, and I consider it beneficial, as it grants those species that cannot use the feeder limited access to sunflower or peanuts. But enough is enough, and a half-dozen goldfinches tossing sunflower seeds over their shoulders is too much. In an hour the feeder is empty, and you have merely fed the squirrels and jays and house sparrows on the ground after all. (For this reason, or merely because they object to the hull buildup on the patio, some people opt to feed sunflower kernels only, which eliminates that tube disadvantage.) The dome feeder's other advantage is that its "hat" also serves as a squirrel baffle, which may have to be installed separately to protect a tube feeder.

Niger can, like sunflower and peanuts, be fed broadcast on the ground. The small northern finches, whose first choice it is, will find it readily, and most of the ground feeders (especially the native sparrows) will relish it also. And, unlike sunflower and peanuts, niger is scorned by the bully birds and squirrels, so competition isn't a consideration. Still, almost nobody feeds niger on the ground. The reason, I suspect, has to do with its cost. Having shelled out the price of ground steak for it, people want to be able to look out the window and *see* that niger, safe and sound in a hanging feeder! The most popular "thistle" feeder is a stamped-out tube feeder, identical to those used for sunflower except that the dispensing holes are very small, appropriate to the tiny, rod-shaped black seed. (One available model, by virtue of plastic hole inserts, can be used to feed either sunflower or niger.) The tube feeder's major competition is the nylon-mesh "stocking" feeder. This feeder suffers by comparison with tube feeders in terms of capacity and durability, but it is very inexpensive and equally acceptable to the goldfinches, siskins, and redpolls. If you choose to feed niger, do accommodate ground feeders by scattering a bit regularly with the mix or cereal grain. And if you have open fields or meadows close by, watch them for wandering winter flocks of snow buntings and horned larks. Should one appear, get your cereal grain and niger on the ground in the most open area available; you may add an unusual species or two to your feeder list.

Suet, the fourth basic food, may be sampled occasionally by just about anything, and hence one sometimes sees an impressive list of species said to be attracted by it. In practice most birds (ground feeders, northern finches, house sparrows, and others) ignore suet altogether. The odd squirrel will take a fancy to the fat, but most won't touch it; this is fortunate, since baffling properly placed suet is virtually impossible. Some jays, chickadees, nuthatches, and titmice regularly feed at suet; others seem never to indulge. Mostly one puts out suet for woodpeckers and, alas, starlings, which are inordinately fond of the stuff; with luck, your suet and/or peanut butter may also attract a brown creeper or two. Suet can be dispensed in any number of ways. It can be stuck (or, after melting, poured) into holes drilled in small logs. It can be secured in an old soap dish strapped to tree trunk or limb. It can be hung in netted bags or variously shaped wire cages made for the purpose. It can simply be wedged into crevices in your trees. However you secure it, suet in trees will be more acceptable to woodpeckers than suet in the open; and remember that the minimum height for any suet is an inch above the top of the jump of the biggest dog in your neighborhood.

It is now time for the obligatory section on suet "recipes," which call for one to melt one's suet (or render one's kitchen fat) and mix in everything from raisins, sugar, and baking soda to seeds and canned dog food. If you don't mind, I'll pass. These recipes apparently make diverting reading for some people, and they certainly make good book filler; but while the satisfaction of this drive to cook, mix, and mold may be of psychological value to the concocter, the birds themselves don't really benefit from it. Our tendency to think of bird food in terms of people food is probably inevitable. That is, after all, how *Sesame Street*'s Big Bird thinks of food:

> *Gonna start right in with a birdseed sandwich*
> *Made on tasty rye . . .*
> *Then top it off with a birdseed cookie*
> *And a piece of birdseed pie!**

Now *there's* a bird who knows how to eat: give him a glass of milk with that and he'd have a real meal. It doesn't seem right to toss an unoffending woodpecker a hunk of fat and wish him *bon appetit* — what kind of a balanced diet is that? So we treat

---

* *From "Shapes of Things to Eat," in* The Sesame Street Storybook *(1971), verse adaptations by Albert G. Miller.*

**The dramatically plumaged evening grosbeak makes quite a splash
when it arrives in numbers at winter feeders.**

him like Little Jack Horner and offer him a suet pudding with treats inside, just as
we offer our seed eaters an attractive and variegated — and hence, by subconscious
assumption, nutritionally complete — birdseed mix.

Now, your downy woodpecker is *not* subsisting entirely on suet. It is also seeking out beetle larvae, pine weevils, grubs, and scale insects, with hop-hornbeam seeds
and dogwood berries on the side, and grape raisins and poison ivy berries for dessert.
It will, regrettably, hammer open the praying mantis egg cases cemented under
your windowsills. It will sample your corn and sneak into your feeders for peanuts
and sunflower, which latter will be wedged into tree or railfence crevice and hatched
open. By all means tempt your woodpeckers further with raisins and dog biscuits,
but why embalm them in fat? Birds are accustomed to foraging for discrete food
items; feeding them *en casserole* means work and expense for you, and is of no benefit to the birds. It is preferable to offer your foods straight, and let the birds do the
picking.

The subject of suet inevitably raises the issue of cold metal as a feeder hazard.

Might plain wire suet feeders, as well as any other metal feeder part, endanger birds by freezing to eye, tongue, or foot? The answer seems to be that this is possible but unlikely. Birds' feet are normally dry, and they take care, as we do, where they poke tongues and eyes. Most commercially available feeders now use nonhazardous perches and plastic- or rubber-coated wire, eliminating the possibility of harm. If you worry about homemade wire feeders, coat them with grease or suet.

Peanut butter is the other controversial feeder hazard. Some have long claimed that this sticky delicacy can choke a bird, or, by clogging nasal passages, suffocate it. Others hotly deny this. Sam Weeks, of Cornell's Laboratory of Ornithology, has argued that the peanut butter found in the mouths of dead songbirds is probably innocent of their deaths; that it just happened to constitute their last meal. People who feed a lot of peanut butter report no evidence that the substance causes the birds any distress. Those who have doubts or simply want to play it safe mix cornmeal in with their peanut butter.

Ordinary house windows are a feeder hazard of a different kind. The feeder birds are eating contentedly when they are panicked by a real or imagined danger; they sweep up and away, and then bang! — one connects with a glass door or window. Sometimes the accident victim bounces off and keeps going; sometimes it doesn't. A stunned bird can be brought into the house and warmed up in a dark box. Usually it will either promptly recover or promptly die. Some species — goldfinch and evening grosbeak in particular — seem to be accident-prone when it comes to windows, while others seem to lead charmed lives. Glass poses two sorts of problems, depending on the angle at which the light happens to strike it. A bird may see a passage *through* your house. This can be corrected by merely drawing a curtain behind the window, or taping dark-colored shapes on it. Often, however, the glass *reflects* the light, and the bird believes it is flying into the landscape behind it. Shapes taped to the inside of your window won't help; affix large shapes of some weatherproof material to the outside glass surface. This should greatly reduce window accidents. If it doesn't, you may have to concede defeat and feed farther from the house.

WHAT DOES ONE DO about feeder pests? Of course, not everyone agrees on what constitutes a pest — the naturalist John Burroughs was fond of downy woodpeckers but drove a hairy woodpecker from his dooryard. The quickest way to start an argument among feeder watchers is to mention evening grosbeaks. There they sit, on or under your sunflower feeders, munching away absentmindedly like cows chewing their cuds, the partly opened bills working the seed so gently that the hulls often drop in one piece, split up one side but hinged on the other. How do you feel about these exotic mechanical sunflower processors? Are they feeder treasures or, as the disgruntled call them, flying pigs? Then, too, our evaluation may depend on numbers. An automatic, unreasoning devaluation of the common is rooted in human nature, and hence we complain about purple finches or goldfinches during an invasion winter and lament their absence the next.

Whatever you wish to discourage, two of the best approaches are the decentralization of food sources and the utilization of selective feeders. Scatter your small grain in several places. Hang a couple of feeders for sunflower, another for peanuts. Rig up a couple of suet feeders, including one near the house where you can more easily discourage starlings. Obviously you cannot feed selectively on the ground. If you live in an urban area or near an active farm, your cereal grain may well attract droves of mourning doves, rock doves, and/or house sparrows. If you object to that, you can either quit feeding small grains or grit your teeth, be thankful you gleaned the corn or bought it cheap, and keep scattering in hopes a tree sparrow, a white-throat, a junco, a towhee, or something else will turn up. Any bird food — especially, although not exclusively, that on the ground — may attract rodents as well as pigeons and house sparrows. Most people don't mind contributing some grain to the native mice and voles, but few people appreciate encouraging house mice or Norway rats. Most house mice are doing fine where they prefer to be, in your house, but rats can be a problem around the property. The first thing to do — and you should do it even if rodents aren't a problem — is to avoid excess amounts of feed on the ground. Scatter your grain, don't dump it. And, since rats like to feed close to home base, scatter it away from outbuildings, porches, and brush piles.

Selective feeders and food-source decentralization, then, will help to slow down your squirrels and larger birds. A third tactic is available, one I have been experimenting with at my northern New England feeders. It entails simple feeding scheduling. Squirrels and jays, you may have noticed, tend to retire for the night well before the smaller birds — probably, again, because of their lower metabolic rate and the advantageous heat-retention factor of their larger bodies. This suggests a plan. Starting in late fall, I feed once a day — about an hour before sunset — after the jays and squirrels have left the area. As the winter progresses, I back the feeding time up as far as I can without attracting jays and squirrels. By midwinter I'm feeding at about 2:30 p.m., which is two full hours before the last of the small birds retire. In the morning, as one would expect, the order of species coming for the remaining half of yesterday's food is reversed, although the lag time is far shorter. Selected arrival times for a recent February morning, for example, were: tree sparrow, 6:09; redpoll, 6:19; chickadee, 6:30; goldfinch, 6:39; first blue jay, 6:44; first squirrel, 8:14. I've found that, among birds of a given size, ground feeders are earlier than tree foragers in the morning, and later in the evening (presumably because seed eaters can find their food in poor light, while insect gleaners cannot). Hence, your first morning arrivals and last evening departees are likely to be native sparrows, something like (depending on where you live) tree sparrow, white-throated sparrow, or dark-eyed junco.*

Whether fox, gray, or red, squirrels are notorious (if entertaining) feeder tyrants across the continent.

The advantage of this feeding schedule is clear. By the time the jays and squirrels hit my feeders in the morning, the smaller birds have had two uninterrupted sessions with the new food supply, and just when they need it most — immediately before and after the long winter night. My cereal grain, sunflower, and niger peter out about midday, after which the birds and squirrels drift away to forage elsewhere. But the small birds know to return for their quiet late-afternoon feeding. To those of you who are veterans of the squirrel-and-jay wars, I'm sure this scheduling busi-

A welcome exception to my feeding-period/bird-size correlation is the cardinal, which, in the North at least, feeds earlier and later than one would expect.

ness will sound too good to be true. I can only say that it has been remarkably successful for me. I cannot guarantee that it will work everywhere, however, because it has not yet been widely tested.* Certainly it is worth a try wherever you live. Since the program is based on *regular* as opposed to *continual* feeding, it will save you money and energy even if it doesn't outfox all your squirrels and jays.

W E NOW HAVE THREE BASIC STRATEGIES for dealing with feeder pests, but something more particular should be said about the infamous gray and red squirrels. *Sciurus carolinensis* and *Tamiasciurus hudsonicus* dominate Feeder Pest files maintained by feeder watchers across most of populated eastern North America. Grackles and blue jays are pushovers compared to these animals. Specialty sunflower feeders handle the birds, but not the squirrels; the latter will jump, climb, or wire-walk to your tube feeder, hang head-down, rear feet clamped over the feeder's top, and feed from those ports in perfect comfort. When you discover this outrage, you bang on the window and swear mightily. This exhibition succeeds in upsetting the rest of your household, but the squirrel, disdainful of your irrelevant blasphemy, continues to dine at his insolent ease.

If mankind has not solved the Squirrel Problem it is not for want of addressing it, and there is no shortage of advice in (and out of) the marketplace. You will be offered baffles — aluminum or plastic disks or domes — to put under your post feeder or above your hanging feeder. Or you can fashion your own out of light metal or old phonograph records. I have a photograph from a correspondent in Pennsylvania whose neighbor baffles his feeding station with an open-bottomed Plexiglas "box," the same size as (and affixed directly to the bottom of) the feeder tray; the squirrel climbs the inviting post only to find itself inside an inverted aquarium. You can coat your feeder post with nonfreezing glycerine. You can grease the wire supporting your hanging feeder, or replace it with nylon fishing line. At least one feeder company sells a squirrel "spooker pole," a steel post with a counterweighted

---

A bird of the Midwest and South, the elegant red-bellied woodpecker has been increasing its range northward.

---

* *It may be that roosting and denning site locations are significant here. If your jays and/or squirrels spend the night in the immediate vicinity of your feeders, it is probably unreasonable to expect that they won't wise up to the late feeding.*

sleeve that drops when a squirrel climbs on, spilling it to the ground. Try any or all of these tricks and products; but don't try the gooey commercial preparations advertised to repel squirrels. They may do that, but they are also a hazard to birds. Once a bird's feathers have become matted with this stuff, it is an instant candidate for death from exposure.

The ever-more-ingenious baffle designs coming out of home and commercial shops suggest that the issue of the ongoing battle between feeder watcher and squirrel remains in doubt, and is likely to continue to defeat winter boredom around bird-feeding houses. Where they are abundant and bold, raccoons may prove a bigger headache than squirrels. They will not only climb for food, but are strong enough to break feeders to get at it. Some people are forced to concede the battle with 'coons, and take their feeders inside every night. Other, more innocent nighttime mammal activity about feeders is likely to go unnoticed. But don't be surprised to find rabbit pellets collecting under your sunflower feeders; tired of nibbling apple bark and chewing prickly ash, the rabbits are gathering to dine on your sunflower hulls. And, with a flashlight and some patience under a tree-hanging suet bag, you may catch a glimpse of one of our two species of flying squirrels, among our most beautiful and least-known common mammals.

This leaves the question of when a feeding program should be initiated, and when it may be terminated. People who can't get enough of bird feeding carry on all year. This is more difficult to justify than winter feeding, since most birds will ignore most feeder offerings during most of the summer, and birds don't benefit much from year-round programs.* A northern winter feeding program can be started anytime during the fall or winter (many begin, of course, with Christmas-present feeders), but obviously it is preferable to begin before the advent of severe weather. Other things being equal, the earlier the feeders are hung, the more birds they will serve through the winter.

W HENEVER YOU START FEEDING, you must be prepared to feed without interruption through the winter. Or that, at least, has been the standard line.

---

* If you do choose to feed through the summer, you should know that two ornithologists doing woodpecker research in the Midwest have found evidence that summer suet can be a problem for birds. It melts during hot days and has been known to saturate feathers, causing distress and head-feather loss due, apparently, to infection.

A birding magazine editor recently put it this way: "You have created an artificial situation and have taken on a moral commitment not to let the food supply fail." Not so, rejoins the author of a recent bird-attracting book: quit whenever you like, the birds will take care of themselves. It's difficult to imagine designing an experiment which would shed much hard light on this newest of the feeder controversies, and in the meantime we're left with more or less educated guesses. I suspect the truth lies between these two positions. Assuming you have the only feeders in the vicinity (obviously your ceasing to feed won't bother the birds if your neighbors are also feeding them), what will become of your birds if you lock up and go to Florida for the month of February? They will not all promptly drop dead. But probably the natural food supply in the area will not support all of them. Some will likely have to move on, seeking new food sources under difficult circumstances. Some of the original feeder birds will undoubtedly survive; some probably won't. How many survive will depend on a number of local variables, especially weather, wild-food-crop abundance, and bird population densities.

The revisionist wisdom holds that the sole benefit of a feeding program is the pleasure derived by the feeder watcher. But I have seen no convincing evidence to reject the conventional wisdom on this matter, which is that the birds benefit as well. Anyone who decides to embark on a winter feeding program should do so, I think, with the expectation of carrying it through the season. And not just into March, when the snow cover recedes, the jays thin out, and the grackles begin to take over. Natural food, especially insect food, does not magically appear with the disappearance of the snow. Feed on through the arrival of the red-wings and robins, the meadowlarks and killdeer, the phoebes and tree swallows. Wait for the arrival of the first warbler, the first vireo, the first kingbird; they come to say spring means business, and it's time to put away the feeders and get out the garden tools.

CHAPTER III

The Christmas Count

. . . Five gold rings,
Four colley birds,
Three French hens,
Two turtle doves and a partridge
In a pear tree.
— from "THE TWELVE DAYS OF CHRISTMAS,"
A Traditional English Song

THE THANKSGIVING TURKEY CARCASSES have yet to receive a decent burial when the radio stations begin playing Christmas carols, the annual signal for aficionados to start getting "up" (as the sportscasters say) for the brief but demanding Christmas Count season, during which thousands of them will be censusing fifteen-mile-diameter circles all over North and Middle America. What these mettlesome souls will be hunting for and counting are birds, including "turtle" doves and "partridge" (gray partridge and chukar are legitimate, if introduced, partridges, and "partridge" is still a common regional name for ruffed grouse), but not French hens, which would be excised by Christmas Count editors as domestic fowl or aviary escapees. Probably you have dismissed "colley birds" as just another illustration of proofreading laxness; most singers sing, and virtually all listeners hear, four "calling birds" in that song. But colley birds they are, the term "coll(e)y" — a close relative of "coaly" and "collier" — signifying black. ("Collie" is another form, the Scottish sheep dog having originally been exclusively black in color.)

Colley birds, then, are nothing more exotic than Old World blackbirds, and, as it happens, our own blackbirds are the major factor in the numbers game of the aggregate Christmas Bird Count. The 1,247 CBCs published from a winter picked at random, for example, totaled just under 121 million birds, of which well over half (68 million) were found on just three counts — Albany (Georgia), Little Rock (Arkansas), and Squaw Creek National Wildlife Refuge (Missouri). What these three counts had in common that particular winter was a sizable blackbird roost. Albany estimated 27 million red-winged blackbirds alone. Little Rock had 10 million each of red-wings and common grackles, and a million starlings. Squaw Creek separated out 19 million red-wings, 800,000 grackles, and 100,000 each of rusty blackbirds and brown-headed cowbirds. (You will notice that the term "blackbird" is here used broadly; it refers to those species of black birds, not all of them blackbirds, that roost together on the wintering grounds.) How do you count millions of birds on a roost? You don't. You count the birds coming *into* the roost in the evening. A counter is stationed under (slightly to one side is hygienically preferable) each major flight line into the roost. Each counter estimates numbers passing over for a brief time, then simply times the flight while sorting out its component species. Then multiply, add the subtotals, and you've got an estimate of the roost size. During the next winter, for example, the Squaw Creek roost counters estimated 500 birds per second in each of six flight lines. The arrival lasted forty-five minutes. Ergo: a blackbird roost of 8,100,000 birds, well down from the previous year's number.

Christmas counters haven't been toting up 100 million birds for very long. That figure would have seemed preposterous to ornithologist Frank Chapman, who originated the CBC idea at the turn of this century. Chapman apparently conceived of

**Great horned (and other) owls (page 53) are prized trophies
on Christmas Counts across two continents.**

the Christmas Count (or "Christmas Bird Census," as he called it) as an alternative to the traditional Christmas "side hunt." This hunt was a competitive sporting event, the participants hieing themselves to woods and fields and waterways to shoot at anything that moved. At the end of the day the bodies were stacked in individual piles, the competitor with the largest winning the day. Chapman introduced, in the December 1900 issue of *Bird-Lore* (a predecessor of *Audubon* magazine), the novel substitute idea of a Christmas Day walk to *count* birds rather than shoot them, and the CBC was born.

FROM THAT FIRST CHRISTMAS COUNT — during which twenty-seven observers conducted twenty-five counts in twelve states and two Canadian provinces — the CBC has grown into a continental phenomenon, *the* major birding event of the year for many birders, and, according to the Audubon Society, the "biggest cooperative birding venture in the world today." The recently undertaken 98th CBC — held from December 19, 1997 through January 4, 1998 — saw something like 46,000 birders censusing about 1,700 count circles, and paying $5 a head for the privilege. (Counts were free until 1940, when a 10-cent contribution was asked to help defray the costs of publishing the results; the fee hit $1 in 1968, and the rest, as the man said, is history.) The great majority of these 46,000 participants were human beings, although, as among the Harvard student body, a few of them were fee-paying dogs, described as contributing "more or less according to their respective abilities."

Whatever your taste in early-winter birding, a count somewhere on a recent CBC circuit could have accommodated you.* If your preference is for warm weather, lush vegetation, and exotic birds, you should have been at the Atlantic Area (Canal Zone) Count on December 30, where, in 90° weather,† counters were kept busy sorting out a continental record 354 species of birds, including things like slaty-backed forest-falcon, great potoo, tawny-throated leafscraper, bright-rumped attila, paltry tyrannulet, and fulvous-vented euphonia.

If you fancy something a bit more boreal, how about the Nanisivik and Pond

* *The data from the collective CBC are published in journal form in 600 three-column pages by the National Audubon Society. The crush of all this data has largely eliminated the personality of the various counts; hence my return to an earlier year for the following vignettes.*

† *Temperatures, here and elsewhere in the book, are given in degrees Fahrenheit.*

A mixed blackbird flock heads for the roost.
Some winter roosts in the South comprise millions of birds.

Inlet counts in the Northwest Territories? Most people think of the Northwest Territories as a huge chunk of godforsaken real estate up near Alaska. It is not. It is a huge
belt of godforsaken real estate extending from the Yukon Territory in the Northwest right across the top of Canada to Baffin Island, just across Baffin Bay from
Greenland. Pond Inlet, as it happens, is 2,000 miles due north of Toronto. Nanisivik, like Pond Inlet, is located on the northern end of rugged Baffin Island, and
its fifteen-mile-diameter CBC circle habitat breakdown reads like this: "Polar rock
desert 60%, frozen sea 25%, frozen tundra 10%, residential 5%."

Had you been counting at Nanisivik on December 16 or at Pond Inlet the next
day, you'd have found moderate winter temperatures (–25° at Nanisivik, –17° at
Pond Inlet) and mercifully light breezes. (When the wind howls down over Lancaster
Sound, the wind-chill factor can easily reach 100° below zero.) Though the weather
was cooperating, viewing conditions, you'd have found, were inevitably less than
ideal. By mid-December the sun hasn't appeared over the Baffin Island horizon for
over a month, and one can see but dimly beyond car and snowmobile headlights in

the midday dark. (Visibility actually improves later in the afternoon, when the moon rises.) You'd have spent your six birding hours scouring the town dump for ravens — which, arctic naturalist and Pond Inlet compiler Kerry Finley believes, survived the long polar night before the days of dumps on the sea ice, scavenging tidbits from polar bear kills — and cruising the sheltered river valleys for rock ptarmigan, which dig feeding craters there in search of the matted, mosslike cassiope shrub. And your day's birding would have produced — one species. The final scorecard: Nanisivik, thirty-three common ravens; Pond Inlet, sixty-five common ravens.

If flatland birding — tropical or boreal — bores you, there is the Bow Summit (Alberta) Count, in Banff National Park. The Bow Summit CBC circle ranges in elevation from 5,700 to 10,741 feet above sea level, and is early-winter home to such interesting conifer and alpine species as spruce grouse, white-tailed ptarmigan, both three-toed woodpeckers, gray jay, Clark's nutcracker, boreal chickadee, and dipper. If cold-weather climbing — Bow Summit's high temperature on December 30 was −20° — is not your cup of tea, Bermuda provides something rather more civilized. Here, on December 31, Christmas counters toured beaches and golf courses on bicycles in 65° weather, and identified seventy-three species (including an immature bald eagle) for their minimal pains. It is even possible to do a Christmas Count without moving a leg muscle. Of the several linear water counts published, the longest and best known is the forty-two-mile pelagic count taken on the ferry run across the Bay of Fundy between St. John, New Brunswick, and Digby, Nova Scotia, where, on December 30, two observers endured below-freezing temperatures and moderate seas aboard the *Princess of Acadia* to tally fourteen species of water birds, mostly diving ducks, gulls, and thick-billed murres.

IF YOU ARE A STAY-AT-HOME TYPE, and have no local count available, the remedy is at hand. Start your own. CBC editors at the Audubon Society in New York will want a map and habitat description of your fifteen-mile-diameter count circle, which you should cleverly locate so as to maximize the variety of good winter-bird habitats, especially any open water that may be available. The rules are few and simple. Your circle must not overlap another count circle (though a few do). Your count must be held during the two-week-plus holiday period whose dates are published in advance each year, and must be conducted within a single calendar day. (A few years ago, a friend of mine was driving home from a pre-count party when, just inside the western boundary of his upstate New York count circle, a large bird collided with his car. He scrambled out of the car, grabbed the stunned bird, held it in front of the headlights, and was sufficiently sober to identify that count's first-ever barn owl. He quickly checked his watch — just past midnight. The bird counted.) Dead birds don't — for obvious reasons — count, but Christmas counters have worried many a corpse in hopes of a last spasm. Birds previously trapped and released on count day are also illegitimate; and, though established feeders can be counted, birds cannot be baited out of the woods by a seed dump prior to count day.

Count participants must know the count's boundaries, and must count only those birds found within them. This rule is, it must be admitted, variously interpreted. Purists don't even look outside the circle. The mostly righteous, upon spotting a good bird perched outside the count boundary, circle around behind it and attempt to chase it into legitimate airspace. Those of equivocal principles operate on the assumption that the circle restricts the birder's body only. They camp *on* the boundary and count anything they can see *in any direction*, a stratagem of great profit, especially when scoping over water. The thoroughly immoral have been known to make quick sorties outside the count circle to pick up scouted rarities or to census promising habitat unrepresented within the circle itself. Needless to say, these latter policies are frowned upon by CBC officialdom.

Now that your Christmas Count is established, you need to recruit fellow observers. You accomplish this by explaining to people that CBCs provide valuable scientific data, but that this is really only a by-product of the event. The real object, you explain, is to have *fun*, which is obtained by getting up before a December or January dawn and beating the bushes in all weathers until dark, writing down the names and numbers of such birds as you may encounter. What *proves* this is fun is that, when it's all over, you pay for the privilege of having done it. Potential recruits may be skeptical at this point, but many will weaken when you hurry on to describe the post-count party — the good cheer, the drinks, the hot food, and the excitement attendant upon the preliminary compiling of the species list.

THE CBC ATTEMPTS TO PROVIDE a wide-ranging aggregate snapshot of North and Latin American early-winter bird distribution. To this end, its most important data are the numbers of individuals of the various species reported. These figures indicate, for example, whether (and if so, where) a particular irruptive species is moving south in numbers, whether northern populations of Carolina wren have recovered from a previous harsh winter, whether starlings are continuing to invade nonurban habitats, and so on. But as a sporting event, which is how most of the faithful see the CBC, a particular Christmas Count succeeds or fails on the basis of the number and quality of species discovered. The goal is not to find a million birds — not every count contains a blackbird roost, or even wants one — but rather to squeeze out of one's circle at least one individual of as many species as possible. Some counts compete in this regard against other appropriate counts; but mostly counts compete against themselves — against their history, against the temporally changing potential of their particular areas.

The species potential for a particular count depends, of course, on where it is. In the good old days, before the NAS began to publish Middle and South American counts, 200 was the magic number, to which only a handful of coastal California, Texas, and Florida counts could aspire. The new south-of-the-border counts have made a shambles of that upper figure. Last winter's CBC species champion was Monteverde, Costa Rica, where 76 field observers identified an astonishing 369 species, including 31 hummingbirds, 46 flycatchers, and 29 tanagers!

Christmas Count results show, as anybody would guess, that species totals decrease as one moves northward. They also remind us, however, of the limits of latitudinal expectations, for open water, especially salt water, is a great equalizer. Before pitying Alaska's Christmas Counts, for example, consider Cordova's eighty-three species, a figure quite beyond the reach of hundreds of counts in the contiguous forty-eight states to the south. Or take New England. The best counts in Rhode Island, Connecticut, and Massachusetts record over a hundred species every year, and those in Maine and New Hampshire have that potential. The poor cousin of the group is Vermont, none of whose counts has, during the present geologic age at least, the remotest chance of attaining that figure. The reason is simple. Vermont is the only New England state lacking an Atlantic coastline, and hence it must do without wintering sea birds and the "half-hardies" which linger well up the northern coasts under moderating oceanic influences.

If what one needs to have lots of winter birds is to be southerly and oceanic, the Hawaiian Islands ought to be a bird — as well as a tourist — paradise. They are not. A basic rule of island biogeography is that an island will have species variety in proportion to two factors: the size of the island, and its distance from a potential colonizing mainland. The Hawaiian Islands may have it all over Bermuda when it comes to size, but they more than lose that advantage in the second regard. Hawaii's

nearest upwind mainland is southeast China, 3,000 miles to the west, while Bermuda's counterpart, the United States east coast, is but 250 miles away. The result is that, despite several introduced species and the presence of strong-flying Pacific migrants which regularly winter there, Hawaii's seven CBCs last winter averaged but twenty-nine species, in contrast to Bermuda's ninety-nine. Only one Hawaiian count managed as many as forty species. That count, Waipi'o's, totaled forty-two, a figure bested by frigid inland counts in Quebec and Alberta (though of course neither Quebec nor Alberta produced a melodious laughing-thrush or a redbilled leiothrix).

WHETHER YOUR NEW COUNT is somewhere in Mexico, with a potential of 250 species, or somewhere in North Dakota, with a potential of twenty-five, you will need help to ferret them out. How many participants are required to cover the 177 square miles of woods, fields, beaches, bogs, bays, or whatever enclosed within your fifteen-mile-diameter circle? The answer is — unfortunately for the scientific value of CBC data — however many can be mustered. In the early days, many counts were conducted by a single individual. (Sometimes help is slow to arrive. Alfred Hargar did the Oxford, Connecticut, Count by himself for the first forty-four years.) Many counts are still small. Of the 1,700 published counts making up last winter's CBC, thirty had a hundred or more participants, but many more had fewer than five. Now, it is obvious that two or three people cannot begin to census a Christmas Count circle adequately; neither can ten people, unless each is competent — and willing — to bird alone. CBC officials at Audubon keep threatening to eliminate those counts which cannot field a minimum number of observers. They haven't had the heart to carry out the threat, however, and their reluctance is understandable. It might be good science to shut those counts down, but it hardly seems fair to penalize the lonely souls doing them simply because their part of the world doesn't produce many birders, or because their counts don't produce the kinds of birds that attract the hotshot birders who travel each year from count to count.

This great discrepancy in the number of observers, along with a smaller discrepancy in the number of field hours put in, results in an obvious problem. When both Count X and Count Y report fifty robins, the unwary might conclude that

Open freshwater, a precious commodity in the North in winter, may host divers, kingfishers, ducks, and even shorebirds.

robins were entering the winter season in those two areas in approximately equal numbers. But that conclusion would clearly be unwarranted if five observers spent six hours birding Count X, while a hundred observers birded ten hours in Count Y. In that event, Count Y's figure ought to represent something close to actual robin numbers, while Count X's figure is *probably* (many variables are at work here) but a fraction of actual robin numbers.

This problem cannot be eliminated, but a way has been found to mitigate the damage. Count compilers are required to submit, along with observer numbers and count duration, party-hour and party-mile figures. Party figures are much more significant than individual observer figures. Twenty observers can cover a count circle fairly adequately divided into ten parties of two each; divided into two parties of ten each, the same twenty birders can't begin to cover the circle. Party-hour and party-mile figures are aggregates of time spent and distances traveled by individual parties, whether large or small. Covering and re-covering a group's territory means keeping on the move — by car, snowmobile, motorboat, canoe, and bicycle; on foot, skis, snowshoes, ice skates, and horseback — so that virtually all party-hours translate into party-miles. The co-compilers of a southwestern count proved, however, that this is not inevitable. They turned in five party-hours in bed, spent, one assumes, in a sleeping bag or under an open window ("It was the Nightingale, and not the Larke, / That pier'st the fearefull hollow of thine eare . . ."). A bold-faced coded figure appended to the published account of each CBC represents that count's party-hour total. These numbers enable researchers to deal with the mountains of CBC data in terms of the number of birds recorded per party-hour rather than in the misleading terms of raw bird totals.

CHRISTMAS COUNTS DIFFER in more than topography, temperature, number of participants, and numbers and species of birds to chase. They differ importantly in terms of organization and seriousness of approach; they differ in style, in personality. Neither my wife nor I grew up with Christmas Counts, and it was not until we were college students on the west coast that we got our first experiences with the event. We innocently applied to assist on a top California coastal count, and were gently grilled on our birding experience and expertise. A few of the most prestigious counts won't even consider walk-ons; participation is by invitation only. This particular count was less exclusive, but our area assignment made it clear that we would have to serve an apprenticeship before being allowed to bird a "good" area, i.e., one on the coast itself. We were sent as a party of two into an area of wild, uninhabited inland range, where, in the course of a long day, we encountered no signs of human enterprise beyond a handful of semiferal cattle and a beast with remote ties to the domestic horse.

What we mostly remember about that day is the killer manzanita thicket. We had been straggling along uphill and down through pathless and largely unproductive savannah for half a day when we came upon a thicketed gully. I wanted to plunge in; my wife declared for circumvention. I argued that this might be the only real cover we'd find all day, that you could never tell what interesting birds might be lurking in such a manzanita thicket, that we owed it to the count to hold up our end, etc., and she reluctantly agreed to be a sport. We worked our way into the depths of that canyon, the thicket getting thicker and thicker, until eventually we found it impossible to proceed — and equally impossible to retreat. We struggled for a time while debating the quality of my judgment, then we sat down and despaired for a while, during which period my wife sought solace in the ketchup bottle full of burgundy which she habitually carries in her daypack and which, to this day, she credits with saving her life. We eventually wormed our way out of that gully — straight up one side on hands and knees — and were able to add to our day's bird list in the amount of one downy woodpecker. (Not a few years have since flowed over the dam, but to this day my wife remains noticeably cool toward the whole concept of the Christmas Count.)

While the two of us were crashing aimlessly about in the manzanita, the rest of the count was going forward with the cool efficiency of a long-established, professional CBC. The best field birders in the region were separated out and stationed in key areas, of which they knew every cubic foot and the probable birdlife therein. Several parties walked marshes for sparrows, bitterns, and rails. A coastal party stopped to work an isolated stand of mature cypress, a traditional barn owl roost. A party stood all day at the end of a narrow spit extending into the Pacific, scoping continually for sea ducks and wandering pelagics. Inland parties hunted the farms, forests, and savannahs.

The countdown party that night was lively but businesslike. The compiler read down the American Ornithologists' Union (AOU) checklist, party leaders responding from their own lists, the considerable crowd indifferent to the yeas directed at common species, but cheering the unusual finds. Rare birds require documentation when the count is forwarded to New York, and on this count observers of those species are led away to appear behind closed doors before an expert Rare Bird Committee. The RBC hears the supplicant out, picks and probes for fine points of shape, plumage, song, behavior, etc., and renders summary judgment, the verdict evident in the face of the emergent birder.

Clearly this was a count that knew what it was doing, and a preliminary check at the end of the evening indicated the species total would be in the 190s, which would assure the count a place among the top half-dozen in North America. The experience had been impressive, but we neophytes found the professionalism of it all a bit overwhelming, even intimidating. (I was relieved that we had told nobody about wasting two hours lost in a gully. Might we have been black-listed for future counts?) So *that*, we said on the late-night drive home, is what a Christmas Count is like.

A year later we discovered that that is *not* — necessarily — what a Christmas Count is like. We were in a midwestern town visiting relatives when we learned that a local CBC would be conducted during our stay. The compiler said she'd be delighted to have us participate, so I signed us up, my wife agreeing to go with the understanding that she would leave the car only if it caught fire. I attended what was called an organizational meeting the night before the count. Five of us sat in the compiler's living room drinking coffee and exchanging birding anecdotes. During a pause I asked how many people were expected on the count. "Seven, counting you and your wife. Oh! and Marge Nyce is joining us for the afternoon. She's baking Christmas cookies in the morning."

The participants looked to be either retired or in their twenties, and the count strategy called for the former to check their feeders and periodically stroll about their respective properties in hopes of intercepting such birds as might be moving through, while the rest of us would split into two groups of two each and hit potential hotspots in the hinterlands. That was in the morning. In the afternoon anybody still game was to join Mrs. Nyce for cookies and a trip across the river to try for more birds over there. What, I asked, was to be our morning assignment? We could, if we liked, cover the "northern" part of the circle, which, vaguely indicated on a road map, appeared to encompass a considerable part of the county. As the meeting was breaking up, I cornered the compiler and asked for some tips. Where in the "northern" area would we find the best habitat? What specialties ought we to concentrate on? "Can't really say," she replied. "As far as I know, that part of the count circle has never been birded."

Needless to say, my wife and I had a good time cruising that virgin countryside, pausing at scattered houses to tote up house sparrows, cardinals, and chickadees; looking over the farms for mourning doves and cowbirds; estimating hedgerow juncos and tree sparrows on the move; watching the sky all the while for a red-tail or a rough-legged hawk. Now and again, while my wife babysat the car, I hustled into a field to kick cover for quail or meadowlark; headed into a woodlot for woodpeckers, siskins, maybe an owl; walked out a railroad track for . . . who knows what. The afternoon birding, on the other side of the river, proved better: a distant-flying pileated woodpecker, two forlorn snipe hunched in a mostly frozen drainage ditch, and several bald eagles perched in riverbank cottonwoods near their traditional feeding spot, the open water below a lock and dam.

It required a scant hour to compile that count, at which point it was discovered that our forty-odd species did not include hairy woodpecker. No hairy woodpecker?! "Call Dick Poah; his feeder is in the count circle." ("I was gone all day. Was the Christmas Count today?") "Call Art Ringer." ("Art's been in bed all day — touch of the flu. Yes, I saw some birds today. What does a hairy woodpecker look like?") "Call Flory Peterson." ("Yes, I'm sure there was a hairy at my feeder this morning. Or was it yesterday morning?")

Whether your Christmas Count is to be a highly professional one, requiring the manpower, energy, organization, and not a little of the expense of a military campaign, or one virtually indistinguishable from a casual group birding day, it will need a compiler. Since this particular count happens to have been your bright idea, that office will inevitably descend upon your shoulders. This need not drastically change your life so long as you make it clear at the organizational meeting that it is the invariable CBC tradition to rotate the compiler's job every two years. This happens to be an outright lie, but it is one well worth perpetrating. Many counts have "permanent" compilers, but the term is a joke. Repeat compilers seldom attain an advanced age, and in the meantime their psychiatric expenses are double the national average.

My own initiation into the mysteries of compilation came some years ago on a San Francisco Bay CBC. A Christmas Count compiler's primary duty is to worry, and this count provided plenty to worry about. For starters it was among the largest of the CBCs in terms of participation. (For a time it was the only count which regularly threw over 200 birders into those 177 square miles on the appointed day; now Edmonton, Alberta, somehow organizes on the order of 600 participants annually.) Organization for the larger counts necessarily begins weeks in advance of D-Day, as the compiler processes the names of hopeful counters. You have to determine, as diplomatically as possible, the birding expertise of people you've never heard of, so that all parties end up with a spread of ability. You have to assign the all-important party-leader positions, which, in a count this large, go to the best twenty or twenty-five birders available. You try to do this without offending anybody, which would be easy were it not for the unfortunate fact that 90 percent of party-leader-caliber people prefer shoreline to inland birding.

Every party leader has to know the exact boundaries of his or her area (straying into a neighboring area is known as "poaching," and is not appreciated), and each of the several people assigned to each party leader has to know exactly where and when to assemble. Finding, juggling, and communicating with a hundred or two hundred scattered birders is personnel problem enough, but it's the little individual problems that test the compiler's stability. There is the man who calls the day before the count to say that he has no car and has just discovered that no bus happens to be going from east Oakland to the Berkeley fishing pier at 6:00 a.m. tomorrow, and could you arrange for somebody to pick him up? Or the little old lady from El Cerrito who calls ten minutes later to say that you have assigned her to a Redwood Regional Park party, but would it be all right if she went with her cousin to the Emeryville waterfront instead, and could she take her dog?

And there are more than personnel problems. There are access problems. You have to arrange to get into good birding areas that are, for one reason or another, off limits. In the Bay area this means making a formal request to the Municipal Water District for permission to enter, and get a boat on, the major reservoirs beyond the East Bay hills. These reservoirs hold municipal drinking water, and they and their wooded watersheds are fenced and patrolled against human access. But these lakes are important to the count, the best chance for common mergansers and wood ducks and such things. The Municipal Water District, properly approached, has traditionally granted one-day access to a named and numbered party, and it does so again. One down, two to go.

The Albany dump is a tougher nut to crack. Dumps are likely to be good — if unpleasant — birding spots anywhere, but they are doubly important on the coast; for it is here that the gulls congregate, and the patient and expert gull counter can sort through the glaucous-winged, western, California, ring-billed, Bonaparte's, and mew gulls for the scarcer species — Thayer's, say, or Heermann's gull. But dump officials, one finds, are something quite different from the pushovers down at Municipal Water. What we got at the Albany dump is what you are likely to get at yours — a flat refusal. They give you the insurance line ("Your bird watcher would get himself run over by a bulldozer and converted to landfill"), but one always suspects they're afraid somebody will notice thirty-four infractions of municipal dump rules, and write a letter to the editor. The dump, once again, would have to be censused from outside the fence.

Then for a go at Treasure Island, that mysterious exit nobody takes halfway across the San Francisco Bay Bridge. The reason nobody takes that exit is that Treasure Island is a secure military enclave, and locals and tourists are equally unwelcome. But the count circle extends into the Bay as far as the island, and it would be nice to get a small party onto it, even if only for an hour. We broached the matter through proper military channels, and in due time a base official spoke to us. He did not exactly say no, but he had conditions. An Audubon-authorized individual might be allowed on the base, to be accompanied at all times by military police. The individual would have to pass a security check. No cameras; no binoculars. "No *binoculars?!*" So much for Treasure Island. I informed the boat party planning to spend the day cruising the Bay for diving ducks and possible stray pelagics that they would have to try to get close enough to the island to pick up any shorebirds on its rocky fringe. I did not share with party leader or boat captain my hunch that any boat slowing off Treasure Island to enable people to stare with binoculars would probably draw automatic-weapons fire from the base. To do so would only have subjected them to unprofitable worry.

Worry, after all, is the business of the compiler. It is the periodic worry that gives him or her, over the years, that sad, detached look which sets compilers apart from the ordinary run of birders. I was young and inexperienced in those days, however, and when I retired for a brief nap on the night of Friday, December 16, I believed my worries were behind me. Everything was set to go. Feeder watchers' feeders were filled, their alarm clocks set. Over one hundred dedicated field observers were also retiring, knowing exactly where they would be at first light. Each party leader knew the specialties his area was expected to produce, and most had done some scouting to locate them. Party No. 8 would get burrowing owls at the Oakland airport; Party No. 17 would get the count circle's only rufous-crowned sparrows in the quarry badlands over the Berkeley hills; Party No. 27 would get a barn owl roosting under the University of California's football stadium. High on the list was

**Snow geese (including "blue" phase birds) winter in great
concentrations on saltwater and in protected valleys.**

the university's Botanical Gardens, where a western flycatcher, which ought to have
been in Mexico or Guatemala, was wintering for the second straight year, making a
living flycatching seeds off bushes in the Central American plantings section. Boats
were ready on the Bay and inland reservoirs. The circle's only decent remaining
marsh would be intensively covered. Some of northern California's best birding
eyes would be on the Bay shore at dawn, some of the best birding ears in the wooded
East Bay hills. Several of us would be owling independently after midnight; and
somebody would go out for missed owls tomorrow evening. The hall had long
since been reserved for the post-count party, the vats of pea soup and the cartons of
French bread long since arranged. In short, I went to bed Friday night feeling good.
I had, I informed my wife, organized that Christmas Count to within an inch of its
life; there was no way we could fail to set a new species record.

AWAY WAS FOUND. Two ways, actually. Subsequent official meteorological records show, as those of us on the count noticed at the time, that on that Saturday it rained in the East Bay for a total of twenty-three hours and forty-six minutes. During a fourteen-minute break in the early afternoon it merely threatened. Now, even a steady rain need not wash out a bird count — though the permanently waffled pages of the field guide my wife took out that day remain mute testimony to what it can do to books, and a few sore losers on the count subsequently held me responsible for the green mold that thereafter appeared on the inner surfaces of their binocular lenses — but it does "depress," both figuratively and literally, many species of birds. They call less, move around less, cease to feed, and hence are more difficult to locate. Songbirds don't respond to "pishing,"* or owls to tapes. (I ruined a perfectly good rain suit climbing in the dark over the seven-foot barbed-wire fence protecting Cal's football stadium, but any barn owls roosting under that cavernous structure refused to respond to any of the wide variety of vocal stimuli offered by a desperate man.) Aerial insect eaters are literally depressed by foul weather: the rain clears the air of insects, and the birds simply don't fly. Hence, for example, there was simply no chance of seeing any of the few white-throated swifts probably lingering in the area.

The second thing that cost us a species record was a shortage of marsh birds. That puzzled me, since marsh species are unlikely to be bothered by rain. A year later, in casual conversation with a friend of the man who had covered our only good marsh, I found out what had happened. It seems the counter had birded the marsh some in the morning, had gone home for lunch to get out of the weather, had started to watch a football game on TV while awaiting better weather, and, when better weather failed to materialize, had given it up and watched the game through. Allow me to point out, dear reader, that it is considered more than bad form not to hold

---

* *"Pishing" and "shushing" are terms used to describe strange sounds birders make — to the consternation of innocent passersby — in hopes of drawing birds out of fencerow or wooded cover. With teeth held tightly together, one makes a p sound over a sh sound (a "pish"), or the sh sound alone (a "shush") as if one were emphatically calling for silence, all the while rapidly and repeatedly opening and closing one's lips over the teeth, interrupting the monotonic "shhhhhhhh!" (This is easy to do, but difficult to describe.) Both sounds may cause curious or alarmed birds to call and/or fly in to check out the perpetrator. Birds generally respond best during the breeding season, and some species (song sparrow and common yellowthroat, for example) are more responsive than others.*

up one's end on any but the most casual Christmas Count; on most counts, indeed, little short of a coroner's report will serve as an acceptable excuse for not working the designated territory — and working it hard — regardless of the weather. Let me put it another way. Some years ago, while my wife and I were out of the state, someone broke down our back door with a sledge and crowbar and hauled away, in our luggage, everything from a cheese and two pairs of winter pacs to the birding optics and our eight-place wedding silver, all uninsured, of course. We do not, as you may imagine, hold that man in high regard, but I believe it likely that I will forgive him before I forgive the man who undertook to bird that marsh and watched a football game instead.

T HAT CALIFORNIA CBC WAS, on balance, a good one. A number of rarities turned up, and we managed to locate 170 dripping species, one short of the count record. But what a compiler remembers is what might — no, should — have been. The rain cost us five or six species, birder malfeasance two or three more; and that is how easy it is for a spectacular count to turn into a good one (or a good one into a mediocre, or a mediocre into a disaster). And it is the peculiar privilege of the permanent compiler to be shown, year after year, new ways to snatch defeat from the jaws of victory.

Weather alone can turn you into a loser in an astonishing variety of ways. (Mark Twain, it will be recalled, distinguished 136 varieties of weather in a single New England spring day; I have been able to discriminate only thirty-seven kinds in early winter, but thirty-three of them are bad news.) A number of counts on our randomly picked CBC were singled out for special weather attention. Observers at Pinawa, Manitoba, arose on December 30 to find a wind-chill factor of −58°. (Cold affects more than people's comfort and stamina — it wreaks havoc with owling. Tapes and tape-recorder batteries freeze up when it gets much below zero, leaving owlers with their own less effective — and also half-frozen — vocal cords.) The Moss Landing, California, group started their New Year's Day count with sixty-eight participants. They ended the day with sixty-six, two having blown off Mt. Pajaro in a wind gust. (Strong winds have other, less dramatic, effects on CBCs. They completely frustrate owling efforts, as the hoots and whistles simply blow away. And they rearrange waterfowl on lakes and coasts — for good or ill, depending on the configuration of the shoreline — concentrating the birds in sheltered bays.) Sullivan, Missouri, had, like Pinawa, the misfortune to choose December 30 for its count. Twelve observers faced fog and cold rain in the morning, sleet and freezing rain in the afternoon. The compiler summed it up this way: "Only the stout-hearted went out in the morning, and only the daft persisted through the afternoon."

■ Taping the Birds ■

IT HAS BEEN A CENTURY since a German made the first-known recording of a bird's song, but, despite the ready availability of the necessary equipment, the science of recording bird sounds — bill snaps and clacks (associated with nest defense and courtship, respectively, in certain species), woodpecker drums, and the noises made by specialized feather vibration are sought as well as songs and calls — remains, at a serious level, the province of a relatively few people. For recordists, as they are called, need to be accomplished electrical and acoustical engineers among other things, and it is no wonder they sound akin to hi-fi buffs — talking about frequency responses, signal-to-noise ratios, wow and flutter; about open-reel versus cassette recorders; about VU meters and LED meters; about parabolic reflectors and shotgun microphones; about low-frequency "rolloff" and "shaping" distorted signals.

Most birders are content to profit from the recordists' work without suffering the agonies and expenses (a good cassette recorder — the cheaper alternative — costs about $500) involved in recording in the field. One simply borrows or buys (from the Audubon Society or an ecology-oriented store) one of the several dozen records of bird songs made available by the Library of Natural Sounds at Cornell University, the Federation of Ontario Naturalists, and several other organizations, and tapes from the record onto a cassette for use in an ordinary $30 portable cassette recorder, which will provide a sound reproduction quality adequate to birder needs. (The contents of some of these records are also available on cassettes, saving that step.) Most of these record titles are singles, concentrating on the songs of a particular family, or on the sounds of a particular season or habitat. The most useful records for field purposes are the multi-record and tape sets produced at Cornell and keyed to Roger Tory Peterson's eastern and western field guides. These records do not feature all the songs and calls of all North American species — some haven't even been recorded — and a few species are omitted altogether. But it is an impressive collection, just the ticket for the birder who wants to tape owl calls for Christmas Count use or rail and bittern calls for breeding-bird census work.

MORE THAN WEATHER CONSPIRES AGAINST CBC pleasure and profit. In a project of this size, it is inevitable that accident and illness take a toll. Nobody seems to have died in the line of duty on our typical CBC, but the usual complement of counters crashed their cars and skied into trees, and counts in Wisconsin and North Carolina were compiled from hospital beds. Two Harrisburg, Pennsylvania, observers were forced to retire from the count frozen after wading into icy waters to rescue a hapless beagle. Sometimes the birds themselves go out of their way to disappoint. Imagine the joy of Pierre, South Dakota, birders when a vagrant varied thrush appeared in their midst in early December. Imagine the care with which Pierre feeders catered to this cousin of the robin for two weeks. And imagine the birder grief when, on December 16, the day before the Pierre CBC, the ungrateful thrush flew into a window and broke its neck.

A very few counts are canceled due to a variety of catastrophic circumstances, but there can be no doubt that the Rio Corona (Mexico) Count deserves the Most Original Excuse award for this CBC. Compiler Gene Blacklock had driven down to the area several days early to set things up and do some scouting. What he didn't know was that various political factions in the state of Tamaulipas, through which the Corona flows, were at that moment in the process of heating up some run-of-the-mill political unrest. Two days before the count, Blacklock found himself in the middle of a "full-scale rebellion." The courthouse was on fire in Ciudad Mante and people were shooting at one another in the streets. A state of emergency was declared in Mexico City, and federal troops came into Tamaulipas on the double. When the Rio Corona Christmas counters attempted to drive into the area on January 1, they found roadblocks on all access routes. This was probably the first time federal troops have been used to prevent birders from getting to a Christmas Count circle, but they, however vexed, were the lucky ones. Compiler Blacklock spent January 2 — count day — holed up incommunicado off the banks of the Rio Corona, listening not to bird song but to gunfire, wondering which anthem to whistle if discovered.

Bad luck, then, in every conceivable guise from rain to revolution, can and does bedevil Christmas Counts. But bad luck is a passing phenomenon; you get up the next time around and hope for better luck. It is otherwise with the worst enemy of all, whose name has been so often invoked in the conservation movement that we hear it as an abstract term, and no longer feel it in the gut: habitat destruction. The trend among CBCs during the 1960s and 1970s was upward, as more and better birders identified more individuals and more species of birds. But the character of many count circles, especially those in heavily populated areas, is changing, and on some long-established counts the numbers are now heading down. Every year CBC compilers file complaints with their reports — of fields, woods, lake- and bayshore gone to development; of marshes drained, ditched, and burned; of dune buggies on the beaches and dirt bikes on the nature trails.

The army of progress inches forward — and sometimes it doesn't inch, but blitzkriegs. What was our typical CBC like at ironically named New Hope River, North Carolina? "During the previous six months," a correspondent reports, "loggers and bulldozers rolled down the twenty-mile-long future lakebed in the Jordan Dam area, flattening at least half of all the forested bottomland below 216 feet. Some of our best birders refused to count there this Christmas — said they couldn't stand it." Those who did count there found unusual concentrations of pileated and redheaded woodpeckers on the margins of the clear-cuts: "They kept flying out into the midst of the devastation, looking for their homes." There is nothing so sad for the veteran of a particular Christmas Count as watching the draining away of its wildlife in the face of deteriorating habitat, whether the assault is systematic or intermittent, the loss sudden or slow.

Obviously all is not gloom and doom and disaster on Christmas Counts. The sun has been known to shine on CBCs, and the birds do not always flee the area just prior to count day. All Christmas counters who work at it awhile have those minor triumphs that make it worthwhile: glassing every manured field in the territory until a flock of horned larks is located, then patiently scoping the clods and birds and corn stubble until something sparrowlike is discerned among the larks, and you call the others to the scope to confirm what will probably be the count's only Lapland longspur; sneaking out a private point on the big lake, easing up behind a screen of cedars, grabbing your companion's arm and pointing — there, close in, drifting quietly with the canvasbacks, a lovely female redhead, a duck the count misses most years; stopping the car along the creek at the first owling stop fifty yards inside the count circle at 3:00 a.m. when nobody's up but you and the farm dogs, climbing out quietly, fumbling at the tape recorder with already cold fingers to play the screech owl tremolo with no expectation of success when, after the second call, you sense something go by over your shoulder and you keep the tape going while you wait for the cloud to pass the moon, and then you search the dead elms on the streambank until you find a suspicious dark blob on a limb, and you slowly reach the lantern down off the top of the car and lay the beam on the nicest red-phase screech-owl imaginable, now bobbing and softly moaning on its perch.

Conscientious scouting before, and hard work during, count day are responsible for most Christmas Count successes. Every year, however, sheer unwonted luck smiles on a few counts, and ours was no exception. There was the green-tailed towhee, for example, that flew into a Roaring Fork River Valley (Colorado) Christmas counter's home and took a comfortable perch on the Christmas tree. Or take the misleadingly straightforward entry on the Ferrisburg (Vermont) Count: *Saw-whet owl, 1.* I happen to have been there, and can report that that bird was neither seen nor heard by anybody on count day, nor, as far as I have been able to discover, on any other day. The twoscore Ferrisburg counters were well on their way to recuperation from the December 16 count when a rumor surfaced to the effect that a retired couple living in the count circle had awakened the morning of count day to find the outlined impression of a small owl on their living-room window. I had seen photographs of such impressions, apparently caused by some special property of owls' feathers, and made arrangements to see for myself.

Four days had elapsed since the bird struck that window, yet the spread-eagled imprint was remarkably clear. Each fanned primary feather on the fully extended wings was clearly distinguishable, and body length and wingspread measurements confirmed my suspicions. The bird had been too small for either boreal or screech-owl, eliminating every eastern owl except saw-whet, which the measurements fit perfectly. But when had the owl hit the window? The couple had retired at 11:15 the night before count day, and had discovered the impression in the morning. They were sure the collision had not occurred before they retired; they had spent the evening in the living room, and had heard no thud. I generously allowed the couple fifteen minutes to get to sleep, but this still left the awkward half hour between 11:30 and midnight. Now, the odds favor a midnight-to-6:00-a.m. impact over an 11:30-to-midnight impact by twelve to one, but Christmas Count birds are supposed to be more than good bets.

The Ferrisburg Count's founder and compiler had deserted us that winter for Arizona, leaving me with the decision. I finally submitted the saw-whet with full details. I argued that the bird's identity was more than adequately established, but admitted that its status as a count-day bird was not mathematically certain. Then I played my trump card. Even if the owl had hit that window at 11:30 p.m., I argued, the resulting concussion must have produced at least a half-hour headache to sit out before it could think about flying the several miles required to leave the count circle. I was relieved — and a bit surprised — when the bird was accepted.* Perhaps regional and national CBC editors are human after all.

O THER THINGS BEING EQUAL, what most Christmas counters are hoping for out there in the frozen bush is a genuine rarity. Rarities are a mixed blessing, however, to compilers and editors, who inherit the task of establishing the validity of the identification. A few of the more professional counts immediately subject such observations to formal investigation, but on most counts the compilers are left to request written details from the observers. If details are forthcoming, it is the compilers' sometimes touchy job to make decisions based on the expertise of the observers and the quality of the descriptions.

Some compilers simply ignore this work, either from laziness, unwillingness to offend, or ignorance of the status of the species in question. This makes the task of the editors up the line an impossible one: how can someone in New York City judge the acceptability of Function Junction's Louisiana heron if the compiler simply submits it along with the rock doves and downy woodpeckers? This negligence is a sore point with the National Audubon Society, since CBC data must be — and be perceived to be — accurate before any scientific use can be made of them. So every year or two editors plead again for complete documentation of rarities. This is how one editor put it: "We ask every participant, compiler, and sponsoring organization to make every effort to promote accuracy in every detail. Cast out the questionable, question the outlandish, double-check the doubtful, doubt the unusual, make enemies rather than mistakes, and submit counts that you know are sanitary, impeccable, and beyond reproach."

Rousingly put, and, as our CBC shows, ignored as usual, leaving the regional editors to gripe and fume in print. The New York State editor doubts Oneonta's and Letchworth's rose-breasted grosbeaks. The Delaware/Maryland/D.C./Virginia editor doesn't believe Bombay Hook's semipalmated sandpipers. The Illinois/Wisconsin editor bemoans the absence of documentation for Illinois' first-ever CBC

---

* *The reader will appreciate that 999 out of 1,000 Christmas Count birds are identified by sight or by sound. But owl impressions aren't the only other possibility. Several species (turkey and, where it is the only grouse, ruffed grouse are examples) can be positively identified from tracks in snow. Of course, it must have snowed into count morning; otherwise one cannot be certain that fresh tracks were left on count day.*

sanderling, at Calumet City. The Minnesota/Iowa/Missouri editor simply deletes a Missouri count's undocumented fourteen Swainson's hawks. (Some compilers, in hopes of avoiding the embarrassment of published doubts and challenges, have taken to including their phone numbers with their counts, along with instructions to call collect if questions arise.)

While some of the above records may have been genuine, there is no doubt about the validity of other rarities, birds substantiated by pages of description, sketches, and, where possible, photographs. There was the ovenbird subsisting on peanut butter at a Glenolden, Pennsylvania, feeder, and the mountain bluebird photographed at Grenada, Mississippi. There were the four white pelicans that stayed the winter at Albert Lea, Minnesota, and the thirteen mountain (!) chickadees at Morton County, Kansas. A black-legged kittiwake (a pelagic gull) turned up on Fort Peck Reservoir, Montana, while a wrong-continent skylark appeared on count day, and overwintered, at Point Reyes, California. Single great egrets at Point Pelee, Ontario, and Vancouver, British Columbia, were the first ever recorded on Canadian CBCs.

Of course, it is geography that makes rarities — one count's once-in-a-lifetime find is another count's trash bird. This fact is nowhere better illustrated than on the Cordova (Alaska) CBC, where the compiler throws off fifty-two bald eagles, ten yellow-billed loons, and a gyrfalcon without mention, but boldfaces a hairy woodpecker and a white-throated sparrow! But the fact that wintering white-throated sparrows are a dime a dozen from New Jersey to Texas in no way detracts from Cordova's excitement, any more than Cordova's indifference to yellow-billed loons diminishes the sensation one would cause if it turned up in Wisconsin or Virginia. The discovery of rarities has never been the point of the CBC, but certainly rarities will always provide its spice.

By the second week in January you will have your count compiled and in the mail — the forms, the list of participants, a check for observer fees, documentation for any rarities, perhaps a short plea for mercy directed to the editors. This begins a lazy time for many birders. The feeder program has settled into a routine and the Christmas Count is history; now you can sit back and wait for the seed and nursery catalogues, which will prompt some (probably desultory) planning for the garden and spring wildlife planting.

In the meantime, get hold of the last-published CBC and treat your birding friends to an original parlor game. (You may want to try its effects on marginal acquaintances before inviting close friends.) At the end of the 1,500 columns of count results, you will find a list entitled "Summary of Highest Counts of Individuals for Canada and the U.S." Here all birds found on the previous year's North American CBCs are listed in AOU order, along with the name of the count which identified them in the greatest number, and the number itself. The game is simple. Someone picks the names of several common birds at random, and everybody guesses where they ought to be in top numbers in early winter, and what those numbers might be. (Allow your friends to use the range information in their field guides if they wish; this will merely salt their subsequent defeats, and they will learn something about the limits of conventional range information in the process.)

I tried the game on myself out of the 97th CBC, choosing mallard, red-tailed hawk, hairy woodpecker, purple martin, robin, eastern bluebird, cardinal, and tree sparrow. Where would you go next Christmas to see these birds in peak numbers, and what would those numbers be?* I'll forgive you your guesses if you'll spare me mine, and we can move directly to the answers. Here is where you ought to have been during the winter of 1996–97: for mallard — Reelfoot Lake (Tennessee), 145,310; for red-tailed hawk — Crowley (Louisiana), 314; for hairy woodpecker — North Bay (Ontario), 134; for purple martin — Lake Placid (Florida), 5; for American robin — Piedmont (Georgia), 502,979; for eastern bluebird — Mena (Arkansas), 496; for northern cardinal — Millersburg (Ohio), 1,897; and for American tree sparrow — Wilson Reservoir (Kansas), 2,155.

Someone at the NAS should figure a way to score this game and then promote it. Thousands of birders would soon be playing (not a few for money), sales of the CBC issue would skyrocket, and Audubon might make some money.

---

* *Of course, high counts move around some from year to year, especially where large roosts are involved, but for many species high numbers and locations are remarkably consistent.*

CHAPTER IV

Establishing Habitat:

A PLANTING PRIMER

*Keep wildlife in mind when you select annual and perennial plantings.
Adding to the diversity and abundance of vegetation on your lot should
attract more wildlife.*

*— from an official publication of New York State's
Department of Environmental Conservation*

In most cases, planting trees is one of the worst things you can do for wildlife.

*— from an official publication of Vermont's
Department of Fish and Game*

ALTHOUGH THESE TWO AGENCIES may not see eye to eye on all matters, the disagreement here is more apparent than real. New York's Department of Environmental Conservation is talking about the ordinary
urban or suburban property, which is long on lawn and short on habitat. Vermont's
Fish and Game is talking about a woodland situation, where the problem is likely

to be too *much,* or the wrong kind of, habitat. As the woods on the Northeast's abandoned farmland matures, this becomes an increasing problem. On federal land, the U.S. Forest Service increasingly wages war on habitat, chopping it down or burning it up. A Forest Service document called "Managing Woodlands for Wildlife" pulls no punches on the subject: "The chain saw is the best wildlife management tool yet invented."

The town dweller, trying desperately to grow a couple of shade trees and a few ornamental shrubs on his development lot, may find this problem difficult to comprehend. But as a forest matures — and particularly an even-aged or monocultured forest, one managed for wood products — the one or several climax species shade out most of the rich understory, eliminating browse and food-producing shrubs and vines. (This is just what the move to intensive, "clean" farming had done on America's agricultural land between the world wars, with the elimination of hedgerows and the grazing of woodlots.) Early-successional plant communities support a greater variety of wildlife, including game species, than do climax communities, which is why the hunters teamed up with the lumber and off-road-vehicle interests against conservationists during the unhappy RARE-II* battles of the late 1970s and early 1980s. The hunters weren't against *woods,* but rather *mature* woods, where you don't find many grouse, rabbits, or deer.

If, then, you are in the unusual and enviable situation of living in the middle of hundreds or thousands of acres of mature woods, you can attract and feed a greater variety of wildlife by simply cutting a sizable opening or two to provide some "edge" — that wildlife-preferred interface where two disparate habitat types meet. You can then set about planting things if you like, or, having let the sun in, you can simply leave it alone, and let natural plant succession take over. The highly mobile, opportunistic herbaceous plants will come in immediately, followed shortly by early-succession woody plants — brambles, red cedar, aspen, bird-planted hedgerow species such as dogwood, cherry, viburnums, and so on. If you periodically burn or

---

Plants provide cover for nests (page 78) and also protection from weather and predators. A mockingbird (page 79) with a red chokecherry.

---

* The countrywide Roadless Area Review and Evaluation process seems mostly to have shown that the idea of leaving areas of undeveloped woods to mature unexploited — to develop, once again, small parcels of "virgin" forest — is not at present a widely popular one.

mow the central part of your opening and let the margins grow up to these shrubs, vines, and small trees, you'll quickly have the best kind of wildlife sanctuary imaginable: one supporting birds and other animals characteristic of open, mixed, and forested habitats.

For most of us, alas, this deep-woods paradise is an unreachable dream, as remote as the bad-art scenes on the Christmas cards sold by some conservation organizations. Our problem, whether we live in city, town, or suburbia (or even in the country), is not too much habitat, but too little. What we need is not a chain saw, but a spade. It is the purpose of this chapter to introduce a wide range of plant species — trees, shrubs, vines, and ground covers — selected for their attractiveness to wildlife in general and birds in particular. Plants attract birds, of course, because they provide two basic animal requirements, cover and food.

■ Cover ■

IT IS USEFUL TO DISTINGUISH THREE SORTS OF COVER: weather cover, nesting cover, and escape cover. Weather infiltrates and permeates, and it follows that only thick vegetation will have much weather-cover value. Foundation plantings of any kind are good, because it is the house rather than the vegetation that provides most of the protection. Out around the property, however, weather cover — and especially winter weather cover — is virtually synonymous with coniferous planting. A spruce, cedar, fir, or pine is good; a clump or hedge of them is better.

It is widely believed that good nesting cover means the thick, the tangled, and the thorny, so that something like a hawthorn overgrown with grape becomes the ideal nesting situation. Probably this notion derives from the fact that certain popular songbirds do in fact prefer this kind of nesting cover; if it's good enough for cardinal, mockingbird, and brown thrasher, it ought to be good enough for other birds. But birds nest under every conceivable circumstance: on the ground (in tall grass, short grass, and no grass); in shrubs (thick and thin, upright and prostrate); in vines (spiny and otherwise); in trees (tall and short, coniferous and deciduous, dead or alive); not to mention in sandbanks, telephone poles, and mailboxes, or on, in, and under buildings and junked cars. *Anything* you plant will provide potential nesting cover; by the same token, no one can guarantee that a particular bird (or *any* bird) will nest in any particular plant on your property.

Escape cover, too, is conventionally thought of in terms of impenetrable tangle.

The notion is not merely a popular one. A recent book on bird-attracting plantings, written by two professional biologists, perpetuates the myth. Lots of checks appear in the "Cover" column for such species as balsam fir, red cedar, American holly, and brambles, but none at all for deciduous trees such as hackberry, flowering dogwood, sweet gum, or American beech. But what is a bird supposed to use for escape cover in a beech/maple woods, a common climax type in the Northeast and one under which little understory grows?

We are talking, of course, about escape from avian predators. A bird doesn't need cover to deal with a cat or a snake — it simply flies away. But how to handle an accipiter or a falcon? The term "escape cover" is part of the problem — it implies flight to a sanctuary providing a good hiding place (taking, that is, the ostrich strategy one step further). This implies, in turn, that a hawk can secure what it can see. Both assumptions are plausible, and both are quite wrong.

How does hawk predation on birds work? I recall a typical example of attempted predation during a recent fall hawk watch. Three blue jays had dropped out of a migratory flight to rest in a nearby maple. A sharp-shinned hawk subsequently did likewise, landing in another tree. She quickly spotted the jays, and proceeded to do some hunting. She made a dash into their maple, the jays responding by moving to the far side of the tree. She watched them; they watched her. After a time, she made another quick flight around the tree at the jays. They moved, almost nonchalantly, to the opposite side. The hawk's only hope for a capture was to flush a jay from the tree, run it down in flight, and ride it to a perch to kill it. The jays weren't budging, however, and after a half hour's trying, the sharpie gave up and moved on.

Other things being equal, most birds prefer to forage in or near good cover. But consider the plight of the several species of woodpeckers that habitually forage on dead trees in open farm country, often at considerable distances from heavy cover. What does the woodpecker do when a goshawk drops by? Anyone who has watched a woodpecker feeding when a shadow goes over knows. Instinctively the bird dodges to the side of its branch away from the shadow-thrower. Usually the shadow proves to be that of a pigeon or something equally benign, and the woodpecker goes back to work. If it does prove to be a predator, the bird presents its bill, perhaps lifts its wings in defense posture, and prepares to dodge around that tree branch while

---

Baltimore orioles preferred to nest in elms prior to Dutch elm disease; now they use a variety of deciduous trees.

strength remains. The goshawk will try, again, to flush the woodpecker; the latter will take its chances sitting tight and dodging. (This, by the way, is just what a squirrel will do under the same circumstances; as well as the small boy who, caught alone on the playground by the school bully, dodges around the jungle gym rather than breaking and running, buying time until the bully gets bored or someone's mother happens by.)

The typical strategy of avian predators — whether a merlin after shorebirds, a Cooper's hawk after a robin, or a shrike after house sparrows — is to surprise a bird on the ground in the open or force a bird to fly; either presents a good purchase for killing.* The intended victim hasn't much choice in the way of predation-avoidance strategies. It can flee, and probably be run down; or it can sit tight in whatever cover is available to it. (On coastal beaches there is no cover, and in response shorebirds have evolved the compensatory strategy of wheeling up and down the beach in compact flocks, presenting the predator with a too-large target, the individual shorebird using the flock itself as cover.) Songbirds, then, sit tight where they are surprised; that is, among the vegetation on or near which they customarily forage. Since birds forage on all kinds of plants, it follows that all sorts of plants are utilized as escape cover. An open autumn maple tree or a dead elm limb may not be your idea of escape cover, but they will do quite nicely for the jay and the woodpecker. Permit me a redefinition. Escape cover is *anything* that stands, hangs, leans, sits, or lies upon the landscape, and which can be interposed between predator and intended victim. It includes not only your plantings, but also your TV antenna and your swing set. You may not think of your shed or garage as wildlife cover, but it probably provides all three kinds: weather cover for the house sparrows that roost within or under the eaves, nesting cover for robin, phoebe, or deer mouse, and escape cover in the form of an obstacle for a pursued songbird to duck around.

When planting for cover, then, the guidelines are simple. For weather cover, the thicker the better; conifers a must. For nesting and escape cover, everything counts. Go for as wide a variety of food-producing plants as possible, and nesting and escape cover will take care of themselves.

---

* *Occasionally hawks — and especially the audacious goshawk — will wade into cover after prey; dramatic chases and battles sometimes ensue, and the stories of witnessed encounters gain wide circulation. My own favorite, reported over a half century ago by the New England naturalist Edward Howe Forbush, tells of a determined goshawk that pursued a terrified chicken under the skirts of an unnerved Maine housewife.*

■ Food ■

THERE ARE TWO BASIC SOURCES OF INFORMATION concerning the food habits of birds and other animals. Recorded observations are an obvious and important source. Much of the early bird information is available in A. C. Bent's multivolume *Life Histories,** which are, among other things, a compilation of the observations of scattered ornithologists. Observations are necessarily sporadic, and may not tell us what a given species prefers to eat or mostly eats; they do at least tell us what certain individuals of that species *have* eaten at particular times in particular places.

The other main source of diet information derives from the analysis of droppings and, especially, stomachs. It was just over a century ago that the U.S. Biological Survey (later the Fish and Wildlife Service) began the systematic examination of birds' stomach contents, collecting tens of thousands of gamebirds, raptorial birds, and songbirds for the purpose. That was in the days of "economic ornithology," the point of which was to study birds, especially in terms of diet, in order to discriminate the "good" birds from the "bad" ones. We have pretty well gotten beyond that approach to ornithology, but the data produced by those stomach analyses remain a valuable part of our imperfect knowledge of the food habits of birds. Stomach-contents analyses are not, however, without biases. Some plant-food parts are more persistent in the gut than others; the food parts of some species are more readily identifiable than those of others. And another very important point has to be kept in mind. When Martin et al.† rate a particular plant's importance to wildlife, they are telling us perhaps more about the plant's abundance than about its palatability to wildlife. A plant that consistently, shows up in stomach analyses and observations will be both common and palatable; but a plant which shows up infrequently may not be unpalatable, but only unavailable.

---

* Bent's Life Histories of North American Birds *was published a volume at a time from 1919 to 1968. Most ornithologists expect Bent to be replaced by a new multivolume work — the* Handbook of North American Birds, *edited by R.S. Palmer; as of 1997, however, only five volumes have been published, taking us through the raptors, and it doesn't look as if the songbird volumes will become available in our lifetime.*

† *The several books referred to in the text are identified in the Notes on the Charts section at the end of the chapter.*

In the species accounts that follow, I briefly indicate the kinds of birds and mammals, often by genus or family, that are known to make frequent use of the particular plant species. This list is intentionally short; it is meant to suggest the range of probable use, and in no way pretends to be exhaustive. Species-by-species bird lists constitute good filler for books, but they are of little value. I have before me, for example, several documents which claim to list all birds known to eat the fruits of common elder(berry) in the Northeast. These lists vary in length from forty-seven species to 118 species! We have, alas, no very certain notion of what birds utilize the fruits of *Sambucus canadensis* or of most other plants. We know from observations and stomach analyses that a number of species have used elder berries; but then it is probably safe to say that *every* species of bird has, under one circumstance or another, eaten *every* plant food geographically and anatomically available to it. When both North American vultures have been recorded eating at bird feeders, what bird can we safely say does *not* at least occasionally partake of maple seeds or elder berries?

But the interesting questions remain: Where is a particular bird likely to eat a particular plant food? When? Under what weather (or other) circumstances? In what amounts? After what other foods are exhausted? With what nutritional implications? We can answer many of these questions for two groups of birds that have been intensively studied in terms of diet — gamebirds and birds whose feeding habits have a major economic impact (house sparrow, blackbirds, etc.). But we haven't enough evidence in the case of most songbirds to tackle these questions with any confidence. The moral of all this is simple. Plant a variety of the bird-attracting trees, shrubs, vines, and ground covers treated in this chapter, and *see what comes.* Then permanently affix a notebook in a convenient window; it's going to take time to top 118 species for common elder.

■ Propagation ■

How is one to obtain the plants he has chosen? Nursery purchases and free transplants are the two obvious answers. Nurseries, particularly those specializing in native plants, can provide many of the species treated in this chapter. With some investigation, many of them can probably be had free from a friend's property or along a roadside. It has been claimed that nursery plants do better than wilding transplants — that they will grow faster and fruit better and earlier. A university botanist neighbor of mine doesn't believe that is generally the case. He points out the kitchen window to two ten-foot maples and a twelve-foot oak. "I dug those up down the road three years ago. Dug as big a ball as I could handle, dragged the tree up here and plunked it in the ground. I watered them down and trimmed the branches back a third. That's it." He says 90 percent of his wilding transplants flourish. Certainly these are pictures of health.

Some plants may be unavailable at nurseries, or too expensive; they may also be unavailable as wilding transplants, or may not transplant well. These plants can be propagated by seed or asexually, by means of cuttings, budding, grafting, layering, even micro-propagation. But what are the seeds' dormancy requirements? Is stratification or scarification required? And what sort of cutting works best — root, soft-wood, hard-wood, or leaf? Plant propagation is an exacting and technical science. If you mean to propagate by seed or asexually, get a good book on the subject, such as Hudson T. Hartmann and Dale E. Kester's *Plant Propagation: Principles and Practices,* 3rd edition (1975). It will explain both the theory and practice of plant propagation, and will indicate the specific procedures used to propagate many species of fruit and ornamental plants. Read the book, then go out and make friends with somebody who's been propagating for thirty years.

■ Landscaping ■

A LOT OF INK HAS BEEN DEVOTED to the question of where to put the plants once you've got them. Having considered the plants' own requirements — in terms of soil moisture, sun, and so on — where can they be placed to best effect? The basic principles of landscaping boil down to a few common-sense guidelines, such as: (1) Plant the tall things in back of the medium things, and those in back of the low things, so that you can see everything from the interior of your property. (2) Plant your large evergreens on the north, where they will provide shelter for the house; plant only deciduous trees on the south, as conifers would block the winter sun. (3) Plant things with their mature height and crown width in mind; seedling oaks planted five feet apart will look fine for a decade, then you're in trouble. Beyond these general guidelines, you are free, if you so desire, to play with size, shape, texture, and color variables in infinite combinations. What medium-sized foreground plants will best break up the solemn military formality of a row of spruces? What back-drop will best show off the winter red-osier dogwood stems or the white snowberries?

**Even a tidy town property can support plantings that will provide
birds with food, cover, and nesting opportunities.**

Where would the aspen quake to best advantage, and the mulberry fruits drop to
least annoyance?

Keep in mind, while working on your plantings, that the landscape taste of
wildlife leans toward (and beyond) the Romantic rather than the Classical. Leave
your property as scruffy as town ordinances and your own constitutional fastidi-
ousness quotient will allow. Let the vines run rampant on the fences. Clip and
prune no more than you have to. (Consider: cardinals like to nest in the kinds of trees
and shrubs commonly used for foundation plantings, at a preferred height of five
to eight feet; how many millions of cardinal nesting opportunities are squandered
by the accidental fact that the convenient topping height for a five-foot-ten-inch sub-
urbanite wielding hedge clippers is four feet?) Leave some dead snags for the woodpeckers to work. Don't mow more lawn than you need.

You will notice that there are no annuals or biennials on the following species list.
This is not because the grasses and forbs are of little food value to wildlife, but
rather because you don't have to plant them. Just leave some odd sunny corners of

your property (or several acres if you have them to spare) alone, and the grasses, "weeds," and wildflowers will blow in fast. But even if the forbs and grasses didn't self-plant, who would waste time urging people to cultivate them? Stomach analyses suggest that the four favorite herbaceous plant groups for northeastern songbirds are ragweed, bristlegrass, crabgrass, and panicgrass.

▓ Wildlife Problems ▓

I T HAS BECOME OBLIGATORY, in essays on wildlife attraction, to issue a discreet warning with regard to the hassles you may be in for if your program succeeds. Federal and state conservation agencies now employ people called "urban wildlife specialists," who spend a lot of time responding to complaints about life- and property-threatening birds and mammals. This is how *they* come to see the results of a wildlife planting program: Your hedge-protected and ground-cover-decorated bank attracts a denning woodchuck, who proceeds systematically to wipe out your garden. The rabbits, who make themselves at home in your new brush piles, help the woodchuck with your garden, and also find time to girdle your young trees. The brushy fencerow provides cover for rodents and skunks; the former gnaw on your telephone cables, while the latter dig up your lawn for grubs. The dead trees you thoughtfully spared attract woodpeckers all right, and their spring drumming on your metal gutters drives the family to distraction. The squirrels attracted to your nut trees chew their way into your attic, and terrorize the bird feeders all winter. The robins flock to your mulberry or cherry tree, then fly over your clothesline and poop on the sheets. A raccoon, lured by the frogs in your new pond, decides to den in your chimney, whence he occasionally issues through the fireplace to run amok in the family room. When your conifers are young, they will host the noise and mess of nesting grackles; and when they mature, they will turn each fall into a shrieking starling/grackle roost. In time the marauding wildlife will exhaust the resources of your property, after which they will use it as a base from which to attack your neighbors. This will shortly put an end to your cocktail-party invitations, and litigation is by no means unlikely. . . .

But not to worry. This horror story represents what foreign-policy strategists call a "worst-case scenario." Anyway, it will probably take a lifetime to have this much bad luck, and won't things be interesting in the meanwhile!

■ Species Accounts ■

MOST OF THE FOLLOWING SPECIES of trees, shrubs, vines, and ground covers have been chosen because they provide good to excellent wildlife food value, based on the evidence of stomach and droppings analyses and on published and personal observations.* Some additional species of moderate food value have been included, usually because they provide excellent weather cover or food during a critical part of the year. Well over a hundred species of plants are treated, a sample large enough to provide a variety of plants suitable for virtually any conceivable soil/water/topographic/climate combination found in the greater Northeast. Plants are listed, within the major groups, alphabetically by common name. This procedure violates botanical convention, which dictates that plants be arranged according to family relationships or alphabetically by scientific genus name. It was adopted because it enables the reader unfamiliar with Latin and Greek designations and taxonomic relationships to find his way around without resorting to a cumbersome system of cross-references.

Common names of plants are notoriously slippery. Popular names differ widely for many species, and botanical authorities themselves disagree on proper designations for some. Sometimes the disagreements are trivial — is the proper vernacular name for *Liriodendron tuilpifera* tulip tree, tulip-tree, or tuliptree? But often the alternatives are importantly — and confusingly — different. Some authorities, for example, call *L. tulipifera* yellow-poplar, others tulip-poplar, even though it is a magnolia rather than a poplar. I have called *Ostrya virginiana* and *Carpinus caroliniana* American hop-hornbeam and American hornbeam, respectively. A popular field guide calls them hornbeam and ironwood, respectively. They are also called ironwood and blue beech, respectively. The nomenclature here is so tangled that, if someone mentions "hornbeam" or "ironwood," you simply have to look him in the eye and demand to know whether he refers to *O. virginiana* or *C. caroliniana*. Like it or not, scientific names are absolutely necessary when talking about plants. Otherwise, there is no way of knowing whether an apparently innocent reference to "snowberry" refers to an evergreen creeping ground-cover shrub *(Gaultheria hispidula)* or to an entirely dissimilar deciduous upright shrub *(Symphoricarpos al-*

---

* I have elected not to treat good wildlife plants that are also potential health hazards to humans; these plants — among which poison ivy is most infamous — are fortunately few in number.

bus). (Scientific names aren't perfectly uniform either, but they shouldn't be much bother unless your botany text or field guide bears an older copyright date.) The plant designations in this chapter do not follow any particular authority. I have judged each case individually, choosing names with an uneasy eye on both traditional usage and contemporary nomenclature.

■ Trees ■

A S H E S (*Fraxinus* spp.). White ash *(F. americana)* is best known, famous as the wood of choice for sports implements (baseball bats, hockey sticks) and for its gorgeous purple and mauve fall foliage. Red ash *(F. pennsylvanica),* along with its variety green ash, and black ash *(F. nigra)* are smaller trees that are hardy farther north. Ashes like rich, moist soil, and plenty of sun (though white ash will do well in partial shade). White and red ashes are always, and black ash often, dioecious; that is, they produce flowers of only one sex on a given plant. Hence you need a female plant, or you'll have no canoe-paddle-blade-shaped fruits (samaras, "keys").* Ashes don't seem to feed a wide variety of wildlife (several mammals, gamebirds, and songbirds utilize ash twigs and fruits), but anyone lucky enough to watch close up as a flock of wintering pine grosbeaks works one will never lose his fondness for the tree. The birds space themselves out over the tree, each perched above a drooping cluster of keys. The grosbeak dips its head and pulls off a key. If the seed is not well formed, the fruit is instantly dropped. If the seed is good, the bird quickly maneuvers the key to a seed-end-in, wing-out position, so that the bird appears to be chewing on a miniature tongue depressor. In two seconds the wing falls away, and the observer assumes the bird has clipped off the samara's seed end. It has not. The grosbeak has split the wing covering up the seed end and has neatly extracted the half-inch-long seed (which looks like a pointed-ended long-grain rice kernel). The bird then munches the seed for several seconds, and the head dips for a new fruit. Pine grosbeaks feed patiently, persistently, the flock keeping up a soft, quavering, liquid conversational note all the while. At close range, the multitude of key crackings from an ash full of grosbeaks produces a sound like a light sleet falling on crusted snow; and the continually falling

---

* Dioecious species will be identified as such in these pages. It is safest to obtain these species from nurseries, where, because of asexual propagation, the sex of young plants is known. If you transplant wildings, you'll have to take potluck.

wings drift out of the tree like a miniature leaf fall. Suddenly the flock takes alarm. The birds switch to the familiar loud, clear, bell-like two- or three-note whistle, and then go bounding off cross-country, looking for another ash.

ASPENS (*Populus* spp.). Many country people call both quaking aspen *(P. tremuloides)* and bigtooth aspen *(P. grandidentata)* poplar or popple, and generally despise them as weed trees, good for nothing but matchsticks and pulp. Aspens are pioneer trees, rapidly germinating in burned or cut-over forest areas, where they serve as short-lived nurse trees for later and slower-growing species, while adding brilliant yellows to the late-autumn woods. Quaking aspen is famous for its shimmering, chattering leaves, constantly in motion because of flattened leafstalks. (This talkative-leaf habit has led the male-chauvinist French to call the similar European trembling aspen *langue de femme* — "woman's tongue.") The quaking aspen, generally claimed to have the widest natural range of any North American tree, grows over the whole Northeast and much of the West, invading the northern tundra along stream margins. The bigtooth (or large-toothed) aspen grows entirely within our Northeast region. Both species are dioecious; both male and female flowers form on pendulous catkins, the female catkins maturing tiny (500,000 to the ounce) "cotton"-borne seeds. Aspens attract fewer birds than many other trees, but they provide important winter and spring food. Prairie chicken and ruffed and sharp-tailed grouse eat buds and catkins; northern finches eat buds. Bark and twigs provide mammal browse, and aspen is the beaver's favorite building-material and food (the bark) tree. The soft wood is utilized by several woodpeckers for nesting cavities.

BEECH, AMERICAN *(Fagus grandifolia).* Beech is a well-known eastern forest climax tree, easily identified by its uniquely smooth, gray bark, which, on mature trees, is inevitably decorated with some half-wit's initials. (An inscription on a particular beech along Carrol Creek in Tennessee has been generally forgiven, for it indicated the spot where "D. Boone Cilled A Bar . . . In Year 1760." The message was legible for over a century, and when the mammoth beech fell in 1916, the Forest Service estimated its age at 365 years.*) *Fagus* derives from the Greek verb "to eat," and

---

* *The scope of this chapter does not, regrettably, allow for extensive excursions into the historical lore of American trees. The reader interested in this subject will find a wealth of fascinating information in my present source, Donald Culross Peattie's* A Natural History of Trees of Eastern and Central North America *(1948).*

when the nut crop is good (every second or third year) the beeches set a table for virtually everything in the woods. Squirrels and black bears rely heavily on beech mast, as do gamebirds (grouse, turkey, wood duck), songbirds (jays, chickadees, tufted titmouse, blackbirds), and others (especially woodpeckers). But attendance at the beech feast is light compared to what it was during the glory days of the eastern deciduous forest, when its most faithful guests were the roving hordes of passenger pigeons.

B I R C H E S (*Betula* spp.). Probably a thousand people can correctly call a tree a birch for every individual who can identify to species our five common birches. (Quiz: what are the mature trunk-bark colors of gray birch, yellow birch, and red birch? Answers: white, red-brown, and gray-black, respectively.) Common names are more than usually confusing. Our northernmost birch, *B. papyrifera,* is called white, paper, and canoe birch. Most birches are medium-sized trees, but our small birch, *B. populifolia,* is variously known as gray, white, fire, old-field, and poverty birch. Our only southeastern birch (Hardiness Zone 6), *B. nigra,* is called both red and river birch; while *B. lenta* passes as either black or sweet birch. Our last common birch has pretty well settled down to yellow birch, but botanists can't decide on a *scientific* name for that one (the choices being *B. lutea* and *B. alleghaniensis*). Whatever you call them, the several birches are valuable wildlife trees, supplying browse for moose and deer; buds and catkins for grouse; seeds (tiny butterfly-shaped samaras) for songbirds, especially siskin and redpolls; nest-building material in the form of bark for vireos, warblers, and tanagers; and breeding sites for such cavity nesters as black-capped chickadee, titmouse, and several woodpeckers.

C E D A R ,   N O R T H E R N   W H I T E *(Thuja occidentalis).* This long-lived, aromatic denizen of northern cedar/tamarack bogs and the Appalachian chain is cultivated and pampered on many an estate of the wealthy, where its admirers are likely to call it arborvitae. Extensively planted as ornamental hedging, northern white cedar provides excellent wildlife cover. Its half-inch-long cones mature in autumn, the woody, leaf-shaped scales opening to release tiny oval samaras, reminding one of miniature elm fruits. White-tailed deer browse the curiously flat foliage fronds, and squirrels and several species of songbirds are known to eat the seeds.

C E D A R ,   E A S T E R N   R E D *(Juniperus virginiana).* Red cedar — not a cedar at all but a juniper — is familiar over a wide area of the Northeast as the compact, cone-shaped evergreen scattered across abandoned meadows and pastures, wherever birds happened to pass cedar-berry seeds. Red cedar wood refuses to split under sharpening, making it the long-favored material for pencils; it is aromatic, and has long been used to line chests and closets; it resists rotting, and the term "cedar posts" has become interchangeable with "fence posts." Another good nesting- and weather-cover species, red cedar also provides emergency browse for deer; and its dark-blue "berries" (cones, actually) are relished by many species of birds — including gamebirds, several flycatchers, mimics, thrushes,* finches, sparrows, and the cedar waxwing (whose very name apparently derives from its association with the tree). Red cedar is usually dioecious. It is also, unfortunately, an alternate host for apple rust, which, while not dangerous to the cedar, is damaging to apple trees. It is therefore not a good idea to plant eastern red cedar within a mile of an apple orchard; in some states, indeed, it is illegal to do so.

CHERRIES (*Prunus* spp.). Pin cherry *(P. pensylvanica)* and common chokecherry *(P. virginiana)* are small trees, hardy right up to Hudson Bay. Like aspen and gray birch, pin cherry pioneers on burned and clear-cut areas (it is also known as fire cherry), and, like them, it is short-lived. Chokecherry, which sometimes matures in shrub form, is longer-lived. And black (or rum) cherry *(P. serotina),* less northern-hardy, is a much larger tree which may outlive its planter twice over. Pin cherry and chokecherry mature their bright medium-red and dark-red fruits early (French Canadians call pin cherry *cerises d'été,* or "summer cherry"), while black cherry's larger fruits mature purple-black a bit later (French Canadians call the tree *cerises d'automne).* People find the fruits of black cherry quite palatable; the fruits of the other two species are relegated to jellies, the usual response to taking them straight being indicated by the name chokecherry. The whole question is academic, however — the birds will eat all the cherries whether you like them or not. Gamebirds, woodpeckers, flycatchers, corvids, mimics, thrushes, waxwing, vireos, grosbeaks, finches — everything turns fruit eater when the cherries are ripening. And bear, raccoon, foxes, rabbits, squirrels, chipmunk, and mice clean up under the table. Cherries are among the best of wildlife-attracting plants, and even the smallest property can support a pin

---

* The term "mimics" stands, in these pages, for at least two of our three eastern mimids — northern mockingbird, brown thrasher, and gray catbird. "Thrushes" represents three or more of that group, usually robin and bluebird plus one or more of our spot-breasted thrushes.

An eastern red cedar, a good cover and food tree for a
variety of songbirds, hosts this northern cardinal.

cherry (also, inevitably, called bird cherry) or a chokecherry. You will not, however, want to encourage any cherry in a pasture. The bark and leaves contain hydrocyanic acid, which is poisonous to livestock.

CRABAPPLES (*[Pyrus] Malus* spp.). "Crab" is said to derive from the Norse *skrab*, meaning "scrubby." Scrubby or not, crabapples are lovely in blossom and in fruit, and they attract a wide variety of wildlife as well. From the hundreds of species and varieties available, many of them introduced from Asia, the following can be recommended because they bear annually and the fruits tend to persist through the winter. Siberian *(M. baccata)* is a large crabapple, hardy well north into Canada. The Soil Conservation Service recommends "Midwest" Manchurian crabapple (a variety of *M. baccata)* for planting in the north-central states. Dorothea *(M. "Dorothea")* and Japanese flowering *(M. floribunda)* are mid-sized crabapples, hardy to Zone 5. Sargent *(M. sargentii)* is a tiny crabapple which produces quarter-inch red fruits, half the size of Dorothea's yellow apples. It too is hardy to Zone 5. Like cherries, apples and crabapples attract insectivores and granivores (seed eaters) as well as fructivores, and, in addition, they are favored nesting trees for a variety of both open- and cavity-nesting birds.

D O G W O O D ,   F L O W E R I N G *(Cornus florida)*. George Washington planted flowering dogwood at Mount Vernon, Thomas Jefferson at Monticello, and lesser property owners have followed suit ever since. Probably everyone living within the tree's range knows it by the showy white petal-shaped bracts (which are usually miscalled flowers) in the spring and the clusters of brilliant red fall fruits, shaped like blunt torpedos. Scores of species of gamebirds and songbirds, as well as many mammals, have been recorded eating flowering dogwood fruits; if the robins and starlings get there first, however, there may not be much left.* This small tree is not only attractive to people and wildlife, it has the added advantage of prospering in shade as well as in sun.

E L M ,   A M E R I C A N *(Ulmus americana)*. The stately, storied American (or white) elm, a familiar and much-loved shade tree, is seldom thought of in terms of wildlife attraction. To be sure, it is first choice as nesting tree for the Baltimore oriole, and dead elms are a boon to woodpeckers as well as to country dwellers with wood stoves. Beyond that, however, American elm is an important seasonal food tree for squirrels, several gamebirds, and a score of songbirds. And the season, curiously enough, is late-winter/spring, when the elm flowers and fruits, respectively. Rose-breasted grosbeak relishes the tiny reddish flowers, while chickadees and purple finch sample the buds and the small, flattened, oval, notch-tipped, hairy-margined samaras, which end up heaped in their millions along the curbs of elm-shaded town and village streets throughout the East. Or did, at least, before the Dutch elm disease changed utterly the look of those streets and those towns.

F I R ,   B A L S A M *(Abies balsamea)*. Anyone looking for a medium-sized tree

---

* A researcher monitoring fall and winter wild fruit use by birds on a New Jersey forest site found the autumn use of flowering dogwood so heavy that, by early November when most migrants had moved on, only 10 percent of the original berry crop remained for wintering birds. For an interesting discussion of the amount (and sequence) of usage by birds of common fruiting plants in a typical fall/winter eastern temperate forest, see John W. Baird's "The Selection and Use of Fruit by Birds in an Eastern Forest" in the March 1980 issue of The Wilson Bulletin.

to put in a cool, moist location out of strong winds would do well to consider the fragrant, exclusively northern balsam fir. This elegant, spire-shaped conifer provides favorite nesting sites for a number of songbirds; the foliage is important winter browse for moose, deer, and spruce grouse; and the fruits — looking like broader-winged red maple keys, but half as long — will, if found, be utilized by a variety of northern birds (chickadees, jays, finches) and small mammals. But even if you never see boreal chickadee or crossbills working your fir cones, you will have ready access to something equally special, something nothing but balsam fir can provide: the aroma of Christmas.

HACKBERRY *(Celtis occidentalis)*. If the natural range of balsam fir defines the northern half of the Northeast (as broadly designated in this book), that of hackberry defines its southern half. Though scattered over a third of the United States, hackberry is a little-known species. Early writers referred to it as the "unknown tree," which happens to be a literal translation of *bois inconnu,* its French Canadian name. Hackberry is considered a near relative of the elms, but leaf shape and venation, bark texture, and tree form are different; and rather than bearing its seeds in the form of paper-winged samaras, hackberry produces a round, berrylike, purplish drupe. This fruit (often called a sugarberry, the tree's alternate common name) is readily eaten by gamebirds, woodpeckers, mimics, thrushes, and finches, so that, although the "berries" persist into winter, they seldom have a chance to outlast it.

HEMLOCK, EASTERN *(Tsuga canadensis)*. The pyramidal eastern hemlock is often planted as a specimen tree on tailored estates, a far cry from its cool, moist native haunts in the northern woods and along the Appalachian chain. New Englanders are familiar with it as the conifer that invades beech/maple woods down the north sides of rocky hills, where, as elsewhere, it thrives in heavy shade. Hemlock groves are good nesting and weather cover for a variety of northern birds (including several warblers) and mammals, while deer browse the foliage and porcupines relish the bark. The winged seeds do not seem to attract a wide variety of birds, but they are readily taken by chickadees, siskin, goldfinch, and crossbills.

HICKORIES *(Carya* spp.). I asked an exurbanite friend the other day to name three uses for hickory wood. He leaned his hickory-handled axe against the shed wall and carried in a couple of high-priced hickory sticks for the fire while contemplating the question, and then, as our families sat down to hickory-smoked ham, admitted he couldn't do so. The variety of uses for which tough, heavy, shock-resistant hickory is the wood of choice is astonishing, so that the food value of hickories is almost incidental. Yet William Bartram found the Creek Indians storing thousands of bushels of shagbark hickory nuts, which they smashed and boiled, collecting the oily milk ("as sweet and rich as fresh cream") to use in their cooking; and cracking hickory nuts long remained a common winter pastime among the Indians' successors. Among our several northeastern hickories, mockernut *(C. tomentosa)*, pignut *(C. glabra)*, and shagbark *(C. ovata)* — listed in order of ascending size — are good wildlife trees. The problem with the nuts of these trees (unlike those of pecan, the best-known southern hickory) is that they are tough to crack, as witnessed by the name mockernut, which derives from the early New York Dutch *moker-noot* ("heavy-hammer nut"). Gamebirds, woodpeckers, chickadees, nuthatches, cardinal, and other birds relish hickory meats, but how are they to get at them? It has been claimed that they utilize squirrel-opened nuts; but surely virtually every squirrel-*opened* nut is also a squirrel-*eaten* nut. Probably you are going to have to gather some to put out, smashed, as a feeder item. (Hint: the best smashing tool is an antique flatiron.)

HOLLY, AMERICAN *(Ilex opaca)*. American holly grows only in the southern part of our region, where it has the distinction of being the only broad-leaved evergreen. It is often called Christmas holly, as it is a much-used decorative green during that season. This is unfortunate for the species, as holly pickers strip the fruiting branches from female trees (the plant is dioecious), often killing them. Given a chance, American holly is a long-lived tree; several of those planted by George Washington two centuries ago still thrive at Mount Vernon. Woodpeckers, mimics, thrushes, and cedar waxwing are fond of the red holly "berries," and they assist the tree's spread by voiding the drupes' bony nutlets. American holly is insect- rather than wind-pollinated; hence female trees are unlikely to fruit unless a male tree grows nearby.

HOP-HORNBEAM, AMERICAN *(Ostrya virginiana)*. All the common names for this tree — hornbeam, hardhack, ironwood (and the latter's French Canadian counterpart, *bois de fer*) — refer to its extraordinarily hard wood, harder than that of ash, oak, persimmon, and hickory. Hop-hornbeam is a small, unassuming, understory woodland tree, identified (if at all) by its shreddy bark and, in season, by its clusters of curious paper-bladder, hoplike fruits. The tree is a near relative of the hazels, so it is not surprising that the nut within the bladder looks like a miniature hazelnut, but stretched to make it elongate rather than squat. Several woodland gamebirds and songbirds, as well as squirrels and mice, are known to eat the nuts. Undoubtedly the buds and catkins are also consumed to some extent.

HORNBEAM, AMERICAN *(Carpinus caroliniana).* Like the last species, to which it is related, the American hornbeam is scattered throughout virtually the whole eastern half of the United States. It too is a small understory woodland tree, often called ironwood, blue beech (because of its smooth, gray-blue bark), and musclewood (due to the muscular bulges characterizing its trunk). The prominently ridged oval nutlets are set at the base of an odd, three-pronged leafy bract, looking rather like a ball stuck in the pocket of a misshapen baseball mitt. The fruits line up along a drooping stem, forming a strobile. The nutlets of hornbeam are eaten by the same birds and mammals that utilize hop-hornbeam.

MAPLES *(Acer* spp.). No genus is more famous in the Northeast; indeed three maples (black, striped, and mountain) grow native nowhere else, and sugar maple barely escapes the region. Among full-sized maples suitable for wildlife planting, sugar *(A. saccharum)* and red *(A. rubrum)* provide the spectacular foliage sought by the legions of autumn leaf-peepers. Silver maple *(A. saccharinum)* and Norway maple *(A. platanoides)* are also widely planted as ornamental shade trees. Maples tolerate a wide range of soil-moisture conditions, but silver and red favor the moist end of the range, Norway and sugar the middle. Ashleaf maple *(A. negundo),* more often called boxelder, is disdained by the landscape gardener because of its ungainly form and brittle branches; but as a wildlife tree it has much to offer. Although shorter-lived, it is faster-growing and earlier to fruit than the above maples; it is also hardy farther north and drought-resistant on the plains. Perhaps boxelder's chief advantage has to do with fruit availability. Silver maple's keys are available in spring only; red maple's in spring/summer; sugar maple's in summer/fall; and Norway maple's in fall only. Boxelder's samaras mature in late summer and persist on the tree straight through winter. Except for boxelder, which is dioecious, these maples are sexually confused. The technical term is polygamodioecious, which means that the flowers may be unisexual or bisexual; when pistils and stamens form on separate flowers, one or both may occur on a particular tree. All of which means that a particular maple tree may or may not be able to produce fruit on its own. Maples provide browse for deer and moose, nesting sites for various songbirds, and food in the form of buds, flowers, and seeds for chipmunk and squirrels, gamebirds, and seed-eating songbirds. When sunflower seeds are unavailable, wintering evening grosbeaks, for example, will work boxelder keys, clipping the wings and eating the seeds.

MOUNTAIN-ASH, AMERICAN *([Pyrus] Sorbus americana).* The American mountain-ash is a small, cool-climate tree, growing in the North Woods and down the Appalachian chain. It is also called the rowantree, an alternate name borrowed from its cousin the European mountain-ash *(S. aucuparia),* now itself a widely planted ornamental in the Northeast. The rowan derives its name from Gaelic and Norse words for "red," and the mountain-ashes are famous for their scarlet autumn leaves and flat-topped fruit clusters. As these trees are members of the same family that includes apples and hawthorns, it is no surprise that its "berries" are actually pomes — miniature apples. Whatever you call them, the fruits of mountain-ash are relished by a number of birds, including sharp-tailed and ruffed grouse, red-headed woodpecker, mimics, thrushes, waxwing, and grosbeaks. Fruits persist, if uneaten, through the winter. Moose are inordinately fond of mountain-ash bark, a circumstance which explains (though it cannot excuse) the tree's preposterous North Woods name: missey-moosey.

MULBERRIES *(Morus* spp.). The native American red mulberry *(M. rubra)* and the introduced white mulberry *(M. alba)* — the tree long cultivated for the silkworm industry — are now both widespread in the East. Some mulberry trees are monoecious, some dioecious; female trees of the latter group may set fruit without male pollination. The familiar elongated fruits, called syncarps, are composed of a number of tiny pulp-covered seed-like achenes. Mulberry fruits are favored by many of our most welcome summer songbirds, and Margaret McKenny (in her 1939 book *Birds in the Garden and How to Attract Them)* has written that all other wildlife planting "may be considered a prelude to choosing a site for a mulberry tree." I recall as a child admiring the rose-breasted grosbeaks that ravened the red mulberry in our midwestern backyard. Other constant visitors include several woodpeckers, a couple of flycatchers, blue jay and crow, the mimics, thrushes, waxwing, vireos, orchard as well as Baltimore oriole, tanagers, cardinal, indigo bunting, and several other finches.

O A K S (*Quercus* spp.). There are over thirty species of oaks in the eastern woods, few of which grow north of the U.S.–Canadian border. (Of the species listed below, only northern red oak is hardy in Zone 4.) The white oak *(Q. alba)* is king of the white oak group, and indeed many people believe it to be king of all North American trees, whether on account of its great lumber value, its great size (a specimen at Wye Mills, Maryland, has a crown spread of 165 feet), or its great longevity (the life spans of just four white oaks stand between us and Julius Caesar). From the larger red oak group we may single out scarlet *(Q. coccinea),* pin *(Q. palustris),* northern red *(Q. rubra),* and black *(Q. velutina)* oaks. On the soil-moisture continuum, scarlet and black oaks thrive toward the dry end, pin oak toward the moist, and northern red and white oaks in the middle. Oaks in the red group tend to do poorly out of the sun; white oak tolerates partial shade. The authors of *American Wildlife & Plants* consider oaks the most important woody plants for wildlife in the Northeast. Much of this ranking is due, of course, to mammal use. Oaks provide, mostly in the form of acorns, the main staple in the winter diet of black bear, raccoon, mule and white-tailed deer, chipmunk and white-footed mouse, and gray, red, fox, and flying squirrels, in addition to supplementary food for red fox, hare and rabbit, opossum, and beaver. But many birds rely on acorns also, whether they swallow them whole (ducks, turkey) or peck them to pieces (most smaller birds). Heavy users of various trees' acorns include mallard and wood duck, ruffed grouse and pheasant, bobwhite and turkey, crow and jays, red-headed and red-bellied woodpeckers, flicker and grackle, white-breasted nuthatch, brown thrasher, tufted titmouse, and rufous-sided towhee. Fortunately, oaks are capable of bearing heavy crops. It requires, for example, just seven middle-aged northern red oaks to produce a hundred pounds of acorns. Unfortunately, most oaks bear heavily only one year in three or five or eight, and poor crop years — especially now that the chestnut is gone — can mean a serious mast shortage, and hard times in the winter woods.

P E R S I M M O N, C O M M O N *(Diospyros virginiana).* Common persimmon is a southern tree (indeed, it is a member of the tropical ebony family), growing north into our region from New York west along the Ohio Valley. The dioecious persimmon is a distinctive tree, with its glossy, leathery leaves and its curious dark bark, furrowed and cross-furrowed into small, irregular blocks. But, of course, it is the fruit for which the tree is famous. *Diospyros* means "fruit of Jove," and many people agree that a fully ripened fruit from a good persimmon is a gourmet item. Since most of the fruits we call berries are something else, I suppose it follows that the p'simmon, which nobody calls a berry, is. Peattie describes the manner after which the southern Indian tribes made bread of the fruit, and points out that Confederate soldiers boiled the seeds as a coffee substitute. Other mammals make more use of persimmon now than man, it being a favorite food of deer, fox, raccoon, skunk, and our only marsupial, whose attentions have given *D. virginiana* its other common name, possumwood. Birds relish the fruits too; turkey, bobwhite, woodpeckers, mimics, thrushes, waxwing, and yellow-rumped warbler are often recorded at persimmon trees.

P I N E S (*Pinus* spp.). Compared to the West and South, the Northeast is pine species-poor, yet the white pine (*P. strobus,* our most famous lumber tree of all), red pine *(P. resinosa),* and pitch pine *(P. rigida)* are notable trees that grow native only in the Northeast; and the introduced Scotch (or Scots) pine *(P. sylvestris)* is now widely distributed in the region. Pitch pine is the small tree of the group, and white pine the patriarch, with red and Scotch pines not far behind. Pines typically tolerate a wide soil-moisture range, but pitch and red do well on dry soils, Scotch prefers the middle range, and white thrives on moist soils. The red, Scotch, white, and pitch pines are hardy through Zones 2, 3, 4, and 5 respectively. Pitch pine, the characteristic tree of New Jersey's pine barrens, is useful for planting on poor soils; it and red pine are especially prolific seeders. All pines are valuable cover trees, and provide nesting sites for everything from hawks to woodpeckers to warblers. And pines are among the most valuable food trees we have. Deer and spruce grouse browse the needles; beaver and snowshoe hare eat the bark; and the tiny winged seeds are staples for mice and squirrels, chickadees and nuthatches, woodpeckers and grosbeaks, crossbills and finches, several warblers (especially pine warbler), creeper and brown thrasher.

S A S S A F R A S *(Sassafras albidum).* The sassafras is, like the persimmon, a dioecious southern tree, likely to be small in stature in our area. An autumn sassafras is a lovely sight, with its orange foliage setting off red-stalked dark-blue fruits. But it was the aromatic oil, obtained mostly from root bark, that made the tree famous,

---

The familiar American robin often nests in a lilac or apple tree; but pines (and other conifers) will do as well.

for the orange/vanilla-flavored substance was long thought to cure or prevent every disease imaginable. Though some country people still call it aguetree, the medicinal claims for sassafras are few in these latter days, and the flavorful oil has been demoted to a soap and perfume ingredient. The ripened oval drupes, at any rate, remain in favor with the birds. Turkey and bobwhite eat them, as do several woodpeckers and flycatchers, mimics and thrushes, vireos and warblers.

SERVICEBERRIES (*Amelanchier* spp.). *Amelanchier* comprises a large and confused group of shrubs and small trees in the rose family. *A. arborea, A. canadensis,* and *A. laevis* are characteristic and widespread species. All are variously known as serviceberry, sarvissberry, juneberry, and shadbush. *A. arborea* is a bit larger than the others, *A. canadensis,* ironically, a bit less northern-hardy. All tolerate a wide range of soil conditions, though *A. canadensis* prefers a moist habitat. The clusters of lovely white flowers light up the drear woods in March and April, when, presumably, the shad run on the coastal rivers — hence the name shadblow. The fruits, too, are early — hence the name juneberry. The serviceberries bear good crops most years, the purplish pome reminding one of the fruit of that other rose, the hawthorn, except half as big. Serviceberries receive some attention from foliage- and bark-eating mammals, but more from the birds. Woodpeckers, eastern kingbird, mimics, thrushes, waxwing, orioles, grosbeaks, scarlet tanager, red-eyed vireo, and cardinal have been recorded feeding on the tiny apples.

SPRUCES (*Picea* spp.). Our spruces (which we clear-cut for pulp, then turn around and pamper as specimen trees on our lawns) provide half the name for a major North American forest type: the spruce/fir forest of the North. White spruce *(P. glauca)* and black spruce *(P. mariana)* are trans-Canadian species, growing in a belt extending from Newfoundland to Alaska. Red spruce *(P. rubens),* on the other hand, is largely restricted to the Maritimes and New England. Black spruce is usually a short tree of boggy habitat; the other species are medium-tall, and grow under a variety of environmental conditions. White and red spruce are often used as ornamental plantings, as are two imports — Colorado (and its variety "blue") spruce *(P. pungens),* native to the Rocky Mountains; and Norway spruce *(P. abies),* a European tree. Our native spruces are a major component of the North Woods, and, as one would imagine, they provide forage and cover for most northern wildlife. Deer, snowshoe hare, and porcupine browse and bark the trees, while woodpeckers, thrushes, kinglets, warblers, and finches nest in their trunks or among their boughs. Spruce grouse feed heavily on the prickly needles, and the tiny winged seeds are gleaned by squirrels, woodpeckers, chickadees, red-breasted nuthatch, grosbeaks, finches, and crossbills.

SWEETGUM *(Liquidambar styraciflua).* One suspects the sweetgum was designed as a joke or a carnival prop, for it is little more than a collection of botanical oddities. The twigs support queer corky wings. The leaves are formed of five or seven regular, sharp-pointed radiating lobes, like the product of an overachieving maple. Both common and scientific names refer to the "fluid amber" gum exuded by a wounded tree — a gum, it is claimed, both fragrant and chewable. The fruit matures to a round, woody, pointy-shaggy capsule, which looks like a persimmon-sized sea urchin or a sycamore fruit wearing a "natural," and which hangs singly on a long stalk through the winter, like a bizarre Christmas-tree ornament. Withal it is a lovely tree (especially in autumn, when the leaves turn yellow, gold, orange, crimson, scarlet, *and* deep purple); and the seeds are eaten by gray squirrel, bobwhite, mourning dove, blackbirds, cardinal, purple finch, goldfinch, pine siskin, dark-eyed junco, and white-throated sparrow.

TULIPTREE *(Liriodendron tulipifera).* The Greek and Latin genus and species names mean "tulip tree bearing tulips," so that one would have thought the common name inevitable. Not so; many books continue to call the tree yellow-poplar. *L. tulipifera* is not a poplar, but a magnolia; its genus, widespread in earlier geologic periods, is now restricted to our eastern American tree and another (or perhaps the same) tree in central China. While easterners may take the tuliptree for granted, outsiders are dumbstruck by this tallest of North American hardwood trees — the distinctively fissured columnar trunk raising the narrow crown 150 feet or more into the sky, the trunk of a woodland tree branchless for perhaps half that height. It is a lovely tree, too, with the huge, upright, cup-shaped green and yellow flowers decorating the crown in late spring, and the four-lobed leaves turning gold in the fall. The fruit ripens as a hard, three-inch-long pointed conelike structure, which disintegrates to release samaras the size of ash keys. A variety of birds nest in the tuliptree, and the seeds are eaten by squirrels, native mice, cardinal, purple finch, Carolina chickadee, and grosbeaks. The ruby-throated hummingbird is said to visit the flowers for nectar, while the yellow-bellied sapsucker utilizes the sap.

T U P E L O , B L A C K *(Nyssa sylvatica).* If you know sassafras, pignut hickory, and flowering dogwood, you probably also know black tupelo, for the native ranges of the four trees are virtually identical. *Nyssa* is the name of a water nymph in classical mythology, so that the refreshingly poetic scientific name means "water nymph of the woods," suggesting tupelo's preference for damp woods. (A more southerly relative grows in standing water, and is appropriately named *N. aquatica.*) The usually dioecious black tupelo, also known as blackgum and sourgum, is marked by shiny, leathery, tropical-looking leaves, which, in early fall, turn orange, scarlet, then burgundy in a still-green woods. The dark-blue fruits, oblong drupes about the size and shape of black olives, grow in clusters of two and three. The bitter flesh of these fruits is relished by black bear, foxes, squirrels, gamebirds, woodpeckers, mimics, thrushes, waxwing, starling, and summer and scarlet tanagers.

◼ Shrubs ◼

SHRUBS ARE LESS WELL KNOWN THAN TREES, and probably less appreciated. One common landscape ideal, in fact, holds that a properly planted property consists of specimen trees and manicured lawn, period; all "bushy" growth is eliminated. In terms of wildlife attraction, this is a great mistake. Shrubs not only provide more food and cover per square foot of land invested than most trees, they also fruit more consistently. And they have a much faster payback. Although a few small trees begin producing fruit quite young (four years for American holly, six for flowering dogwood, American mountain-ash, chokecherry, and some crabapples), you will probably have to wait a decade for sassafras or red mulberry to fruit; fifteen years for American elm, American hornbeam, tuliptree, or balsam fir; a quarter century for American sweetgum, American hop-hornbeam, or mockernut hickory; and a third of a century or more for American beech, eastern hemlock, or white oak. In pleasant contrast to these figures, most of the shrubs treated below fruit at three to five years, a few earlier yet; so that, if you are buying two-year-old nursery plants, or digging two-year-old wildings, you should be feeding birds from your own shrubs in about two years.

A L D E R S *(Alnus* spp.). Speckled alder *(A. rugosa)* and smooth alder *(A. serrulata)* are thicket-forming streambank and wet-meadow shrubs. Speckled alder is hardy farther north, and tolerates a bit more shade. Alders are little used for ornamental plantings, but they are useful for damp areas. Alder thickets are good cover for game-birds (woodcock nests in them) and other wildlife, and the seeds dropped by the woody cones are eaten by sharp-tailed grouse, redpolls, siskin, and goldfinch.

A U T U M N - O L I V E *(Elaeagnus umbellata).* The Soil Conservation Service calls this oriental member of the oleaster family "one of the most versatile shrubs for conservation use in the Northeast." It grows well in poor, acid, and sandy soils, and hence is often used to line roadbanks, gravel pits, and the like. Autumn-olive is an attractive plant, too, with its fragrant yellow flowers, its green-and-silver foliage, and the great clusters of silver-dotted, red, juicy, round drupes. Humans find these fruits quite palatable, as do several gamebirds, tree swallow, mimics, thrushes, waxwing, cardinal, and other finches.

B A R B E R R Y , J A P A N E S E *(Berberis thunbergii).* The spiny stems, reddish twigs, and bright-red oblong fruits of Japanese barberry are familiar to many people, as it is a standard town and suburban hedge planting throughout its introduced range. Two similar barberries — European and American — are also planted, but they are alternate hosts of the black stem rust, and ought not be planted in wheat-producing regions. Barberries are valued as ornamentals partly because birds don't care much for the berries; hence they hang on the plants all through the winter, and serve as emergency food for wildlife if other, more palatable sources are depleted.

B A Y B E R R Y , N O R T H E R N *(Myrica pensylvanica).* Bayberry is best known as a sand-dune plant forming thickets along the Atlantic Coast, but it grows under a wide range of soil conditions. A dioecious member of the waxmyrtle family, bayberry produces tight clusters of odd gray, waxy, hairy, aromatic, nubby berries which persist on the stems a year or more. These wax-coated nutlets are utilized by gamebirds, woodpeckers, starling, meadowlark, bluebird, and, most notably, tree swallow and "myrtle" warbler, which two species frequent the bayberry dunes in astonishing numbers during fall migration.

B L U E B E R R I E S *(Vaccinium* spp.). Among the many species and varieties of blueberries in our region, highbush *(V. corymbosum)* and lowbush *(V. angustifolium)* are widespread, useful species. The low, spreading lowbush blueberry is the more

**A song sparrow nest, holding an incomplete clutch of eggs,
nestles prettily in a blackberry bramble.**

northern of the two; highbush blueberry has, as befits a tall shrub, the larger leaves and berries. Lowbush blueberry favors dry upland sites, while highbush blueberry prefers moist conditions. Both species do best in full sun. Highbush blueberry probably won't bear until about eight years of age. The fruits are much sought after by a great variety of wildlife, including spruce and ruffed grouse, turkey, several woodpeckers and flycatchers, jays and mimics, thrushes and waxwing, orioles, tanagers, towhee, and sparrows. Parts of the plant are also utilized by black bear, red fox, cottontail, skunk, deer, chipmunk, and mice. The several blueberries constitute, in short, one of our most valuable general wildlife-food shrub groups.

B R A M B L E S (*Rubus* spp.). An interesting little book on New England shrubs and vines published nearly a century ago says, with regard to blackberries and dewberries: "This group is especially to be commended to the systematic botanist who is seeking problems." Add raspberries and you've got some hundreds of species of plants collectively known as brambles, still a fine choice for anyone "seeking problems." It would be pointless to introduce particular species, and dangerous to attempt generalizations. But: (1) raspberries such as *odoratus, occidentalis,* and *idaeus* are mid-sized brambles tolerating some shade; (2) blackberries such as *allegheniensis* and *canadensis* are taller brambles tolerating little shade; and (3) dewberries (or is it groundberries?) such as *hispidus* and *flagellaris* are low prostrate or trailing brambles. Of those species mentioned, *idaeus, canadensis,* and *hispidus* are the more northern-hardy. Most brambles grow on dry, often poor soils, but *hispidus* is a denizen of bogs and other wet places. Bramble roots are long-lived, individual canes usually dying after two years. Brambles reproduce by seeding, thanks to the birds, and vegetatively (tip layering, suckering), often forming impenetrable thickets, important low cover for birds and small mammals. And virtually everybody agrees with the Fish and Wildlife Service that brambles "rank at the very top of summer foods for wildlife." Deer and rabbits browse them, and the fruits are taken by small mammals and just about every species of bird you can think of from pheasant to yellow-breasted chat to summer tanager to fox sparrow.

CHOKEBERRIES (*[Pyrus] Aronia* spp.). Red *(A. arbutifolia)* and black *(A. melanocarpa)* chokeberries are obscure members of the rose family growing in eastern woods and hedgerows. Red chokeberry is generally the taller plant, black chokeberry the more northern-hardy. Both grow on a wide range of soils, though both seem to prefer moist situations. Both are attractive shrubs, with their small, white, five-petaled, roselike flowers, red leaves in the fall, and round berrylike fruits of the color indicated in their respective common names. Several mammals are known to eat these fruits, as well as spruce and sharp-tailed grouse, bobwhite, black-capped chickadee, mimics, thrushes, waxwing, and eastern meadowlark.

CURRANT, AMERICAN BLACK *(Ribes americanum)*. Much like the familiar garden currant, the wild black currant grows throughout most of the Northeast. The drooping racemes of pale-yellow trumpet-shaped flowers mature shiny black berries during the summer months. A variety of mammals (including coyote) have been recorded feeding on currants, as have several game-birds, flicker, mimics, thrushes, waxwing, and finches. Unhappily, wild currants are alternate hosts of the white pine blister rust, and should not be planted if there are pines in the area.

D O G W O O D S (*Cornus* spp.). *Cornus* derives from the Latin *cornu,* or "horn," suggesting the extreme hardness of the wood. A European member of the genus was the traditional choice for butchers' skewers, hence that tree's common names of skewerwood and (from the Old English *dagge,* or "dagger") dagwood; and hence our own form dogwood (not to mention the name of Blondie's thickheaded consort). Our northeastern shrub dogwoods are attractive and valuable wildlife plants, and fortunately there is at least one species to fit virtually any situation. Red-osier *(C. stolonifera)* and roundleaf *(C. rugosa)* dogwoods are hardy to Zone 2, alternate-leaf *(C. alternifolia)* and gray *(C. racemosa)* dogwoods to Zone 4, and silky dogwood *(C. amomum)* to Zone 6. Alternate-leaf and roundleaf dogwoods will tolerate medium-heavy shade, the other three species light shade. All are hardy on a variety of soils, but red-osier and silky dogwoods are usually found in moist situations, roundleaf dogwood in dry situations, and the other two in the middle. The white (or, in the case of alternate-leaf, cream-colored) flowers appear in mostly flat-topped clusters, which subsequently mature blue or white drupes. Birds spread the seed, and new plants (especially of gray and red-osier species) tend to form colonies by means of stolons or root suckers. These hedgerow and woods-border thickets provide fine nesting and feeding cover for wildlife; and the abundant dogwood fruits are favorite fall food for everything from moose to mice, from wood duck to warbling vireo. Gamebirds, woodpeckers, flycatchers, mimics, thrushes, waxwing, cardinal, and grosbeaks are all heavy feeders on dogwood "berries."

E L D E R S (*Sambucus* spp.). The elders, or elderberries, are familiar as a traditional source of wine and jam — at least American (or common) elder *(S. canadensis)* is. The fruit of red (or scarlet) elder *(S. pubens)* is not relished by humans. (Its flowers aren't much appreciated either, as witness another common name, stinking elder.) Both species are lovely in bloom and fruit; common elder produces dense, flat clusters of fragrant white flowers and dark purple berrylike drupes, while red elder develops cone-shaped clusters of yellow-white flowers and bright-red fruits. Elders are very important, mostly late-summer food plants for wildlife, being utilized by most of the same species that feed on dogwood. Common elder thrives in full sun, usually on damp locations; red elder is more northern-hardy, and grows well in partial shade as well as full sun.

F I R E T H O R N *(Pyracantha coccinea).* The firethorn is an exotic and looks it, with its narrowly oval, glossy green, semi-evergreen leaves and its showy autumn clusters of orange-red fruit (each with a star-shaped indentation on the blossom end). This import is much planted as an ornamental in the southern part of our region, where it has escaped to fencerows and thickets. The mealy, bitter fruits are persistent through the winter, and are eaten by pileated woodpecker, mimics, thrushes, waxwing, purple finch, and several sparrows.

G O O S E B E R R Y, P A S T U R E *(Ribes cynosbati).* Pasture (or prickly) gooseberry is a denizen of rocky woods throughout most of the Northeast. *Cynosbati* means "dogbramble," and another common name for the plant is dogberry; apparently the shriveled calyx, which adorns the berry, looks to some people like a dog's snout. It is, whatever you call it, a forbidding shrub, with spiny stems and prickle-guarded fruits. The red-purple berries are, nevertheless, sweet to the taste, and they are eaten by the same birds and mammals that utilize the related American black currant. Wild gooseberries also host the white pine blister rust.

H A W T H O R N S *(Crataegus* spp.). There are reportedly over a thousand different species, subspecies, hybrids, and varieties of hawthorns in the U.S., though which are which seems to be anybody's guess. Hawthorns are called thorn apples by many country people, and farmers consider them a nuisance in the pastures (where cows spread them by eating the fruit and depositing the seeds in their dung). Wildlife enthusiasts appreciate them, however, for the winter food and summer nesting sites (for mimics especially) they provide. Deer and livestock and rabbits browse hawthorns, and gamebirds, woodpeckers, mimics, waxwing, thrushes, and finches eat the haws. The following species are good bearers of persistent fruit. *Phaenopyrum* and *crus-galli* are tall hawthorns, *beata, brumalis,* and *populnea* mid-sized, and *levis, compacta,* and *porteri* small. Hawthorn fruits are not a favorite item of many species, but they provide valuable emergency winter food. Probably you will have to choose between hawthorns and eastern red cedar, however, since the two are alternate hosts of rusts which will destroy the hawthorns.

H A Z E L S *(Corylus* spp.). Hazels, or hazelnuts, are inconspicuous early-succession woodland shrubs. American hazel *(C. americana)* is more southerly than beaked hazel *(C. cornuta),* and may be distinguished from it in spring by the outrageously long male flower catkins. The nuts of the two species are very similar, but the thin husks that enclose them are not: that of American hazel ends in a short, ragged fringe, while that of beaked hazel ends in a long proboscis. This odd growth gives the latter plant both its common and scientific (*cornuta:* "horned") names; but neither is very descriptive, and I hereby propose "trunked hazel" as a more accurate designation. Everybody agrees, at any rate, that hazelnuts (or filberts) are excellent eating. Squirrels, chipmunk, gamebirds, woodpeckers, and blue jay eat them with relish, while moose, deer, hare, rabbit, and beaver utilize other plant parts. Fruit production varies radically in hazels. An Alberta study reported in Gill and Healy found that beaked hazel per-acre nut production varied from 13,000 to forty-four in consecutive years. American hazel is thought to fruit heavily more frequently than beaked hazel.

H O L L I E S (*Ilex* spp.). Three of our native holly shrubs make attractive wildlife plantings. Common winterberry *(I. verticillata)* is northern-hardy to Zone 3, smooth winterberry *(I. laevigata)* and inkberry *(I. glabra)* to Zone 5. The two winterberries sometimes grow taller than inkberry, and they prefer wet-to-moist soils. Inkberry, or gallberry, is an evergreen holly, and does well on drier soils. These species are usually dioecious, and furthermore the female plants require a male pollination source within ten yards or so. A single male holly plant of any species will pollinate female plants of the same or other species, so long as the flowers of the two sexes bloom at the same time. The winterberries set small, red, globular drupes; inkberry, as the name suggests, produces black fruits. Gamebirds, woodpeckers, mimics, thrushes, waxwing, and several finches are fond of these holly "berries."

H O N E Y S U C K L E S (*Lonicera* spp.). Among a number of shrub honeysuckles growing in the Northeast, four are good wildlife and ornamental plants: American fly *(L. canadensis),* tatarian *(L. tatarica),* amur *(L. maackii),* and Morrow *(L. morrowi).* (Japanese honeysuckle — *L. japonica* — is a widespread, long-established exotic; it bears well, but is extremely aggressive, and is considered a pest in some areas.) American fly honeysuckle is a native plant, hardy through at least Zone 3. The other three species are imports, still in the process of escaping. Tatarian and amur are apparently hardy to Zone 4, Morrow to Zone 5. American fly is the lowest plant, amur the tallest; the other two are mid-sized. The exotic honeysuckles are heavier bearers than the native species; American fly and amur have the best shade tolerance. The lovely red (occasionally yellow in tatarian and Morrow) berries are available in most species during summer and perhaps early fall. Amur honeysuckle has the advantage here, for its fruits ripen in the fall and persist into winter. Honeysuckles provide some cover for wildlife, and the berries are eaten by gamebirds and several songbirds. Browsing animals utilize foliage and twigs where honeysuckles are available.

HUCKLEBERRIES (*Gaylussacia* spp.). Black huckleberry *(G. baccata)* is our best-known member of the genus, growing throughout the East from Newfoundland to Louisiana. Dangleberry *(G. frondosa)*, also known as tall or blue huckleberry, and dwarf huckleberry *(G. dumosa)* are more southerly and more restricted in range, occurring largely along the coastal plain. Black huckleberry is intermediate in height between the other two, whose names indicate their stature. All three species grow under a variety of soil conditions, but black huckleberry especially is often found on poor, dry soils, where it invades with other berry plants after fire or other disturbance. Huckleberries generally prefer full sun, but black huckleberry tolerates partial shade. Dwarf and (most) black huckleberry plants produce black berrylike drupes; dangleberry's fruits are dark blue. Pies and jellies have been concocted from the sweet fruits of the two larger species, but huckleberries are mostly left to the birds now. Squirrels, turkey, grouse, pheasant, blue jay, mimics, thrushes, waxwing, orchard oriole, scarlet tanager, white-winged crossbill, pine grosbeak, and towhee have been recorded sampling the fruit; deer occasionally browse the plants.

JUNIPER, COMMON *(Juniperus communis)*. Common, or pasture, juniper is a widespread invader of pastures and abandoned fields. Wondering why the prickly plant is usually found growing beside field boulders, a biologist working in Massachusetts pieced together an interesting ecological scenario. Juniper, he determined, is largely planted by migrating fall robins, whose characteristic perches between feeding bouts are bare field rocks. The robins deposit their droppings on the rocks, and subsequent rain washes the juniper seeds down the sloping sides of the boulders, whence, come winter, they settle into frost-heave cracks in the ground. Here the seed is kept moist by the rock's mini-watershed during its two- or three-year dormancy period; and after germination, the boulder protects the seedling from grazing animals. Hence robin plus rock plus weather equals *J. communis.* Common juniper, in return, supplies evergreen cover and small dark-blue berries, which persist on the plant a year or more. The fruits of this often dioecious shrub are eaten by the same species that feed on its relative, eastern red cedar.

R O S E S (*Rosa* spp.). Among the many varieties of roses, one or more of the following will suit just about any situation: rugosa *(R. rugosa),* meadow *(R. blanda),* Virginia *(R. virginiana),* pasture *(R. carolina),* swamp *(R. palustris),* and multiflora *(R. multiflora).* The first and last species are introduced; the others are native roses. The several species are northern-hardy through Zones 2, 2, 4, 5, 5, and 6, respectively. Pasture, or Carolina, rose is ordinarily the lowest of these forms, multiflora rose the tallest. The others usually grow to five or six feet. Swamp rose, of course, thrives on wet or moist soils; most roses do best under medium to dry circumstances. All roses, especially when allowed to form thickets, are valuable cover and food plants; but of all the roses, the oriental multiflora rose is wildlife king. After World War II, federal conservation agencies pushed multiflora for farmland hedgerows — living fences — to provide livestock containment, soil-erosion control, wildlife food, and wildlife-cover avenues, all at the same time. Multiflora did all these things; indeed, an eight-year study of food plants in Michigan (reported in Gill and Healy) determined that multiflora rose received more wildlife attention than any other plant. The only problem with multiflora is its aggressiveness: the birds seed it, then it spreads on its own. It is easy to start but difficult to stop, so that the professional journals now publish more articles about multiflora eradication than about multiflora propagation. Obviously a few small rose plants will not provide the food or nesting cover of a multiflora hedge, but all roses are popular among browsing animals (from deer and rabbits to mice), and the hips are important winter food for gamebirds (especially sharp-tailed grouse and greater prairie chicken in the northern prairie states) and a variety of songbirds, to whom they are available when preferred foods are covered with snow.

R U S S I A N - O L I V E *(Elaeagnus angustifolia).* Russian-olive is also known as wild olive and Jerusalem willow. It is neither olive nor willow, but, like its relative and fellow exotic autumn-olive, an oleaster (which it is also called). Undoubtedly the shape of the mealy drupes accounts for the name olive, while the narrow leaves *(angustifolia)* suggest willow. Russian-olive is drought-hardy and grows practically anywhere; it is widely planted for shelterbelts in the West. Although the species ordinarily grows as a several-stemmed shrub, DeGraaf and Witman report that it will develop into a medium-sized shade tree if only one stem is retained. Russian-olive provides fair cover, and its yellowish/pinkish/silvery fruits are readily eaten by gamebirds, crow, mimics, robin and bluebird, waxwing, grosbeaks, and finches.

SERVICEBERRIES *(Amelancbier* spp.). We have looked at three serviceberries (or shadbushes or juneberries) that usually take the form of trees. Among those that are usually shrubs, we may mention swamp *(intermedia)*, roundleaf *(sanguinea)*, inland *(interior)*, Bartram *(bartramiana)*, Gaspé *(gaspensis)*, low *(humilis)*, and running *(stolonifera)* serviceberries, if only for the fun of comparing common and scientific specific names. It would be futile to discuss soil ecology and stature for particular species, since positive field identification of most of these and other shrub serviceberries is unlikely. If you want to transplant wilding juneberries, you'll have to take potluck and see what develops. The black or purple fruits of these shrubs are eaten by the same species that utilize the larger serviceberries.

SNOWBERRIES *(Symphoricarpos* spp.). The wonderful Greek genus name means "together-borne fruits," and both snowberry *(S. albus)* and coralberry *(S. orbiculatus)* bear their drupes in small, tight clusters. Snowberry's fair-sized fruits are white and waxy (hence another common name, waxberry); those of coralberry are smaller and various shades of coral, red, purple, and maroon. Indian currant is a nice alternative name for the latter species, which is slightly taller and less northern-hardy than snowberry. These shrubs provide good cover where they form thickets, and the fruits are taken by gamebirds, thrushes, waxwing, cardinal, grosbeaks, and probably other birds and small mammals.

SPICEBUSH, COMMON *(Lindera benzoin).* Common spicebush is a shrub you can learn to identify by smell, as any plant part — twig, stem, leaf, fruit — gives off a distinctive spicy aroma when bruised or broken. Formerly the dried "berries" were powdered to substitute for several spices, hence the common names pepperbush and wild allspice. (Boiled spicebush bark was also used as a tonic for the ill, and hence that other common name, feverbush.) Spicebush is a scattered understory plant in mostly moist eastern woodlands. The tiny clusters of yellowish flowers line the stems before leaf-out, to be replaced by oblong red drupes — assuming fertilization is available to this usually dioecious species. The fruits are eaten by several gamebirds as well as by flicker, kingbird and great crested flycatcher, catbird, the spot-breasted thrushes, red-eyed vireo, cardinal, and white-throated sparrow.

SUMACS *(Rhus* spp.). We tend to think of sumacs as oversized weeds growing along railroad tracks, but oriental members of the same family provide us with

Many people consider sumacs the poor cousins of shrubs, but they provide winter food for chickadees and other birds.

cashews, pistachio nuts, and high-grade varnishes. Our own native sumacs have also been useful plants: the Indians smoked the leaves, and whites used the tannin obtained from the bark to tan leather. (These leathers were used to make shoes, and it may be that our word "sumac" started out as "shoe-make"; in any case, the proper traditional pronunciation of sumac is not "soo-mack" but "shoe-mack.") Our staghorn *(R. typhina)* and smooth *(R. glabra)* sumacs (both often dioecious) are familiar early invaders of waste places, the former somewhat taller and, of course, more richly "velvety" in stem and fruit head. Both species tend to spread out from a central core via root sprouting, so we are accustomed to seeing circular colonies of sumac. (These clones are self-limiting, dying outward from the center after twenty years or so.) The large cone-shaped fruit clusters may go unnoticed among the brilliant orange-red autumn leaves, but once the leaves are down, the fruit heads — each containing several hundred dry drupes — remain like spires. Squirrels and rabbits bark sumac stems; deer feed on both fruit heads and stems during the winter. And sumac fruits are an important winter emergency food for many birds, especially gamebirds, woodpeckers, jays, crow, black-capped chickadee, mimics, thrushes, several vireos and warblers, cardinal, and several finches.

V I B U R N U M S *(Viburnum* spp.). Among our many shrub viburnums, the following are recommended wildlife plantings, listed in order of decreasing hardiness: nannyberry *(V. lentago),* highbush cranberry *(V. trilobum),* and witherod *(V. cassinoides),* Zone 2; mapleleaf *(V. acerifolium),* Zone 3; northern arrowwood *(V. recognitum),* Zone 4; and southern arrowwood *(V. dentatum),* Zone 5. Mapleleaf viburnum is a low shrub, nannyberry a tall one; the others are intermediate. Viburnums grow under a wide variety of soil conditions, with witherod and the arrowwoods often on moist soils, mapleleaf on dry. All these viburnums are border and woodland plants, and all tolerate some shade; the arrowwoods and mapleleaf thrive in considerable shade. Shrub viburnums typically invade a new area by seed, then spread by root suckers or stem layers. These are attractive plants, with their usually flat-topped clusters of white flowers followed by clusters of round or oblong drupes. These are either dark blue or black except in the case of highbush cranberry, whose fruits are a glorious red. The fruits of most viburnums are available only in the late summer and fall;

those of nannyberry and highbush cranberry persist into or through the winter. Viburnums furnish important winter browse for deer in some areas, and the fruits are utilized (if not often relished) by small mammals as well as by several gamebirds, woodpeckers, mimics, thrushes, waxwing, and several finches.

YEW, CANADA *(Taxus canadensis).* Despite its scientific specific name, this plant is called American yew by some authorities. (Many people avoid the nationality problem altogether by calling it ground hemlock.) Canada yew is a soft-needled low evergreen shrub found in cool, moist, shady places in the eastern and central provinces and most of the northeastern United States. It is not as common now as formerly, apparently because deer and moose sometimes browse it to death; which seems odd, inasmuch as the plant's seed and wilted leaves are reportedly fatal to livestock. The sometimes-dioecious yew produces odd fleshy red fruits, whose single seeds are visible through a hole at the blossom end. Canada yew provides low understory cover, and its fruit — though sparse most years — is eaten by ruffed grouse, mockingbird, robin, wood thrush, and several sparrows.

■ Vines ■

VINES ARE A GOOD FOOD SOURCE FOR WILDLIFE, and vine tangles provide excellent cover. Fences, walls, stumps, and dead snags are both more useful and more attractive with vine cover. And don't burn your shrub and tree cuttings. Pile them up in an odd corner and plant half a dozen vines around the perimeter. In two years you'll have the most luxuriant brush pile imaginable.

AMPELOPSIS, HEARTLEAF *(Ampelopsis cordata). Ampelopsis* is Greek for "grapevine-like," and certainly this plant's attractive cordate leaves resemble one of several standard grape leaf shapes. A ripe ampelopsis berry might be mistaken for a small grape, also, unless you tried to eat it. Some species of birds, however, are known to eat the dry blue fruits, including pheasant, bobwhite, mourning dove, flicker, the mimics, and bluebird.

BITTERSWEET, AMERICAN *(Celastrus scandens).* Unlike ampelopsis, bittersweet produces no tendrils, but rather climbs by twining. Bittersweet can develop inch-diameter stems and climb fifty feet high, but it is usually a smaller plant. Vines sometimes outlive their host trees, or climb dead trees, and people jump to the conclusion that the vines have choked, strangled, or smothered them. Although this is seldom the case, French Canadians know bittersweet as *bourreau des arbres,* "the trees' executioner." The ripened fruits of this usually dioecious species, red berries set off by the orange, split-back capsule cover, are well known as autumn table decorations; you would do well to plant your American bittersweet out of sight from the road. The berries are eaten by gamebirds and several species of songbirds, including mimics, thrushes, and cedar waxwing. The New Jersey study mentioned earlier found cardinals and white-throated sparrows heavily dependent on bittersweet during the early winter months.

C R E E P E R,   V I R G I N I A *(Parthenocissus quinquefolia).* The Greek genus designation means "virgin's ivy," and French Canadians know it as "virgin's vine." Americans call it virgin's (in the form of Virginia) creeper, or simply woodbine. This climbing vine clings to walls and other smooth surfaces with the help of holdfasts, small adhesive disks produced at the tips of the branched tendrils. The palmately compound leaves turn a gorgeous scarlet in fall, making this species of unusual ornamental value for a vine. The blue berries, borne on bright-red stalks, are readily taken by several small mammals as well as by woodpeckers, several flycatchers, tree swallow, chickadees, white-breasted nuthatch, mimics, thrushes, several vireos and warblers, scarlet tanager, and several finches.

G R A P E S *(Vitis* spp.). Of the many wild grapes we may mention three that are common in the Northeast. Riverbank grape *(V. riparia)* is the most northern-hardy of the three; as its common and scientific names suggest, it does well in damp locations. Summer grape *(V. aestivalis)* and fox grape *(V. labrusca)* — the source of many of our cultivated grapes — grow best under moist conditions, but both grow on wet and dry soils as well. These two species are winter-hardy through Zone 5. Wild grapes climb well up into the overstory, the stems of older plants developing into large, Tarzan-style "trunks," whose weight sometimes breaks down smaller trees. Grapes are probably our most valuable wildlife vines. Birds use the shreddy bark in their nests, often located in grape tangles. Deer browse the foliage and stems. And the familiar fruits are utilized by black bear, foxes, opossum, raccoon, skunk, squirrels, gamebirds (wood duck, ruffed grouse, pheasant, turkey), cuckoos, woodpeckers, blue and gray jays, mimics, thrushes, waxwing, vireos, warblers, blackbirds, grackles, orchard and Baltimore orioles, scarlet and summer tanagers, cardinal, and several finches. Probably every non-raptorial terrestrial species of bird in the Northeast has tasted grapes, either in their juicy fall form or as winter "raisins," and A.C. Martin et al. list this vine group as among the top ten woody wildlife plants in the region.

GREENBRIERS (*Smilax* spp.). Greenbriers are mostly southern plants; of the several growing in the Northeast, common *(S. rotundifolia)* and cat *(S. glauca)* greenbriers are widespread and abundant. Both are dioecious, thorny, climbing vines, which tend to spread via new canes produced by underground stems. Of the two species, common greenbrier (also called horsebrier and bullbrier) is somewhat more shade-tolerant, more northern-hardy, and produces heavier thorns. The greenbriers often form tangled, thorny thickets, which make them either an "obnoxious pest" (Fernald) or excellent wildlife cover, depending on your point of view. Greenbriers are browsed by deer and rabbits, and the blue-black berries are eaten by several small mammals as well as by several gamebirds, fish crow, several woodpeckers, mimics, thrushes, cardinal, and several sparrows.

TRUMPETCREEPER, COMMON *(Campsis radicans).* Trumpetcreeper is a conversation-piece plant. There is always something to point out — the huge, orange-red, trumpet-shaped blossoms, the aerial rootlets (by virtue of which the vine climbs), or the six-inch-long, slender pod fruits (catalpa trees are in the same family). Although common trumpetcreeper is seasonally stunning, nobody has ever claimed it is of much interest to wildlife. The notable exception is that post-breeding ruby-throated hummingbirds flock to the blossoms, and the plant has been included here on the basis of that special use.*

■ Ground Covers ■

GROUND COVER PLANTS ARE SO CALLED BECAUSE, spot-planted, they spread (via rhizomes, runners, stolons, creeping branches, or stems) to cover an entire area. Ground covers are handy to have for areas where you either don't want lawn or can't grow it. They are typically used, for example, under large conifers,

---

* *Hummingbirds, hummingbird plantings, and the relationship between them are subjects addressed in Chapter 7.*

where the soil is likely to be moist, shaded, and acidic. All ground covers are attractive, but if you take carte blanche from your nurseryman you'll probably get a sterile ground ivy or something — just as so many people have ended up with privet for hedging. If you can obtain one or several of the following northern species, you'll be feeding wildlife as well as covering ground attractively.

B E A R B E R R Y ,   C O M M O N *(Arctostaphylos uva-ursi)*. Both the wonderfully exotic scientific names translate "bear's grape(s)," as does the common French Canadian name, *raisin d'ours*. The widely distributed bearberry is an attractive plant, with its upright stems, spatula-shaped evergreen leaves, and round, red, mealy drupes. As is so often the case with plants that grow most commonly in the far North, little is known about wildlife utilization of bearberry. Deer are known to browse the foliage, bear and grouse to feed on the "berries." Probably a variety of songbirds and gamebirds would also take the fruits if available.

B U N C H B E R R Y *(Cornus canadensis)*. This miniature dogwood produces, like the flowering dogwood, a showy four-bracted white "flower" in the spring. The blossom stands erect above a whorl of typical dogwood leaves; it is replaced in late summer by a compact cluster of scarlet drupes, formerly made into puddings, and currently eaten by a small variety of gamebirds and songbirds, including thrushes and vireos.

C R O W B E R R Y ,   B L A C K *(Empetrum nigrum)*. *Empetrum* means "upon rock," suggesting the rugged coastal and alpine habitats frequented by crowberry. Its narrow, thick, quarter-inch-long leaves are so tiny they are sometimes called needles, but the plant looks more like a heath than a conifer. This sometimes-dioecious species forms attractive mats, the tiny pink-purple flowers lost among the foliage. The berrylike drupes, however, are conspicuous as they turn from purple to black during the summer. Only snow bunting and pine grosbeak have been determined to consume the fruits to any extent, but one suspects the record is far from complete on this plant. Why, for example, are its two common names crowberry and curlewberry?

P A R T R I D G E B E R R Y *(Mitchella repens)*. Partridgeberry is a lovely evergreen trailing plant, the shiny green leaves shaped like round-cornered triangles. The leaves grow in pairs, as do the delicate white-pink, fragrant, trumpet-shaped flowers. The twin flowers share a double ovary, and the resulting red berrylike drupe has two blossom-end "spots," resulting in the plant's alternate name, two-eyed-berry. French Canadians call the species *pain de perdrix,* or "partridge bread." The fruits are known to be eaten by, in addition to "partridge," bobwhite, turkey, red fox, and skunk. Probably songbirds sample them also.

STRAWBERRY, WILD *(Fragaria virginiana).* Of several forms of native strawberry, *F. virginiana* is the common one, growing throughout the extended Northeast. The often-dioecious wild strawberry is much like the domestic strawberry, and its white flowers and red fruits need no introduction. Ruffed grouse, pheasant, greater prairie chicken, crow, mimics, thrushes, waxwing, and several finches are known to eat strawberries, as do several species of small mammals.

WINTERGREENS *(Gaultheria* spp.). Our two wintergreen-flavored ground covers, teaberry *(G. procumbens)* and creeping snowberry *(G. hispidula),* are members of the heath family. Both have egg-shaped evergreen leaves (tiny in the case of snowberry) and tiny white bell-shaped flowers. Teaberry, also called wintergreen and checkerberry, produces round red fruits. French Canadians know creeping snowberry by the delightful name *oeufs de perdrix* ("partridge eggs"), presumably in honor of its oval white fruits (much whiter, by the way, than the eggs of any North American grouse). Deer, bear, and gamebirds are known to make use of wintergreen plants. Probably some songbirds eat the berrylike fruits as well.

■ Notes on the Charts ■

Hardiness Zone. The figures in the first column key to the accompanying zoned map. When the chart entry is for a genus rather than a species, the Hardiness Zone entry may be multiple: "2 to 4," for example, for ashes. This means that the most northern-hardy ash discussed in the text grows in Zone 2, while the most southerly ash discussed is hardy only as far north as Zone 4. Note that the Hardiness Zone figure does not describe a plant's range, but rather defines the northerly limit of that range. Most of the far-northern plants included here will grow, in proper habitat, south throughout our region.

Shade tolerance. A plant with "good" shade tolerance will grow in heavy shade. One with "fair" tolerance will do well in partial sun, while a plant with "poor" tolerance requires full sun. Some genus entries have, again, multiple designations, indicating that the several species discussed in the text have different shade tolerances. Note that a shade tolerance designation does not define a plant's *ideal* growing situation, but rather indicates how much shade it is likely to tolerate. Generally speaking, a tree or shrub with good shade tolerance will grow faster and fruit earlier and better if allowed some sun; similarly, a plant with fair tolerance will usually do better in full sun. All of which only means that most plants are happy to grow in the sun; the trick is to know what plants will be content, if not happy, to grow in the shade.

Mature height. I have here recorded specific mature-height figures for trees and shrubs. This is obviously more than a little foolhardy, since individual plants of a particular species cannot be expected to mature under all circumstances at closely similar heights. But the alternative is to indicate a mature-height range for each species. This sounds like a reasonable course to follow, but it often proves self-defeating. Under rugged timberline conditions, for example, balsam fir matures as a low, wind-sculpted shrub, while a recent American Forestry Association champion specimen found in Michigan's Porcupine Mountains State Park measures 116 feet. Thus an accurate mature-height range for *Abies balsamea* would read "2 to 116." The entry here for the species — 50 — means that an ordinary balsam fir, growing somewhere near the middle of the species' range, under conditions neither optimal nor marginal, will likely mature at fifty feet, more or less. These expected mature-height figures will tell you, at the very least, whether the tree you are considering is small, medium, or large, whether the shrub is low, medium, or tall; and this is often an important consideration in terms of space requirements or landscaping effects. Most genus entries rate multiple designations. The designation for ashes — "50 to 90" — is not, again, a range; it means that the smallest ash discussed in the text matures at about fifty feet, the largest at about ninety feet. (Here, as elsewhere on the charts, the text will indicate which species is which.)

Soil moisture requirements. This rubric is pretty much self-explanatory. Here there are often multiple entries for individual species. Northern white cedar rates a "wet to dry" designation, meaning that the species grows under the full range of soil moisture possibilities.

Tolerates dry, sandy soil; Salt-tolerant; City-"hardy." These rubrics are self-explanatory. The first two were developed with reference to sandy, salty coastal habitats. But the first is also useful as an indication of what is likely to grow in poor, sterile soils inland, and the second may be helpful when it comes to planting along roads in those provinces and northern states which follow the unfortunate practice of heavy winter road salting. All three columns provide conservative lists. Undoubtedly more plants belong in each column, but, as relatively little work has been done in these areas, we simply don't know what they are.

Season(s) fruit/seed available. This column indicates when a plant's primary food is likely to be available to wildlife. (Some species also provide important secondary food, such as buds, often at different times of the year; outstanding examples are indicated in the text.) Many plants' fruit availability season is that period when the fruit is ripe and on the plant, but this isn't always the case. Beech nuts and the fruits of some hawthorns, for example, remain important forage on the ground right through winter, even into spring. Of course, some wildlife species can utilize fruits or nuts on a tree but cannot do so under two feet of snow; for other species, the opposite applies. Nor can the seasonal periods indicated here be guaranteed. If the beech crop is poor, or if, for a variety of reasons, there is great wildlife pressure on the beech mast in the fall, then beech nuts will not be an important food that winter in that area. Members of a given genus tend to mature similar fruits at about the same time. When there are important species differences in this regard, the chart entry will so indicate.

I have omitted one feature often included on planting charts. I have not assigned plants an "ornamental value" rating.* Although it is obvious that some plants are showier than others, I am uncomfortable about categorizing them as Beautiful, Middling Plain, and Downright Ugly, which is really what an ornamental-value-rating system does. Our business here, at any rate, is with *food* values rather than ornamental values. I suspect most people interested in birds will be more than willing to allow space to an undistinguished shrub or tree with little to recommend it except that it sometimes holds a warbling vireo's nest, or has proved an indigo bunting's favorite singing perch, or attracts siskins or waxwings in the winter.

---

* *This information can, if desired, be culled from field guides, or found in list form in various books. Leon C. Snyder's* Trees and Shrubs for Northern Gardens *(1980), for example, lists plants under such rubrics as "showy flowers," "fragrant flowers," "brilliant fall color," "colored fruits," "unusual shapes," even "interesting winter bark."*

I HAVE RANSACKED NUMEROUS DOCUMENTS while compiling these charts. Both the text and the charts have benefited from many of them, including bulletins and pamphlets from various university and governmental extension services, the Wildlife Management Institute, the U.S. Forestry Service, and, especially, the U.S. Department of Agriculture's Soil Conservation Service. A variety of books — field guides to trees and shrubs, treatises on silvics and the history of the eastern forest, tomes on plant propagation, bird-attracting manuals — have proved useful. M.L. Fernald's *Gray's Manual of Botany* (8th edition, corrected printing 1987) is, of course, a standard reference for the region. Three books address the question of wildlife and plant foods directly and at length, and these have been most helpful of all. Alexander C. Martin, Herbert S. Zim, and Arnold L. Nelson's *American Wildlife & Plants: A Guide to Wildlife Food Habits* (1951) sums up what had been learned about wildlife food habits by midcentury, largely on the basis of government-agency stomach analyses. The book treats the whole of the United States, and attacks the subject both by animal and plant species. Not all birds or plants are treated; of those that are, some receive impressively thorough treatment, others not, depending on the number of observations and stomachs available for analysis. The book has inevitable shortcomings, but it remains a valuable source of plant-food data for mammals, fish, amphibians, and reptiles as well as for birds.

Two books with more restricted focuses are the USDA Forest Service General Technical Report NE-9, entitled *Shrubs and Vines for Northeastern Wildlife* (1974), compiled by John D. Gill and William M. Healy; and Richard M. DeGraaf and Gretchin M. Witman's *Trees, Shrubs, and Vines for Attracting Birds: A Manual for the Northeast* (1979). DeGraaf and Witman treat some 160 species of plants, Gill and Healy's authors a little over half that number in more detail. Both books describe the plants, treat range, habitat, and life history matters, and discuss propagation techniques at some length. The former sums up bird and mammal uses of the various plants; the latter lists bird species believed to use the plants for food, cover, and nesting. Both books have been compiled after an extensive examination of the scattered literature and the resulting wealth of information has greatly benefited this chapter.

■ TREES ■

	Hardiness Zone	Shade tolerance	Mature height (feet)	Soil moisture requirements
Ashes (*Fraxinus* spp.)	2 to 4	fair to poor	50 to 90	wet to dry
Aspens (*Populus* spp.)	1 to 4	poor	50	moist to dry
Beech, American (*Fagus grandifolia*)	3	good	75	moist
Birches (*Betula* spp.)	2 to 4	fair to poor	30 to 75	wet to dry
Cedar, northern white (*Thuja occidentalis*)	2	good	50	wet to dry
Cedar, eastern red (*Juniperus virginiana*)	4	fair	50	moist to dry
Cherries (*Prunus* spp.)	2 to 4	fair to poor	25 to 60	moist to dry
Crabapples (*[Pyrus] Malus* spp.)	2 to 5	fair	10 to 50	moist to well-drained
Dogwood flowering (*Cornus florida*)	5	good	35	well-drained
Elm, American (*Ulmus americana*)	3	fair	100	moist to well-drained
Fir, balsam (*Abies balsamea*)	3	good	50	moist
Hackberry (*Celtis occidentalis*)	4	fair	50	moist to dry
Hemlock, eastern (*Tsuga canadensis*)	4	good	70	moist to well-drained
Hickories (*Carya* spp.)	5	fair	50 to 75	well-drained
Holly, American (*Ilex opaca*)	6	good	45	moist to well-drained
Hop-hornbeam, American (*Ostrya virginiana*)	4	good	30	moist to well-drained
Hornbeam, American (*Carpinus caroliniana*)	4	good	30	moist to well-drained
Maples (*Acer* spp.)	3 to 4	good to fair	60 to 80	wet to dry
Mountain-ash, American (*[Pyrus] Sorbus americana*)	2	fair	30	moist to dry
Mulberries (*Morus* spp.)	5	fair	50	moist to well-drained

Tolerates dry, sandy soil	Salt-tolerant	City-"hardy"	Season(s) fruit/seed available	
red			fall/winter	Ashes
X	quaking		winter/spring	Aspens
			fall/winter	Beech, American
gray	white		fall/winter	Birches
	X		fall/early winter	Cedar, northern white
X	X		fall/winter/spring	Cedar, eastern red
black	black		summer/fall	Cherries
		some spp.	fall/winter/ early spring	Crabapples
		X	fall	Dogwood, flowering
		X	spring	Elm, American
			fall/winter	Fir, balsam
X		X	fall/winter	Hackberry
			fall/winter	Hemlock, eastern
pignut			fall/early winter	Hickories
	X		fall/winter/spring	Holly, American
			fall/early winter	Hop-hornbeam, American
	X		fall	Hornbeam, American
boxelder		sugar, Norway	variable (see text)	Maples
			fall/winter	Mountain-ash, American
	X	white (some var.'s)	summer	Mulberries

▪ TREES ▪

	Hardiness Zone	Shade tolerance	Mature height (feet)	Soil moisture requirements
Oaks (*Quercus* spp.)	4 to 5	fair to poor	80	moist to dry
Persimmon, common (*Diospyros virginiana*)	6	poor	50	moist to dry
Pines (*Pinus* spp.)	2 to 5	fair to poor	50 to 100	wet to dry
Sassafras (*Sassafras albidum*)	5	poor	35	moist to dry
Serviceberries (*Amelanchier* spp.)	3 to 4	fair	25 to 40	wet to well-drained
Spruces (*Picea* spp.)	2	good	30 to 70	wet to dry
Sweetgum (*Liquidambar styraciflua*)	6	poor	100	moist to well-drained
Tuliptree (*Liriodendron tulipifera*)	5	poor	120	moist to well-drained
Tupelo, black (*Nyssa sylvatica*)	5	poor	60	wet to well-drained

▪ VINES ▪

	Hardiness Zone	Shade tolerance	Soil moisture requirements
Ampelopsis, heartleaf (*Ampelopsis cordata*)	5	fair	moist to well-drained
Bittersweet, American (*Celastrus scandens*)	3	fair	well-drained to dry
Creeper, Virginia (*Parthenocissus quinquefolia*)	4	fair	moist to dry
Grapes (*Vitis* spp.)	3 to 5	fair to poor	wet to dry
Greenbriers (*Smilax* spp.)	5 to 6	fair	moist to dry
Trumpetcreeper, common (*Campsis radicans*)	5	fair	moist to well-drained

▪ GROUND COVERS ▪

	Hardiness Zone	Shade tolerance	Soil moisture requirements
Bearberry, common (*Arctostaphylos uva-ursi*)	2	fair	well-drained to dry
Bunchberry (*Cornus canadensis*)	2	good	moist to well-drained
Crowberry, black (*Empetrum nigrum*)	2	fair	moist
Partridgeberry (*Mitchella repens*)	3	good	moist to well-drained
Strawberry, wild (*Fragaria virginiana*)	2	fair	well-drained to dry
Wintergreens (*Gaultheria* spp.)	2	good	wet to well-drained

Tolerates dry, sandy soil	Salt-tolerant	City-"hardy"	Season(s) fruit/seed available	
scarlet	white, n. red	pin, n. red	fall/winter	Oaks
	X		fall	Persimmon, common
X	pitch		fall/winter; all year: red, pitch	Pines
X	X		fall	Sassafras
			summer	Serviceberries
white	white, Colorado	Colorado	fall/winter	Spruces
	X	X	fall	Sweetgum
		X	fall/early winter	Tuliptree
			fall	Tupelo, black

Tolerates dry, sandy soil	Salt-tolerant	City-"hardy"	Season(s) fruit available	
		X	fall	Ampelopsis, heartleaf
		X	fall/early winter	Bittersweet, American
X	X		fall/winter	Creeper, Virginia
			late summer/fall/winter	Grapes
			fall/winter	Greenbriers
		X	flower: midsummer/early fall	Trumpetcreeper, common
X	X		late summer/fall/winter	Bearberry, common
			fall	Bunchberry
	X		midsummer/fall/winter	Crowberry, black
			late summer/fall/winter	Partridgeberry
			summer	Strawberry, wild
			fall (snowberry); fall/winter/spring (teaberry)	Wintergreens

■ SHRUBS ■

	Hardiness Zone	Shade tolerance	Mature height (feet)	Soil moisture requirements
Alders (*Alnus* spp.)	3 to 5	fair	15	wet to moist
Autumn-olive (*Elaeagnus umbellata*)	4	fair	12	moist to dry
Barberry, Japanese (*Berberis thunbergii*)	5	fair	5	moist to dry
Bayberry, northern (*Myrica pensylvanica*)	4	poor	8	wet to dry
Blueberries (*Vaccinium* spp.)	2 to 4	fair to poor	2 to 12	moist to dry
Brambles (*Rubus* spp.)	3 to 4	fair to poor	1 to 9	wet to dry
Chokeberries (*[Pyrus] Aronia* spp.)	2 to 5	fair	5 to 10	wet to dry
Currant, American black (*Ribes americanum*)	3	fair	5	moist to dry
Dogwoods (*Cornus* spp.)	2 to 6	good to fair	10	wet to dry
Elders (*Sambucus* spp.)	2 to 4	fair to poor	10	wet to well-drained
Firethorn (*Pyracantha coccinea*)	6	fair	12	moist to well-drained
Gooseberry, pasture (*Ribes cynosbati*)	3	good	5	moist to dry
Hawthorns (*Crataegus* spp.)	most: 5	poor	10 to 30	moist to well-drained
Hazels (*Corylus* spp.)	3 to 4	fair	9	well-drained
Hollies (*Ilex* spp.)	3 to 5	fair	10	wet to dry
Honeysuckles (*Lonicera* spp.)	3 to 5	good to fair	5 to 14	moist to dry
Huckleberries (*Gaylussacia* spp.)	2 to 6	fair to poor	1½ to 6	wet to dry
Juniper, common (*Juniperus communis*)	2	poor	4	well-drained to dry
Roses (*Rosa* spp.)	2 to 5	poor	4 to 10	wet to dry
Russian-olive (*Elaeagnus angustifolia*)	3	poor	20	well-drained to dry
Serviceberries (*Amelanchier* spp.)	3 to 4	fair	5 to 30	wet to dry
Snowberries (*Symphoricarpos* spp.)	3 to 4	fair	4 to 6	moist to dry
Spicebush, common (*Lindera benzoin*)	5	good	12	moist
Sumacs (*Rhus* spp.)	4	fair to poor	10 to 15	well-drained to dry
Viburnums (*Viburnum* spp.)	2 to 5	fair to good	5 to 20	moist to dry
Yew, Canada (*Taxus canadensis*)	2	good	3	moist

Tolerates dry, sandy soil	Salt-tolerant	City-"hardy"	Season(s) fruit/seed available	
			fall/early winter	Alders
	X	X	fall/early winter	Autumn-olive
X		X	fall/winter/early spring	Barberry, Japanese
X	X		all year	Bayberry, northern
lowbush			summer	Blueberries
many spp.			summer	Brambles
	red	red	fall/winter	Chokeberries
			summer	Currant, American black
		gray	late summer/fall	Dogwoods
		American	summer/early fall	Elders
		X	fall/winter	Firethorn
X			summer	Gooseberry, pasture
		most spp.	most: fall/winter/ early spring	Hawthorns
			fall/winter	Hazels
inkberry	inkberry	inkberry	fall/winter	Hollies
Morrow	tatarian	most spp.	amur: fall/winter; others: summer	Honeysuckles
black			summer/early fall	Huckleberries
X	X		all year	Juniper, common
many spp.	some spp.	most spp.	fall/winter (most spp.)	Roses
X	X		fall/winter	Russian-olive
		many spp.	summer	Serviceberries
coralberry		both spp.	fall/winter	Snowberries
		X	late summer/fall	Spicebush, common
X			fall/winter/spring	Sumacs
	witherod	most spp.	late summer/fall to fall/winter/spr.	Viburnums
			summer	Yew, Canada

USDA HARDINESS ZONE MAP

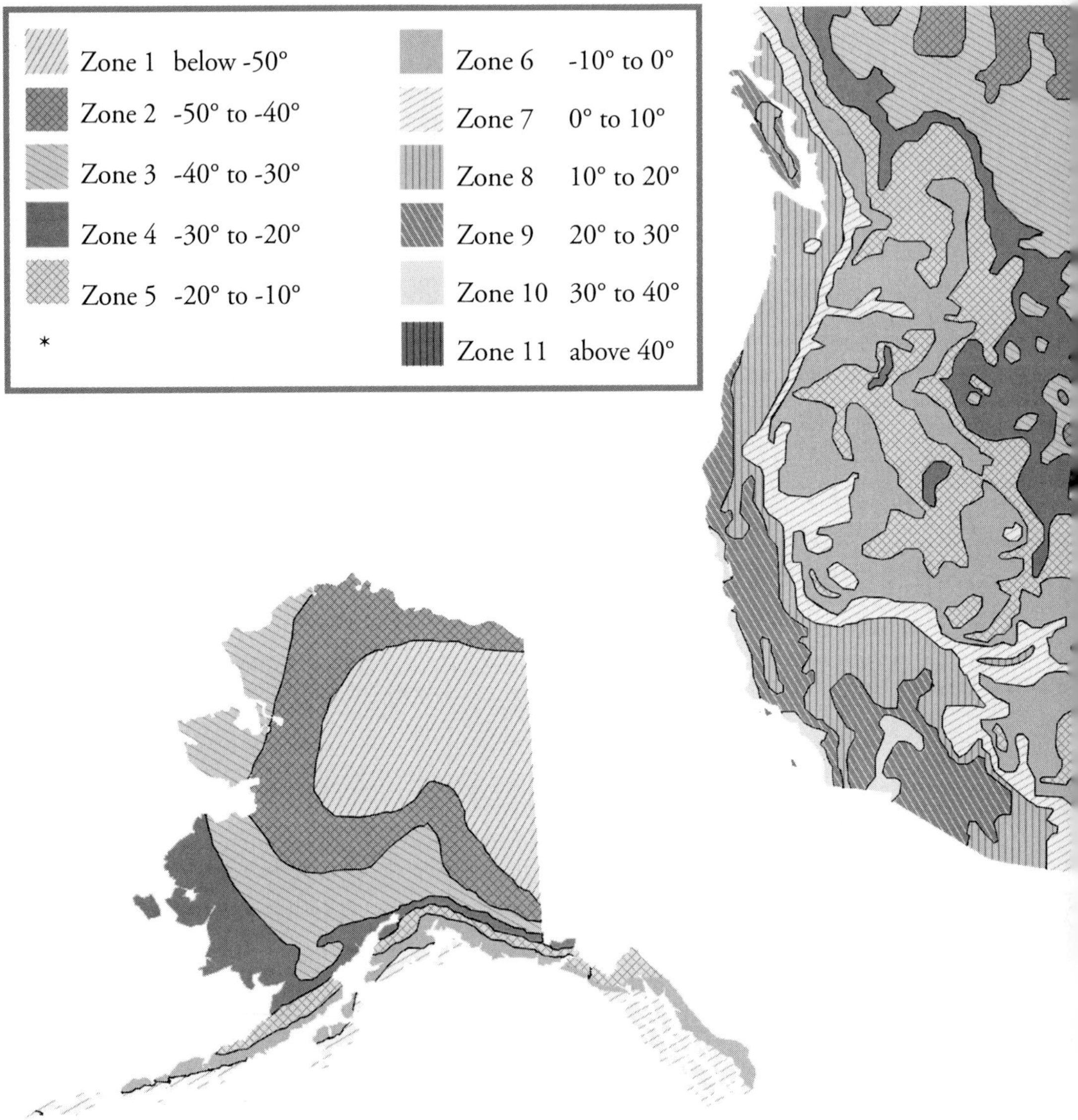

Zone 1 below -50°

Zone 2 -50° to -40°

Zone 3 -40° to -30°

Zone 4 -30° to -20°

Zone 5 -20° to -10°

*

Zone 6 -10° to 0°

Zone 7 0° to 10°

Zone 8 10° to 20°

Zone 9 20° to 30°

Zone 10 30° to 40°

Zone 11 above 40°

* Approximate range of average annual minimum temperature (degrees Fahrenheit).

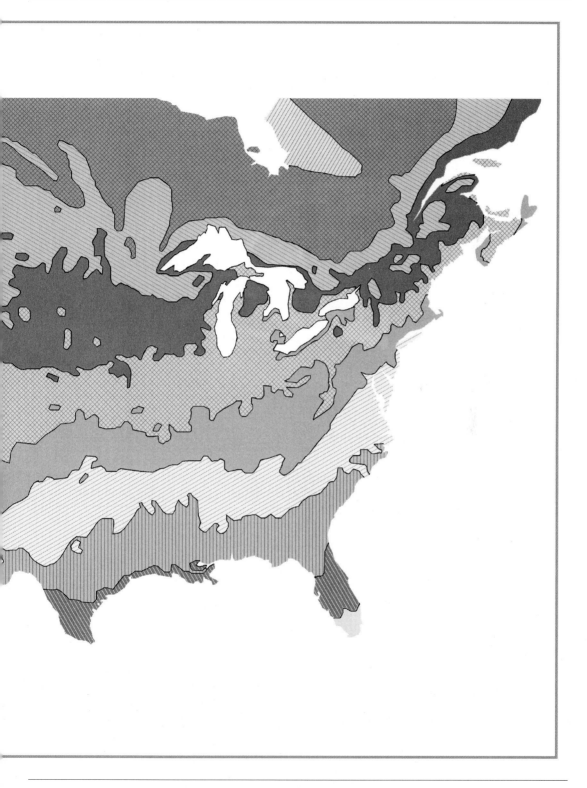

Big Day Doings

*1. All teammates must sign the pledge, signifying, on their honor, that
(a) all rules were read at the count start, (b) all rules were complied with,
(c) all rules were reviewed again by all at the count end, at which time
(d) any questionable identifications were deleted and the pledge was signed by all.*

*2. Your pledge also attests that you (a) uninterruptedly maintained direct
conversational contact (no radios) with every other teammate during all birding
and travel periods, (b) made every effort for every person to identify every
reported species, and (c) made your count in a single calendar day.*
    — from the American Birding Association's Big Day Rules

SPRING IS THE SEASON notorious for prompting gloriously mad, exces-
sive behavior, and the birding institution called the Big Day probably has
more in common with the Maypole of Merry Mount than you might at first
imagine. The point of the Big Day, usually a team event, is simply to identify the
largest possible number of species of birds in a twenty-four-hour period within predetermined geographical limits. The state is the operative arena for most Big Days,

but there are those who also undertake County Big Days, Walking Big Days, and One-Mile Big Days. (A man who apparently found his state Big Day too restrictive recently chartered a Lear jet and set up a Texas, Arizona, and California Big Day; but the weather turned against him, airport problems delayed him, and his Really Big Day ended with a list little larger than the current U.S. One-Mile Big Day record of 102 species.) Most Big Days are scheduled for the peak of spring migration, when most of an area's breeding species are around and singing, and the likelihood of adding migrating northern breeders is greatest.

The official American Birding Association-sanctioned Big Day in Vermont is fairly new. The first one was run in 1975 in the northern part of the state. Two years later, a crack team of four southern Vermont birders challenged the northern team, and the annual Big Day intrastate rivalry was born, the two teams competing with one another as well as against the standing state record. I joined the northern team for a subsequent Big Day, set for May 21. Based on journal notes, here is how it went for that side.

THE NORTH STRAGGLES into Frank Oatman's place in East Craftsbury during the evening of the 20th, Wayne Scott from Middlebury in the Champlain Valley, George and Walter Ellison from White River Junction in the Connecticut River Valley. I'm going along, I offer, for purposes of quality control. The response is a round of hisses and catcalls. (Not only do these expert birders need no help, it is decided that, under the circumstances of the competition, it would be unfair to allow me to offer any; I am relegated to the role of mere journalist, a restriction I strive to honor during the course of the day.) Over a spaghetti and asparagus supper, we assess our prospects (not good — it's been a bad waterbird spring, and nobody has detected much migratory action the last few days) and the weather (not promising — the radio says 70 percent chance of rain). We settle down to catch some rest shortly after 10:00 p.m.

1:30 a.m. Alarm clocks announce the Big Day. A breakfast of cold cereal proves inadequate, and a skillet of scrambled eggs is whipped up. The weather doesn't look at all bad; maybe the rain will hold off. This Big Day, like many "insider" birding events, has been scheduled for a weekday. Too much traffic on weekends; too many

---

Big Day tactics include birding from cars (page 134).
A great horned owl (page 135) is always a challenge to spot.

people hanging around the lakes, asking questions, hassling the birds. Much serious birding is done during the week, and it follows that few serious birders, especially of the younger generation, hold conventional jobs, which can interfere alarmingly with a birding career. Some birders live on nothing, and decline work altogether. Others take jobs which conflict minimally with birding. One man I knew in California dealt blackjack in a gambling parlor all night and birded all day; he seems not to have slept at all.

Only one member of the current northern team holds what most people would call a regular job. George is a district court judge, and has wangled a couple of days off. His son, Walter, just graduated from college, hasn't decided whether to apply to graduate schools or bird around the world for a year. (Walter is wearing his lucky sweatshirt, decorated with a large Ross' gull in acrylics, commemorative of his co-discovery of the famous Ross' gull off the Massachusetts coast several years ago.) While working on an M.S. degree at Middlebury College, Wayne serves as a teaching assistant in the biology department. Frank, on retainer with a bird-tour company, leads groups to such exotic places as New Zealand and Guatemala. Like Wayne, he is working on a master's paper with an ornithological subject.

Breakfast done, the gear is loaded into the station wagon, and George climbs behind the wheel.

2:36 On the road, heading for the Island Pond area of the Northeast Kingdom for warblers and boreal specialties. The first wildlife we see in the headlights is a black cat. Its decision not to cross our path is roundly cheered. The troops relax in the darkness. Walter has recently returned from a birding trip to Mexico; he and Frank, a Mexican specialist, are talking about fan-tailed warblers, bumblebee hummingbirds, and bat falcons. Frank recalls a high point of his birding career, a dawn chorus of rare slate-gray solitaires on a Mexican mountain top.

2:46 Quick stop at Caspian Lake to play the loon tape. No loon replies. Back on the road, we spot another black cat, and this one crosses the road ahead of us. Groans. A second bad omen. (The first: Wayne has forgotten his tape recorder, and for some reason Frank's will play at half-volume only. This will be a problem.)

3:21 Road stop produces our first bird, a great horned owl calling in the distance. A probable Lincoln's sparrow sings in the distance, but a troublesome wind prevents positive identification.

3:37 Road stop. Things are still quiet, but a kingbird buzzes somewhere down the road. The moon is rising.

3:57 We arrive at the town of Island Pond, over which the barn swallows are already chattering.

4:05 Stop on Route 105 outside town, at what is probably the best whip-poor-will location in the state. Two are calling, as well as several common yellowthroats, a swamp sparrow, and a white-throated sparrow. From overhead comes the otherworldly sound of a winnowing snipe, courtship flying in the dark sky. Things are tuning up.

4:10 Road stop. From high over a field we cannot see comes that peculiar jumble of chippering notes identifying a woodcock at the top of his remarkable courtship flight. A catbird and a song sparrow are just beginning a long day of singing.

4:15 Road stop. First robin. Several tree swallows are flying and hollering. We try to hoot up a barred owl. No response.

4:21 Road stop. The down-spiraling veery song issues from a wet woods. Another snipe. A *peent*-ing note locates a strutting woodcock. More white-throats singing.

4:32 We leave a logging road off the highway to walk through spruce and fir woods around Moose Bog. Buxton's Pond is lovely under cloudy half-light from the moon. Walter's barred owl call echoes grandly off the two unnamed mountains beyond the pond. Singing yellowthroats are unperturbed, and no barred owl replies. Singing yellow-rumped warbler and golden-crowned kinglet are identified.

4:43 A wooded swamp along the logging road produces a Nashville warbler and a northern waterthrush.

5:00 We hit the trail into Moose Bog. Veeries are singing everywhere, and warblers are getting into the act: blackburnians, Nashville, Canada, magnolia. Fresh moose tracks and grouse dusting holes decorate the trail. From spruces to the left comes a hoarse, burry *chick-a-dee* call. Boreal chickadee! That's one the South will never get! Wayne flushes a large bird off the trail. Maybe a spruce grouse. (The team is getting hungry for boreal specialties.) Ruffed grouse will rocket away when flushed; spruce grouse will likely fly up into a nearby tree. The North fades into the woods to search for a perched grouse in the predawn half-light. No luck. Grackles fly overhead out of Moose Bog. The birds are coming fast and thick now. Four cedar waxwings, scarce in the state this spring, fly over calling. We hear the hoarse-robin song of the scarlet tanager, the odd protracted conversational song of the ruby-crowned kinglet, the *chebunk* of the yellow-bellied flycatcher. Two chimney swifts chatter overhead. (Do they feed this far from Island Pond, or will they nest in isolated cabin chimneys or hollow trees in the area?) A ruffed grouse drums. Frank plays a black-backed three-toed woodpecker drum; no response. The bog has been pro-

**Overlooking common species is the bane of Big Days,
but there is little chance of missing the vocal gray catbird.**

ductive, but boreal chickadee remains our only northern specialty. No three-toed woodpecker, no spruce grouse, no olive-sided flycatcher.

5:45 The troops emerge from Moose Bog. The sun is just lighting up the tops of the tallest spruces. The North has identified thirty-some species (it's bad luck to begin toting up too early) by sunup. Of these we have *seen* perhaps four or five. (This may suggest one reason many birders, especially the young turks, don't like the term "birdwatcher.")

6:10 We drive into the other side of Moose Bog. Cowbirds. A crow calls. A short walk into the bog itself. We go in quietly, hoping for a few ducks or shorebirds. Nothing on the water. Red-winged blackbirds are active, and a rose-breasted grosbeak sings from the woods beyond the water. The sweet jumbled song of the northern-nesting Lincoln's sparrow rings out from the far end of the bog. Our first heron, a great blue, flaps over.

6:27 Heading back out of the bog. Hold it! A small finch just landed in that fir — white-winged crossbill? Sorry: purple finch.

6:37 Returning for a second pass at Buxton's Pond, windows open for songs. An argument develops over a trill picked up from a roadside tree. Some say dark-eyed junco, others chipping sparrow. It sounds like sparrow, but the habitat is junco. Walter insists the road creates enough edge for chipping sparrow; the others doubt it. I hike back from the next stop to check: chipping sparrow. (So much for habitat birding.) Cape May warbler and winter wren are singing. And then a distant but unmistakable *hic*-THREE-*beers* brings a general sigh of relief. Finally an olive-sided flycatcher.

7:00 Buxton's Pond is better this time. Singing solitary vireo; bay-breasted, Cape May, and blackpoll warblers. Flicker and hairy are added to the woodpecker list. A raven flies overhead. A red-breasted nuthatch calls, and, in the distance, the sad descending whistle of a wood-pewee. A small drab shorebird flies stiff-winged along the pond edge: add one spotted sandpiper.

7:15 Back on the highway, listening out the windows as we head for the logging road birders call "Three-toed Road." The list continues to grow. Parula warbler. A kingfisher rattles. Chestnut-sided warbler. We stop to listen, and pick up a singing alder flycatcher. Then a distant drumming woodpecker — a medium-length drum, the taps slowing down at the end. *Three-toed!* The troops head into the ferns and spruces, hoping for a glimpse. The three-toed drum is played on the tape recorder, but the woodpecker leads us deeper into the woods. The team reluctantly gives up the chase, and heads back for the car. Black-backed three-toed woodpecker. Good bird! We'll take it!

7:30 Back in motion. We collect red-eyed vireo and black-and-white warbler, but there is rising concern over still-missing gray jay, rusty blackbird, and mourning warbler.

7:50 Driving along Three-toed Road, we pick up the ascending buzz of a black-throated blue warbler, and the first of scores of singing Baltimore orioles. The team is discussing how much time to spend trying for gray jay, rusty blackbird, and mourning warbler when, on cue, comes the latter's welcome *churry! churry! churry!* Then, from the other side of the road, the electronic spiraling song of Swainson's thrush.

8:10 We come suddenly upon a vast area in the throes of clear-cutting. Mordant jokes about forestry-management practices. At least it'll be good mourning warbler habitat in a few years. But the day is coming along, and the troops are cheering up. The total count is low at this point, but we're doing well on northern specialties, now lacking only spruce grouse, gray jay, and rusty blackbird. The common stuff will be picked up later. It is pointed out that we're just about warblered out. We lack only pine, cerulean, golden-winged, and Louisiana waterthrush among possible warblers, and the first three have been scouted and staked out at later stops.

8:19 We stop in good habitat to play the gray jay tape. Nothing. We stop again, play the tape, and stare into the woods. (Unlike most birds, the gray jay seldom has the decency to *answer* a tape. More likely it will materialize at the forest margin, take a look, and disappear in total silence.) Again the tape. Come on, gray jay! Nothing.

8:28 We run up on a logging truck being loaded. We can't get around, and can't afford a half-hour wait. Damn! George manages to get the car turned around, and we head back for the highway.

8:40 Wayne drops off, oblivious to team remonstrances.

8:44 Almost hit by a logging truck. Wayne wakes up.

8:48 Stop to listen to red-eyed vireo songs, hoping to detect the similar song of the Philadelphia vireo. No such luck. We pick up our first phoebe.

9:00 Heading back to Island Pond. Field sparrows are scarce in the Champlain Valley this spring, so we stop along the highway where the bird has nested previously. No field sparrow, but we pick up goldfinch and a singing, skylarking bobolink.

9:09 Since willow flycatcher isn't back at Dead Creek yet, we make special stops for that and field sparrow. A brown thrasher sings along the highway, and a snipe perches forlornly on the Canadian National Railroad track.

9:17 Our first starling. Hyperbolic acclaim.

9:21 Stop at a dry field for field sparrow. Success this time, as the progressively faster monotonic bouncing-ball song rings from somewhere upslope.

9:35 We pull up to the back side of Island Pond to check the water. A loon floats on the far side. Good. A killdeer starts and stops on the bathhouse lawn. A house wren sings.

9:43 Second swing through the town of Island Pond produces more new birds. House sparrow. (Congratulations all around.) Rock dove. (More congratulations.) As we pull into a gas station, Wayne spots cliff swallow nests under the eaves of a restaurant across the street. A quick check of the barn swallows hawking insects overhead reveals several cliffs among them. But the gas station, the only one open in town, has a sign saying $3 limit, and the attendant won't even sell us that: "Sorry, regular customers only." Fuming, the team drives on. "Why didn't you pull rank on the guy, George? Haul him into your court." ("The prisoner, having been found

guilty of refusing to sell gas to the presiding judge and other Big Day birders, shall be taken from this court to a place of lawful execution. . . .")

9:56 The North stops at Cathy's Corner Restaurant for pie (renowned among area birders) and coffee.

10:20 Back in the car, having left Cathy's short by three chocolate-cream, three pecan, and one each pumpkin and butterscotch-cream, we head northwest for Lake Memphremagog.

A stop at Seymour Lake produces only a ring-billed gull. But, walking back to the car, George spots three hawks soaring over a distant ridge. One large and two small buteos; likely a red-tail and two broad-wings. We hold the glasses on the large bird, which finally turns, showing wing windows and tail barring. Red-*shouldered* and two broad-wings. Good — we'll pick up red-tails in the Champlain Valley. Or right up the road, where George and Walter know of a red-tail nest in a large birch high up a cliff off the highway. We stop and look. No adult in sight. Maybe we can see young in the nest. Scopes are trotted out. Nothing moving. While waiting, a small flock of songbirds flies east way up along the top of the ridge. One vote each for evening grosbeak and cedar waxwing. Much discussion of tail-body proportions and wing-flap rhythm. The birds are all but out of sight before the rest of the team get a look, and there are no replays in this business. No consensus, no bird.

10:57 Hallelujah! A gas station happy to serve foreigners. The French Canadian woman not only has gas, she has a bird nesting behind the store. What kind of bird? She doesn't know the English name. *Les hirondelles* she calls them. Sure enough: she lifts a protective metal cover to reveal a tree swallow nest perched on a propane tank!

11:03 On the road for Memphremagog again. It begins to mist. Don't look now, but it looks awfully like rain in the west.

11:05 Stop at a plowed and freshly harrowed field to look for horned larks. The farmer and his son stare at our car from the field as we stare at their field from the car. Good — there's a lark. And a second on the other side of the road. A savannah sparrow sings somewhere down the fence line.

11:15 Newport on Lake Memphremagog. Our weather luck is holding; the pavement is wet, but it isn't raining now. We pull up on a residential street with plenty

---

**The white-throated sparrow's plaintive *Old Sam Peabody,*
Peabody, Peabody rings through northern forests.**

of apple trees and lilacs, hoping for a ruby-throated hummingbird. A warbling vireo sings its lazy, repetitive warble from the shade trees, and purple martins are hawking insects over the neighborhood. But no hummingbird.

11:30 Newport Beach. A quick scan: nothing new. The troops are heading back to the car when Walter points out several inconspicuous shorebirds far down the beach. The banded bird is a semipalmated plover; the others are small sandpipers, but which "peep" are they? A quick stalk down the beach. Fairly brown, and, yes, light legs: four least sandpipers. We move closer to double-check; there may be a semi-palmated sandpiper among them. But all have light legs: least sandpipers. The mood is subdued as the North returns to the car; careless haste has nearly cost us two shorebirds.

11:44 Frank has a pine warbler staked out in mature pines on Indian Point. Several great crested flycatchers are *weep-weep*-ing, but where's the warbler? We case the area and are about to give up when the bird trills once. Another close call.

12:18 p.m. Checking various lookout points on the lake. Frank plays tapes for bitterns and rails at the mouth of the St. John's River. Often a productive stop, we find nothing new today.

12:40 Four gulls are perched on a rock well out in the lake. Scopes show two larger than the others. If the smaller are ring-billed, the larger are almost certainly herring, but the plumages are atypical. Much discussion about immature gull plumages and bill colors. Big Day objectives urge that time not be wasted on these gulls. But birders are birders, and the troops hate to leave this identification problem unsolved. The bills on the larger birds seem too small for herring. What about Thayer's? Reluctantly we give it up, and go back to work.

12:58 A notorious Memphremagog birding stop. Driving down the lane by the Old Lady's summer house, everybody caws in screeching falsetto: "What are you boys doing?" "This is private property!" "You get out of here!" Most owners are happy to let birders use their property briefly once intentions are stated, but the Old Lady is less than rational, and she has long been vigilant to evict birders even from property not her own. I was here with Wayne and Frank a few years ago when the old termagant was neutralized. We had searched our wallets for official-looking cards, selecting one with small print. Wayne strode over to the shrieking, rake-waving woman in his most official manner, flashed the card, and informed her that we were scanning the lake for narcotics smugglers out of Canada (the U.S.–Canadian border bisects Memphremagog to the north). Suddenly the lioness was a lamb, urging us to come back often and help curb crime of various sorts on the lake. Birders have been welcome ever since; presumably she associates the binoculars and scopes with the forces of law and order. Unhappily, this day we find no new species to record.

1:22 Headed for our last stop on Lake Memphremagog. A lone black duck, winging along the far shore, is bird No. 100. And South Bay Marsh proves fantastic. The birds are, as birders say, falling nicely. Two minutes into the marsh, walking the railroad track, an American bittern flushes. Our first black terns appear almost simultaneously, and then the sneezy *fitz-bew* note of the willow flycatcher completes a slam on flycatchers. No way the South can match that! Wayne calls a common gallinule, but the bird slips out of sight among the reeds before anyone else can find it. (This is not good; Big Day purists play by the 95 percent rule, which dictates that each member of the team identify 95 percent of the entire team list.) We continue out the roadbed, playing rail tapes. Finally — a half-hearted response from a sora. Things are looking up as we head back out of the marsh, and, to cap a very productive stop, the mad *kek-kek-kek* note delivers gallinule to the rest of the team.

2:14 The North pulls up at a Newport deli for lunch. George and I have brought honest-to-god food from home, but the others are more typical birders. Preoccupied with more important matters, most serious birders — no matter how "organic" in belief — habitually patronize delis and fast-food joints when hunger interferes with birding. Frank turns up with a three-course meal, consisting of a sour vinegar, olive, and hot-pepper salad, potato salad, and a box of donuts. Walter returns with potato salad and Fritos, Wayne with blueberry yogurt, Fritos, and a Coke.

2:30 We park at a marsh outside Newport to eat. Frank hangs his half-volume tape recorder out the window, secured by a strap over the door lock, and an obliging Virginia rail answers halfway through his olive and hot-pepper salad. The list of species is read off; the team wants to see what we lack, and to decide where to go next. As we take stock, we find some good news and some bad news. The good news is that the Northeast Kingdom has yielded over a hundred species. That's better than it produced the year the North set the standing state Big Day record. The bad news is that we have been too long about it. It's getting along in the afternoon, and the weather looks grim in the west. Birdwise, we are in bad shape in three categories: waterfowl, shorebirds, and "southern" specialties. Waterfowl and shorebirds would normally dictate trips to Missisquoi refuge and the islands in northern Lake Cham-

**A great blue heron sails down over a lake, its head
forward as it prospects for a landing place.**

plain. But the lake is high and the land is dry this spring, resulting in a lousy waterfowl and shorebird season; most of these birds have obviously overflown the state.
Missisquoi has produced the most exciting birds in past Big Days — things like
glossy ibis and great egret — but it might well prove a bust this year. The troops
decide to give up on the northern lake, do what we can with lake birds at St. Albans Bay and Sand Bar State Park, then head down the Champlain Valley to close out
the day hunting southern specialties in the Dead Creek area.

2:40 Time (and past time) to head cross-state for Champlain. We slow down to forty
along a stretch of Route 100 through a hayfield, where Frank has had a pair of upland sandpipers in the past. We are checking fence posts and gazing hopelessly over
all those acres of thriving meadow grass when that beautiful and delicate upland
shorebird miraculously appears, racing the car in its distinctive flutter-flight. The
car explodes. Too much!

3:25 The grim part of the day: the middle of an hour-and-a-half trip through unproductive country, time we can ill afford to waste. The North has better habitat

variety than the South; it also has greater distances to cover getting from one to another. The troops settle back to rest, and talk turns to other Big Days. Back to 1977, when the same North team capitalized on late birds (horned grebe, snow goose, greater scaup) and rare birds (double-crested cormorant, great egret, ruddy duck, Wilson's phalarope) to set a Vermont Big Day record of 144 species.

Of course, Big Day records from the northern interior states are small compared to those from more southern and, especially, coastal states. While we labored in the Vermont woods, the national Big Day record was held by a determined four-man California team, which started birding for owls at Mt. Palomar at 12:01 a.m. and threw in the towel at 11:20 p.m. (when flashlights failed to produce kittiwakes off the Santa Monica pier, but did irritate couples preoccupied with other springtime activities), having completed a carefully scouted 675-mile itinerary that included the Salton Sea, Anza Borrego State Park, the Cuyamaca Mountains, Old Mission Dam, the Santee Lakes, the mouth of the San Diego River, Point Loma, La Jolla Point, San Diego Bay, and Marina del Rey. The record count: 231 species in a calendar day.

When the state Big Day no longer seems sufficiently challenging, it's time to move up to the North American Big Year or even to the World Big Year, which provide more time and geographical scope.

▪ The Big Year ▪

PROBABLY THE NORTH AMERICAN BIG YEAR will never be a very popular participatory event, simply because few people can afford to spend most of a year traveling and birding. Big Year records, however, which used to stand for years, toppled regularly during the glory days of the 1970s as a result of the expanding listing mania, a burgeoning where-to-find-rare-birds literature, a growing bird-tour business, more and better telephone rare-bird alerts and hotlines, and increasing attention by birders to strategy and the exploitation of local birding expertise.

Probably no subsequent Big Year competition has matched the drama (and generated the interest) of that between Kenn Kaufman — long-haired and jobless, a veteran birder at nineteen — and Floyd Murdoch, an "establishment" graduate student in his thirties. The year was 1973. While Murdoch traveled, birded, ate, and slept conventionally — that is to say, expensively — Kaufman hitchhiked around North America, spending under $1,000 for the entire year's living and traveling expenses. (Murdoch spent more than that on airplane tickets alone.) Kaufman grubstaked himself by cashing in his life insurance; when that money ran out he sold his blood. During hard times he subsisted entirely on dried pet foods (he recommends Little Friskies and Gravy Train).

As a seasoned hitchhiker, Kaufman knew the year would not be without incident. It was not. In a brief article he wrote about the experience (called "Under My Thumb but Almost Over My Dead Body," *Birding,* May/June 1974), he alludes to the usual "hair-raising rides with traumatic drunks," the "disgusting perverted characters I had to punch out," and the "grillings by suspicious cops." He was not prepared, however, for the two-day stint in a Virginia jail (for hitchhiking), or for the "pleasantly insane young widow" who kidnapped him in Maryland.*

The trouble with any Big Year effort is that it pays increasingly diminished returns. The magic number in 1973 was 650 species, and both Kaufman and Murdoch had reached 550 by the end of spring migration. From then on the pool of new birds becomes, like the birder, increasingly exhausted. The two ran into one another on a pelagic trip off the coast of Washington State on October 7. Murdoch had recorded 666 species, Kaufman 656. They thought about declaring a tie and hanging it up. But too many people were involved — scouting, advising, pushing, or just looking on — and they had no choice but to carry on. November ended with Murdoch leading 668 to 665. And then December — time for the last push. Murdoch traveled a desperate 12,000 miles, but added only one new bird, a blue tit discovered in Ontario. (It was later concluded that the bird was more likely an escapee than a wanderer, and hence not countable.) Kaufman, meanwhile, dropped into Baja California (which the American Ornithologists' Union considers part of North America, while the American Birding Association excludes it), adding five new species.

When it was all over, the men had birded from the Dry Tortugas off the tip of Florida to St. Lawrence Island, in the Bering Sea within sight of Soviet Siberia. Floyd Murdoch had traveled over 100,000 miles and had birded in 47 states. His tentative list of 669 species was a new ABA North American Big Year record. Kenn Kaufman had recorded just over 80,000 miles of travel, 69,200 of them by hitchhiking (some thousands of which he drove himself, without benefit of driver's license). His tentative list of 670 species set a new AOU North American Big Year record.† (A friend of mine remembers bumping into Kaufman shortly after the or-

---

* *Kaufman has since written a book on that remarkable Big Year,* Kingbird Highway *(1997).*

† *Some species from both lists were subsequently disallowed.*

deal was over, and Kenn said he'd like to go around again and take time to see what all those birds looked like.)

The 1973 Big Year is yet to be surpassed in terms of dramatic interest; many birders thought the records coming out of it couldn't be surpassed either. They were wrong. In 1979 a forest-management consultant named Jim Vardaman, a self-styled intermediate birder, set out to break 700 species, or nearly seven-eighths of all the birds that have *ever* been identified in North America (including several that are now extinct). That list includes 116 "accidentals," birds such as shy albatross, Chinese egret, white-tailed eagle, paint-billed crake, Temminck's stint, jungle nightjar, Bahama woodstar, hoopoe, eye-browed thrush, melodious grassquit, and ant palm swift, exotics that have showed up once or twice (presumably under their own power) somewhere in North America. Only seven birders had been able to record 700 species in North America in their entire lives; Vardaman describes a 700 Big Year as the equivalent of a 3:30 mile.

Vardaman began to plan his assault in the fall of 1977 with the help of a brain trust of seventy-five hard-core birders and a six-man insider Big Year Strategy Council (one of whom was Kenn Kaufman). They determined where and when one had the best chance of finding every possible North American bird, and laid out a detailed itinerary for the year. An expert local birder was set to squire Vardaman at every stop; a widely disseminated periodic newsletter urged birders all over the continent to call him collect immediately (code name: Birdman) upon discovery of a rare bird. He would, he said, go anywhere at any time for a "visitor" or an "accidental."

The Big Year started off on a sour note, as the *Sports Illustrated* writer sent to cover the assault died of a heart attack. Vardaman was not to be deterred. He and his Florida guide were out on New Year's Eve. They camped under bird No. 1, a barn owl, and counted it one second into 1979. By the end of January he had birded in five time zones and had traveled over 12,000 miles. His sighting ledger — he counted only those birds identified by himself and at least one witness — had been signed 294 times.

The Big Year proceeded nicely, and Vardaman broke the standing North American Big Year record with an ironically common American woodcock — bird No. 658 — found in a ditch outside Chicago. He birded everywhere — sneaking up on grouse leks in Colorado, beating the bush in Minnesota, watching for Asiatic strays from remote Attu in the Aleutian chain, cruising both oceans in rented planes and boats for pelagics. The numbers mounted, and by the time the bulk of fall migra-

tion was over, he had logged 690 species. Only ten birds to go, and three months in which to track them down. But only strays were left to be counted, and you can't track strays; you sit back and wait for one to turn up somewhere, and hope you'll hear about it if it does.

Early December. Vardaman and his south Texas guide find a white-collared seedeater, a tiny Mexican ground finch, along the Rio Grande. Bird No. 698, and three weeks to go. But the phone isn't ringing, and Vardaman is getting desperate. He puts out the word to the south Florida press: a $100 reward for a confirmed sighting of a blue-gray tanager. Nobody responds. He spends a quiet Christmas with the family. Too quiet. Then, with New Year's looming, a last flurry. A great skua has been sighted off the Maryland coast. A Middle American golden-crowned warbler has appeared in Brownsville, Texas. And a stripe-headed tanager has found its way from the Bahamas to Miami. Vardaman charters a plane and goes after the skua, a species on which he has already spent over 1,000 miles of searching by plane and boat. This time he gets it. He is on his way to Brownsville by way of Miami when he gets the bad news — both tanager and warbler have gone. It is New Year's Eve. He says the hell with it and goes to bed.

Vardaman's record 699-bird North American Big Year cost him over 160,000 miles of travel (mostly by plane, but including 20,000 miles by car and over 3,000 miles by boat) and enough money to buy a house. He says it was worth it.* (One recalls Kenn Kaufman's comment summing up his Big Year: "It was a ridiculous amount of effort, but anything can be fun if taken to extremes.") What the media people gathered around Vardaman wanted to know was what he planned for an encore. He was thinking, he replied, about planning for an all-out *World* Big Year. The goal would be 5,500 species, more birds than anyone has ever recorded in a lifetime. His wife, Virginia, says he'd better be kidding. As she put it to a reporter: "I don't know how he'll be able to afford the trip and the alimony, too."

A common flycatcher, the eastern phoebe appears on Big Day lists from Newfoundland and Georgia west to Alberta and Texas.

---

* *Vardaman's adventures can be followed in detail in his book,* Call Collect, Ask for Birdman *(1980).*

Tᴴᴇsᴇ ᴀᴍᴀᴢɪɴɢ Bɪɢ Yᴇᴀʀ ᴛᴏᴛᴀʟs would not be possible, of course, if listers were not willing to rush great distances after birds someone else has discovered (known as "blitzing"), and able to count them when found (known as "buying" birds). These practices are not sanctioned by everyone in the birding community; but then competitive listing itself is controversial. Some birders consider listing a valuable and exciting part of field ornithology; others believe it an aberration. There is little doubt that the American Birding Association, founded in the late 1960s to "promote the hobby and sport of birding," is in part responsible for the subsequent upsurge in listing activity. The ABA writes the rules for, supports, and publishes the results of the various events. *Birding,* the ABA's journal, boasts, in addition to the usual staff positions, an All-Time Records editor, an Annual List editor, a Big Day editor, a Listing Supplement editor, and a Statistical editor. It publishes, along with the various Big Day and Big Year lists, Annual State lists, Annual Provincial lists, All-Time Reported State and Provincial Year lists, cumulative State and Province lists, as well as Annual and Life World, North American, Contiguous States, Canadian, Mexican, Central American, and South American lists.

Of course, the number of conceivable bird lists is virtually endless. Some birders work hard on county lists. Many people who don't even consider themselves birders keep feeder lists. And many a confirmed lister has started with an innocent property list, whereon one notes species identified on or from one's own property. (Some property lists are remarkable; Frank Oatman's is now over 200, and includes things like gyrfalcon.) Then there are the more bizarre lists. At least one Californian keeps a wire list, wherein he memorializes species observed perching on wires, leading an irreverent fellow birder to urge the value of the hitherto overlooked hovering-near-wire list.

While the ABA defends the listing game, it is often called upon to apologize for the behavior of its listers. The crush following the discovery of a rare bird can leave the immediate area a shambles, and more than a few property owners have threatened to shoot the resident rarity as the only means of getting rid of the birders. Telephone rare-bird alerts were founded to publicize the discovery and location of rarities; yet the New York Rare Bird Alert, among others, has ceased to indicate the whereabouts of feeder rarities to protect property owners. The rare birds themselves

---

Like other woodpeckers, this downy doesn't sing;
in spring it drums to declare territory and advertise for a mate.

are also vulnerable. Listers play tapes of territorial songs at known locations of rare breeders to get them up and singing (and hence countable). The end result of too much of this is that the birds give up their nesting habitat to the rivals on the tape recorders. The birders get their birds, but the beleaguered birds may cease to breed. And listers are becoming as big a threat to several scarce North American hawks as the falconry community.* A leading southwestern birder mourns the lot of the black hawk and the gray hawk: "besieged by birders day after day, week in and week out," he believes these hawks are being pushed out of the U.S. altogether.

Friends of mine participated in a sad incident illustrative of the vulnerability of rare birds. Perhaps forty birders had showed up at the Benicia, California, marsh during an exceptionally high tide, hoping to flush an elusive black rail out of the flooded salt marsh. The strategy is simple: you form a human line and wade through the water and emergent vegetation, hoping to push up a rail. They succeeded in kicking one up, but, typically of rails, it dived back into the marsh. A friend writes: "Immediately the rail's hiding place was surrounded by a tight circle of birders. Unfortunately, enthusiasm was too great, and the circle of birders was too close. One birder even walked in the middle of the area, attempting to flush the rail. The rail was not found, and it was only after most birders had dispersed that we discovered why. The sparrow-sized bird had submerged itself to escape, and it had been accidentally squeezed underwater by someone's feet. It was found struggling to get its head above water, and it never recovered. Needless to say, all of us who were still around to see what had happened were very depressed for days thereafter."

We are now used to the notion of parks and trails being loved to death, of rare species of plants being collected into extinction; perhaps few will be surprised to learn that scarce birds are being pursued and identified to death. But listing excesses in-

---

* Falconry, of course, is the ancient sport, associated formerly with nobility, of training birds of prey — especially falcons and accipiters, though buteos and even owls are sometimes used — to hunt from the arm. Falconry is illegal over some of North America, but it has been legalized (under the largely illusory control of a licensing system) by some states. Falconry is a practice subject to a wide variety of abuses: illegal species are taken, hawks are taken from protected areas, birds are bartered and sold, hawks are kept as pets, birds are mistreated and injured during training. But falconry would be objectionable to conservationists even without these abuses, simply because, to engage in the sport, falconers necessarily remove hawks from the wild — by trapping migratory birds and by taking young from nests — hence further depleting the reproductive pool of already (in some cases dangerously) diminished populations.

**The drake wood duck is considered by many to be the most
glamorous and exotic of North American waterfowl.**

creasingly offend birders and non-birders alike; and the ABA, as champion of the
sport, will inevitably suffer. Most ABA support comes from a handful of states, and
it appears unlikely that support will increase much elsewhere. Of our Vermont Big
Day teams, four members submit state lists to the ABA, and four do not. In Texas
or California, one would find a higher ratio of allegiance; in much of the rest of the
country, one would expect a lower.

4:10 Arrive Lake Champlain, and the North goes back to work. A single species
has been added during the long drive, a kestrel along Route 105. The promised
cold front blows in out of the northwest on strong winds. The temperature drops
dramatically, and we find whitecaps on St. Albans Bay. But three common terns are
sitting tight in the bay, perched on posts, facing into the weather.
4:25 Rain follows the passage of the front, and the town sewage lagoon produces
only a pair of mallards and a green heron.
4:45 The wind quiets, but now it's raining heavily. The afternoon looks like a

washout. Discussion about the track of this front, relative to how it may be affecting the South, which is heartily wished the cruelest of storms. The troops dive into the flood-plain forest at Sand Bar State Park, and the verb is used advisedly. We trek in the rain through a sodden, lush understory of poison ivy and ferns, surrounded by clouds of mosquitoes. This is not the most pleasant birding, but Sand Bar is important. The state's only breeding colony of cerulean warblers is located here.* There are also blue-gray gnatcatchers here, and we hope for pileated woodpecker and other things. Several gnatcatchers are located, buzzing and feeding despite the rain. The ceruleans, however, are sitting tight, and we haven't volume enough on Frank's tape recorder to elicit a response. The team searches the drenched treetops in vain; the ceruleans are simply not going to show. We finally get a downy woodpecker (by drum), and several brown creepers are detected hitching up tree trunks. On the way out, a singing yellow-throated vireo gives us all the possible vireos except Philadelphia.

6:00 Back on the road, headed south. A quick check indicates our total stands at 116 species. Will we make Dead Creek? We check the water along the road on the move, eventually picking up goldeneye and wood duck. 118. A quick turn into a lakeside parking lot. Weighted down by heavy, wet clothing and hiking boots, the troops run out a half-mile-long, willow-studded sand spit. A two-minute scan at the end produces nothing. Hard run back. Jogging was never like this. The North debates its last destination. Do we head for Burlington or for Dead Creek? Walter and George know Burlington, and it's close. But Wayne and I have golden-winged warbler, vesper sparrow, mockingbird, and bluebird staked out between Middlebury and Dead Creek. And Canada goose is a cinch at Dead Creek, with red-tail probable and turkey vulture possible. The troops admit more is available down south, but it'll be dark in two hours, and we're an hour and a half from Dead Creek.

6:40 The decision is made: we'll head straight into Burlington and get what we can. But it looks like we'll never get there, as the piece of heavy machinery ahead of us declines to pull over to let the line around. We crawl for fourteen minutes through Malletts Bay. Expletives deleted.

7:30 We make the Intervale, a good place for ducks and herons below the Burlington dump. A quick (and illegal) stop along the guard rail for black-crowned night

---

This colony appears as an isolated dot on the cerulean warbler range map in the current edition of Peterson's eastern field guide.

heron. No night heron. A second stop for ducks. Only a couple of mallards. Expletives deleted. Semipanic sets in, and the troops begin to argue over whether we wasted time in the Northeast Kingdom. The South got 120 species last year; we're stuck on 118, and striking out in the rain. The want list is pared to five: night heron, blue-winged teal, nighthawk, cardinal, mockingbird.

7:41 We pull into the small marshy area behind the General Electric plant. Fifty feet off the road, perched like a stage prop on a leaning stub, sits a lovely adult night heron. Whew! 119.

7:50 In Burlington the suspense builds. Walter, who knows the city best, is weighing questions ("Any chance for house finch?") and suggestions ("Let's try the hospital for nighthawk") while giving George directions at every corner. We cruise a rich estate area on the lake at double-time, hoping for singing cardinal and mockingbird. The rain is letting up. Come on, birds, sing! Finally one does — and the familiar song of the cardinal never sounded half so good. 120. Where are the Burlington nighthawks? Perhaps the drop in temperature has put them down.

8:01 George pulls up at a suburban cemetery. The team piles out and heads into the marble orchard, away from the traffic noise, in hopes of hearing a white-breasted nuthatch, a mocker, a Carolina wren, *anything!* Nothing. Expletives deleted.

8:25 We're headed for Winooski for a last shot at nighthawk, when Wayne spots a lone individual hunting the darkening sky. 121. As we stop opposite a school to write down the nighthawk, Frank "shushes" out his window, and a curious male house finch flies right up to the car. 122! It's magic, and as it happens, the last magic we have.

8:30 Quick discussion. Shall we proceed to Middlebury, get Wayne's tape recorder, and head out again for possible night-vocal birds like Canada goose, mockingbird, vesper sparrow, and owls; or shall we try for screech-owl down at Rock Point and call it a day? The consensus is that once we get to Wayne's place and smell Karen's chili, we won't go back out. The North is running out of gas.

8:40 Rock Point. Frank and Wayne both have masterly renditions of the quavering decrescendo, but screech-owls, if present, aren't responding.

8:50 We pack it in and head for Middlebury and the countdown. A stop at a highway gas station briefly rekindles hope. Someone has heard a mockingbird from *over there.* To the amazement of the station attendant, five men burst out of the car, charge to the back of the station, and lean expectantly into the dark. In vain. Many a hawk watcher, after a long day of staring into an empty sky, begins to see things. Apparently the same principle holds for a long day of hard listening.

THE HUNT OVER, the troops settle back for the dark hour's drive to Middlebury, discussing the day and their chances. The North's past superiority has rested on its better water habitat. But with few waterfowl and shorebirds around this spring, that advantage has been neutralized. And we have missed a number of easy birds by not making the central Champlain Valley. We are strong, however, on flycatchers, warblers, and northern specialties. Perhaps the list will stand up. It won't hurt, however, to seek heavenly help, and a team member puts the plea with admirable candor and directness: "Please, God, don't let the South have more species than the North."

There is some question as to whether the South will show up for the Middlebury countdown. They were noncommittal on the phone Sunday evening, and the North seems to feel they won't show for chili unless they've had a good day. As we pull up at Wayne's apartment, however, we spot the South's field car. Uh-oh. Doug Kibbe, Don Clark, Annette Gosnell, and Whit Nichols are already there, waiting on the North and the chili. Greetings all around. Complaints about the lousy weather, the lousy birding. Billfolds come out, dollars are produced, and Wayne goes for a case of beer. The chili is hot, the beer cold. Intermittent cheer covers the apprehension.

Time for the countdown. I read off a checklist, marking identified species in two columns. The South starts out strong, picking up three unanswered waterfowl ("Where'd you get the black scoter?") and three unanswered hawks. Shorebirds end up seven each. The North picks up a counter here and there in the early going, as the South has missed night heron, ruffed grouse, and black tern. Owls come out even, but the South has a hummingbird and a bobwhite. (The latter is probably a hunting-club release, and hence not completely legitimate; but the North, which had counted one in a previous year, is in no position to complain.) The North is several birds behind, but its strong suits are coming up. We score with unanswered yellow-bellied and olive-sided flycatchers, and black-backed three-toed woodpecker. (The South is incredulous: "You took three-toed by *drum?*") The South's rough-winged swallow cancels out the North's boreal chickadee. The South has a mockingbird (groans from the North), as well as gray-cheeked thrush, bluebird, and a rare sedge wren. (Only Doug seems to know about this latter bird, and the North wants to know what the South has against the constant-communication rule.) But the North bounces back, as the South has missed solitary vireo and both kinglets.

We arrive at the warblers, and whoever wins the battle of the warblers will probably win the war. Black-and-white . . . Tennessee . . . Nashville . . . northern parula

. . . yellow . . . magnolia . . . Cape May . . . black-throated blue . . . yellow-rumped . . . black-throated green . . . blackburnian . . . chestnut-sided . . . bay-breasted . . . blackpoll. . . . Fourteen straight warblers get yeses from both teams. The North's pine warbler is unanswered, but the South has a prairie warbler, which occurs only in the southern part of the state. Ovenbird . . . northern waterthrush. . . . The South has a Louisiana waterthrush, the North an unanswered mourning warbler. Common yellowthroat, Canada, and American redstart close out the list with double yeses. Each team has identified twenty-one warblers, a remarkable day's work in the spring woods. And that golden-winged warbler, singing faithfully from the elm on Exchange Street outside Middlebury? The South made Middlebury, but didn't know about the bird. The North, which knew about it, didn't make it.

Down the homestretch, from blackbirds through finches. The South has three unanswered birds — indigo bunting, rufous-sided towhee, and vesper sparrow — birds the North had meant to get in the mid-Champlain Valley. The North's only unanswered bird down the stretch is Lincoln's sparrow. While I add up the columns, the teams banter over each other's misses. "No red-tailed *hawk?!*" "What about ruffed grouse?!" It is pointed out, to everyone's dismay, that both teams have missed pileated woodpecker, evening grosbeak, and, most astonishing of all, white-breasted nuthatch.

Karen checks my addition, and the results are announced: South, 123. North, 122.

The victors are jubilant: the South Will Rise Again, and all that. For the winning team, eighteen hours of running birding following a night of next to no sleep has turned into a pleasant memory. And for the North? The North will remember a black cat and a forgotten tape recorder and Dead Creek beckoning but too far. Nearly midnight, and people have things to do in the morning. The troops pile into cars to head for the far corners of the state. Goodbyes are being said outside, and I find myself alone in the apartment, wishing somebody would point me at a bed. Must be an oldies show on the radio, for a couple of lyrics register through the fog:

An' if that mockin'bird don't sing,
Daddy's gonna buy you a diamond ring.

Doug sticks his head back in the door. "Why not go with us next year? Try a winning team for a change." It's going to be a long year for the North.

CHAPTER VI

Housing Helps

FOR CAVITY NESTERS

*All our cities are furnished with houses for the reception of these birds;
and it is seldom that even lads bent upon mischief disturb the favoured
[purple] Martin. He sweeps along the streets, here and there seizing a fly,
hangs to the eaves of the houses, or peeps into them, as he poises himself in
the air in front of the windows, or mounts high above the city, soaring into
the clear sky. . . . Its notes are among the first that are heard in the morning,
and are welcome to the sense of every body. The industrious farmer rises from
his bed as he hears them. . . . The still more independent Indian is also fond
of the Martin's company. He frequently hangs up a calabash on some twig
near his camp. . . . The slaves in the Southern States take more pains to
accommodate this favourite bird. The calabash is neatly scooped out, and
attached to the flexible top of a cane, brought from the swamp . . . and placed
close to their huts. Almost every country tavern has a Martin box on the upper
part of its signboard; and I have observed that the handsomer the box, the
better does the inn generally prove to be.*

—JOHN JAMES AUDUBON, *Birds of America* (1840–44)

THE MARCH OF CIVILIZATION was kind to most cavity-nesting birds in North America for its first couple of hundred years. Few primary cavity nesters (those that drill their own cavities, mostly woodpeckers) or secondary cavity nesters (those dependent on abandoned woodpecker holes and natural cavities) are birds of the deep forest, and the nineteenth-century thinning of the eastern forests was a boon to the majority of both groups. The typical nineteenth-century family farm was, in fact, a cavity nester's paradise: fields and open woods, lots of standing mature trees (both dead and alive), and those two special sources of natural-rot cavities, the apple orchard and the wood-posted fence. The white man's march has even benefited the sand- and dirt-bank cavity nesters; when one hunts a new territory for kingfisher or bank swallow nests, he starts with quarries and landfills.

Purple martins (page 160) nest in groups, while bluebirds (page 161) need space.
Above: Woodpeckers, such as this red-headed, are designed to drill wood and are difficult to attract to man-made boxes.

But civilization has, in this century, increasingly turned on the cavity nester. The tool of the new age is the chain saw. With it, the suburban property owner cuts out "unsightly" brush and dead trees. With it, the economy-minded new pioneer converts dead elms to firewood. With it, the orchardist cuts the dead wood out of his trees. And with it, the forester cuts the snags out of his woods. (There is a hopeful note here, however; at the federal level, at least, the forestry establishment is beginning to recognize that dead trees are not just bug houses and fire threats, but are indispensable living places for cavity-dwelling mammals and cavity-nesting birds.)

While this concerted move against deadwood was going forward, farmers

**Enthusiastic box nesters, tree swallows are far from
picky about the quality of the construction.**

were switching from wood to steel fence posts. These developments have meant fewer and fewer nesting sites for the woodpeckers, wrens, bluebirds, and others; and for the cavities that do get found or drilled, they have to compete with resident house sparrows and starlings, those two monuments to human ecological ignorance.* The prognosis is not bleak for all species of cavity nesters, as a number of variables are operative here; but prospects are distressing for several, and dim for many others. The property owner can make a local difference by (1) leaving standing dead-

The Brooklyn Institute holds the dubious distinction of having introduced the house (often called English) sparrow — it is not a sparrow at all, but rather a weaver finch — to this continent, with two small releases in 1852 and 1853. Unsuccessful attempts to introduce the European starling were made during the following decades with releases from Pennsylvania to Oregon. Unhappily, one Eugene Scheifflin, a Shakespeare buff whose hope was to introduce into the United States every species of bird mentioned in the Master's plays, succeeded with releases in New York's Central Park in 1890 and 1891. The progeny of those house sparrows and starlings now breed in every one of the contiguous states and in every Canadian province.

wood (whether dead trees or dead limbs on live trees), and (2) erecting birdhouses to supplement or substitute for standing deadwood. Not all cavity nesters breeding in our area will utilize a birdbox. This chapter treats those that will, as well as several non-cavity nesters that will accept man-made nesting shelves.

Almost everybody who decides to build birdhouses makes a bad one before he makes a good one. This is not, on the face of it, such a bad idea. In the first place, a bad birdhouse is cheap, and easy to make; better yet, it is no less likely to attract birds than a good one. If you want to see what a bad birdhouse looks like before undertaking your own project, simply drop by your local supermarket, hardware store, or garden center in the spring. You will probably find a variety of acceptable models.*

To make a bad birdhouse you need only gather some scraps of any kind of wood of any thickness. (Old wood shingles or plywood pieces are ideal.) You tack these together with ordinary wire nails to form a box. You put on a roof of some sort, cut out an entrance hole in the front, hang it on a tree, and you're in business. The first summer a male house wren will cart some sticks into your box. If you're lucky, a female will accept the box, rebuild the nest, and raise a family. So far so good. The second spring house sparrows will discover your box, and will proceed to fill it right up above the entrance hole with sticks, string, pins, and cigar wrappers. Now you have, in lieu of a birdhouse, a box full of trash. Your new yard ornament will last several more years, while the boards warp and the nails pull out. Now the sticks begin to poke out the bottom and sides as well as the entrance hole; by this time you are tired of the family's comments on your craft project anyway, so you take it down and burn it. Now you are ready to build a *good* birdhouse.†

■ Materials ■

WOOD IS THE MATERIAL OF CHOICE FOR BIRDHOUSES, because it is easy to get and relatively easy to work, and because its natural insulating properties

---

A blanket condemnation would be unfair. Several companies and scattered individual craftsmen are selling well-designed and well-constructed houses. The majority of commercially available boxes, however, are junk. It will be easy to tell the difference once you know what to look for.

†*Designing a birdhouse requires more woodworking expertise than birding expertise, and the following account owes much to the detailed advice of master woodworkers Joe Juday, Arlo Keitzer, and Myles Bennett, whose help is gratefully acknowledged.*

moderate cold and hot environmental temperatures. Any conductive material, especially metal, should be avoided; the point of a birdbox is to raise young birds, not fry them. Durability and moderate workability are the most important factors to consider in choosing a wood; and the best woods, in no particular order, are redwood, cypress, white cedar, and western red cedar. You don't need a "clear" grade of lumber. Get a second grade of whichever is available and cheapest. Get it air-dried, or better yet, kiln-dried. Get it rough-sawn, if possible, and get it in ¾-inch (net) dimension. (That particular thickness isn't crucial; but ½-inch wood and thinner tends to split during construction and warp after exposure, while 1-inch lumber is a waste of wood for any but the largest boxes.)

Almost any Cub Scout will tell you that the real fun of building a birdhouse is painting it. Do you paint before or after assembly? Just the outside, or the inside too? What color? Cub Scout masters will appreciate the answer, even if the Scouts won't: don't paint it. Paint does nothing for birds and next to nothing for wood. None of the woods listed above requires any treatment; a birdbox properly constructed from one of them may well outlast the builder. Untreated, your box will weather, in the humid Northeast, to a mixture of dark browns (as the wood extractives migrate to the surface) and dark grays (as the fungal spores and mycelia multiply on the surface).

If you find the aesthetics of weathered wood pleasing, fine. If you find them appalling, or merely wish to minimize surface checking and cracking as the box matures, by all means treat your wood pieces with a water-repellent preservative before assembly. Ask your building-supplies dealer to recommend a clear mineral wax, marine varnish, or whatever; but make it clear that you do not want a product that will turn sticky or produce an odor under any weather circumstances. Any wood preservative will need to be reapplied every year or so if it is to retain its effectiveness. If, for whatever reason, you decide to use a less-durable wood (pine, for example), consider paying more for a pretreated wood. Factory treatment is accomplished under pressure, and hence preservative penetration is far better than that of your brush-on workshop treatment. Again, however, avoid lumber pretreated with products — creosote is one — that will "bleed" out of the wood and/or have a strong smell.

How about hardware? Probably 99 percent of birdhouses are constructed with ordinary wire nails. This was part of the reason our bad birdhouse came apart in a few years. The too-soft, too-thin boards warped as they weathered, and the nails simply pulled out. If you must use nails, use whatever form of rustproof nail (zinc-clad, galvanized, copper, aluminum, stainless steel) is available with a ribbed or twisted shank. The ridge-and-groove design of these specialty nails results in a holding power superior to that of ordinary, smooth-shanked nails. Holding power can also be increased by driving the nails at an angle. Something like 6-penny nails are what you want; or you can bond the joints with a good wood adhesive and secure them with 4-penny nails. (You may use 1-inch lumber for the largest boxes on the chart; if so, you'll want larger nails.) If you have trouble with splitting, try blunting the tips of the nails before insertion. (Blunt tips crush wood fibers, while sharp tips wedge them apart; the latter action produces more splitting.) If the splitting continues, you'll have to go to a smaller nail or predrill your holes.

Proper-size rustproof nails with a ribbed or twisted shank will produce a good sound box. If you are determined to go first-class, however, you will want to use brass screws to assure both rustproofness and maximum holding power. Brass screws (dip them in paraffin to make insertion easier) cost more than nails and, because you have to predrill the holes, take a little more time. *If,* that is, you are an accomplished nailer. If you end up splitting half your wood with nails, screws will prove both cheaper and quicker. Try some of both; see what you're comfortable with.

■ Design and Construction ■

BIRDHOUSE DESIGNS CAN BE MULTIPLIED INDEFINITELY, but there isn't much point in doing so. The design featured here is simple to build and is acceptable to all cavity nesters that will use birdhouses. (Yes, including purple martin.) The various parts of the box look like this:

The *front* is notable for what it *doesn't* feature — a perch. The birds you're trying to attract don't need one. (When was the last time you saw a natural cavity or a woodpecker hole with a perch under it?) A perch on a birdhouse merely encourages house sparrows and starlings to sit in front of the entrance and hassle the inhabitants. If you drill the entrance hole, tack the front piece of lumber to a waste piece to prevent splits as your bit emerges. The top edge of the front (like the back edge of the top and the top edge of the back) may be beveled for a neat fit. If an appropriate tool is not available, no beveling need be done; but be sure your joints lap adequately. If your lumber hasn't at least one rough-sawn side for the inside of the box, take a file or rasp or chisel and horizontally roughen the inside of the front piece below the hole. Otherwise, young birds may have a difficult time getting out of the box.

The *sides*, requiring the only angle cut, should be ventilated by two to four ¼-

A Basic Birdhouse Design

Nesting Shelf

inch holes up under the roof, the number depending on how much sun the box is to receive. You may want to drill these holes after the box is put together. Should your box prove to have a considerable crack between sides and roof, omit the holes. The vents will help to change the hot air that rises to the top of a birdhouse on scorching summer days.

Note that the grain on the *top* runs downhill, like that on sides, front, and back. The checks and cracks that develop during weathering will run with the grain, and hence will help to carry water off the box rather than hold it. Exact dimensions of roofs are not critical, but the roof should extend well over both front and sides to protect entrance hole and vents from blown rain. It takes three strokes of a handsaw to cut a shallow drip line about an inch back from the front edge on the underside of the top piece. This will prevent water from "roof-walking"' into your house, and is particularly important if the slope of your roofline is shallow.

The *bottom* needs to be able to drain any water that gets into the box. Since the birdhouse will probably not be perfectly level when erected, water will tend to slide to one or two sides, making the corners of the bottom the best drain locations. Either buff the corners off before assembly, or drill ¼-inch holes in each. A similar hole in the middle is advisable, in the event a slight "cupping" of the bottom board results in water collecting in the center. Notice in the full box sketch that the bottom is recessed about ¼ inch, an aid in weatherproofing the house.

Remember that a birdhouse that cannot be easily opened quickly becomes a non-functional yard ornament. You have to be able to get into the box to dump the old nest (or sawdust) along with any droppings and parasites.* (The *first* thing to look for when buying a birdbox is an openable part. No box tacked up tight need be further considered.) Any clever teenager can design several efficient ways to make a box's interior accessible. Parts can slide against cleats; hinge and hook-and-eye combinations can be employed. The sketch illustrates a cheap and easy way to hinge the front without using special hardware. One smooth-shanked nail or round pivot screw is inserted high up through each side and into the front piece. Drill these two holes carefully — on a level and straight in. The bottom of the front piece is secured either by a single brass screw or, if removing one screw sounds like too much work, by an L-screw set in a saw-cut notch.

Several species of non-cavity nesters — most notably robin, phoebe, and barn swallow — although they do not use birdboxes, will sometimes utilize a nesting shelf. The sketch illustrates a common and simple shelf design. If the shelf is to be located inside a shed or barn or under eaves, the roof may be omitted.

---

* *Generally speaking, birdboxes should be cleaned out in the fall. Simply dump the contents and scrub down the interior with a stiff brush and water. If lice or mites are in evidence, spray the box (especially the joints) with a miticide before remounting or storing for the winter.*

■ Location and Mounting ■

MANY PERFECTLY FINE BIRDHOUSES NEVER HAVE A CHANCE to attract the birds for which they were intended, simply because of improper location. People want their birds to feel safe, so they put the houses high up among the foliage of trees; and they don't want them to feel lonely, so they put up boxes in bunches. But the latter violates most birds' territorial imperative, and the former is incommensurate with their nest-search image. To take the territorial question first. The colonial purple martin is an exception and barn swallows require little (and tree swallows only moderate) territorial spacing, but other species that use birdhouses need considerable room. Probably you won't want to put up more than two boxes for a given species on a one-acre property; and those two boxes should be placed at opposite corners. Small property owners will have better luck attracting a single pair of several different species, for intraspecific territoriality is more basic than interspecific territoriality.

Now for that wren or bluebird or tree swallow or flicker or red-headed woodpecker house you carefully hid halfway up your backyard maple tree, and which the species in question has ungratefully ignored for three summers. The problem is that these species aren't programmed to search for nesting cavities in your flourishing shade tree. The woodpeckers normally excavate cavities in dead trees; the smaller birds nest in woodpecker holes or in natural cavities in, say, rotted stubs or fence posts. Now, what dead trees and rotten fence posts have in common is a notable lack of foliage cover. The species notes that follow in this chapter will indicate proper habitat for box placement; suffice it to say here that many of our birdhouse species, including those noted above, prefer a perfectly exposed nesting box, however this may violate our notions of security and privacy.

The third common placement mistake concerns height. The assumption that forty feet up is better than ten feet up isn't shared by many birdhouse species. Boxes for most of our common species can be erected from a stepladder or while standing on your own two feet. The dimensions chart indicates a suggested box height for each species.

Boxes can be erected — facing, if possible, away from prevailing winds — in several ways. If the house is to be located on a vertical surface, such as a garage wall or a tree trunk, you have simply to screw a backboard onto the back of the house, and nail or screw through that. No, it won't harm a fairly mature tree to drive a couple of large nails into the trunk. (Consider what maple sugaring does to tree trunks

**Nest box placement is important; people tend to
place them too high and to hide them in tree foliage.**

year after year.) But don't nail into small trees, and if possible use old-fashioned iron nails for attaching houses to living trees. Newfangled nails are coated with various substances, some of which have a greater potential for harming the tree than does the wounding itself.

A pipe makes a good birdbox stand. Simply drive it into the ground, affix an appropriately sized pipe flange to the bottom of your box, and spin the house onto the pipe. If you can't drive the pipe deep enough to achieve stability for the house, set it in concrete. However you erect your house, make it as straight up and down as possible. A bird-attracting book I grew up with diagrams the properly erected birdbox with the front face slanting down, so that a bird looking out sees the ground. Now, it's true that most woodpecker-excavated nesting holes orient somewhat downward — whether because this minimizes water entrance, because such a hole is easier to defend, because the moister micro-environment of the underside of a limb makes excavation easier, or because of other reasons, is unknown. The problem is that in the case of the birdbox, the orientation of the entrance hole bears a fixed rela-

Winter Roosting Boxes

tionship to that of the floor; if you slant the front, you leave the birds with a slanting floor to nest on. In the case of cavity nesters that build no nest, the eggs end up lined along the bottom/front joint, making them impossible to incubate. Remember, too, that your birdhouse has two anti-rain features unavailable to the drilling woodpecker: a roof and drain holes.

What about predation at nesting boxes? Squirrels, rats, and snakes will enter boxes to prey on eggs and young birds. Cats trap adults at the box, and, along with dogs, take young after they fledge. Snakes and rats are seldom a serious threat; cats and squirrels may well be. You can try the same anti-predator measures you use for winter bird feeders. Sleeve or conical baffles may work on posts or poles, assuming they can be placed high enough so they cannot be jumped over. Some people put all their boxes up on pipes and grease the pipes during the nesting season. Low boxes, especially those mounted on fence posts, are extremely difficult to protect. Everybody with rats will, on general principles, attempt to trap or shoot them out. The tough-minded will do the same with problem cats and squirrels; the tender-hearted will perforce rely on their own vigilance and good fortune.

Birdhouses should be in place when the intended tenant species appear in your area. You may want to leave your boxes up all year, so that they can double as roosting boxes during the winter. Keep an eye on them, however, in late winter and early spring. If house sparrows or starlings begin to build in them, you'll probably want to clean them out and block the entrances until the intended species arrive. A new birdbox, especially if it has been treated (whether with paint, stain, or waterproofing solution), may prove unattractive to birds. New boxes obtained or built in the fall or winter should be erected at once, to give them time to weather and mellow before spring.

■ Winter Roosting Boxes ■

NESTING BOXES CAN DOUBLE AS WINTER ROOSTING BOXES, particularly for the larger birds (anything flicker-sized or bigger), which ordinarily roost singly. For the smaller birds, however, which benefit from communal roosting, a box designed for the purpose is better. Roosting boxes come in vertical and horizontal models, which typically look something like the accompanying sketches.

The vertical model looks much like an oversized birdhouse. It can be any height — most are built in the 18-to-24-inch range — depending on how many staggered perches you think you can fill. Perches, usually ¼-inch or ⅜-inch dowels, can either be fixed with glue in holes drilled in one wall, or anchored with glue and/or brads in holes drilled through both walls. The horizontal model can accommodate one or two long perches, depending on how high you build it. Length is optional, but 12 to 18 inches of perch will hold a lot of chickadees. The depth of a one-perch roosting box should be little more than the length of the species you hope will use it, while that of a two- or multi-perch box will have to be more generous in order to accommodate birds on staggered perches.

The door on a roosting box is positioned near the floor, to help prevent the escape of the collective body heat rising from the sleeping birds. The box should be tight, with no ventilation or drainage holes. Obviously you help select your clientele by determining the entrance-hole size. Species likely to use roosting boxes are the same ones that are likely to use nesting boxes. Note those species which winter in your area, and determine your hole-size choice from the birdhouse dimensions chart. You may want to restrict one roosting box to the smaller birds — nuthatches, chickadees, titmice, and wrens. A second box can be designed to accommodate medium-sized species. If you live in bluebird wintering country, it is well worthwhile putting up a roosting box for them. Bluebirds readily pack boxes, and during hard winters in the northern part of their permanent range many will survive only where they are available.

Most blueprints floating about the bird-attracting literature show vertical roosting boxes with a hinged top. This leaves you, come spring, with the difficult chore of threading an arm through a maze of perches with some sort of scrubbing tool to clean the floor. This is unnecessary. Hinging the front instead, after the manner suggested for birdhouses, gives easy access to the floor. Top, front, or bottom can be hinged on the horizontal model. Any roosting box should be located in a sheltered place away from winter gales. The vertical box mounts well on a tree or post, while the horizontal box is designed for use on the side of a building.

■ Dimensions Chart ■

THE FOLLOWING CHART provides box and shelf dimensions for all species likely to use them in the extended Northeast. All but two. Starling and house sparrow will make themselves at home in anything they can get into, which raises a point worth stressing. Over and over in the popular bird-attracting literature one sees the

◾ DIMENSIONS CHART* ◾

Species	Floor of box (inches)	Depth of cavity at front (inches)	Entrance above floor to mid-hole (inches)	Diameter of entrance (inches)	Approximate height box placement (feet)
House wren	4 x 4	7	5	1	6
Bewick's wren	4 x 4	7	5	1⅛	6
Carolina wren	4 x 4	7	5	1⅜	6
Black-capped chickadee	4 x 4	8	6	1⅛	5
Carolina chickadee	4 x 4	8	6	1⅛	5
Tufted titmouse	4 x 4	8	6	1¼	5
Red-breasted nuthatch	4 x 4	8	6	1⅓	12
White-breasted nuthatch	4 x 4	9	7	1¼	12
Downy woodpecker	4 x 4	10	8	1¼	12
Hairy woodpecker	5½ x 5½	14	11	1¾	20
Red-headed woodpecker	5½ x 5½	14	11	1¾	20
Red-bellied woodpecker	6 x 6	14	11	2	20
Northern flicker	7 x 7	16	13	2½	15
Tree swallow	5 x 5	6	4	1½	5
Barn swallow	6 x 6	6	three sides open		8
Purple martin	6 x 6	6	2½	2½	17
Eastern phoebe	6 x 6	6	three sides open		8
Great crested flycatcher	6 x 6	10	7½	2	10
American robin	7 x 7	8	three sides open		6
Eastern bluebird	5 x 5	9	7	1½	4
House finch	6 x 6	6	4	2	8
American kestrel	8 x 8	16	13	3	20
Northern saw-whet owl	7 x 7	15	12	2½	15
Eastern screech-owl	8 x 8	16	13	3	12
Barn owl	18 x 20	18	4	6	18
Wood duck	10 x 10	21	16	4	5 (over water)
					15 (over land)

* Like other published birdhouse dimension charts, this chart is ultimately based on one in "Homes for Birds," put together by the Bureau of Biological Survey and issued as Farmers' Bulletin 1456 by the Department of Agriculture in 1925. I have introduced many changes from that pioneering work.

notion expressed that particular box dimensions are critical, that the bluebird, say, is roaming the countryside looking for something 5 x 5 x 8 inches with an 1½-inch entrance. This is nonsense. Birds that ordinarily depend on natural cavities and woodpecker holes (and to a lesser extent those that drill their own cavities) nest in a wide range of cavity sizes. One of the standard frustrations of building and erecting those huge wood duck boxes is that six-inch starlings move in. (Researchers at the Patuxent Wildlife Research Center in Maryland were relieved to find that cylindrical boxes with a 4 x 11-inch semicircular entrance, mounted horizontally, deterred starlings; but purple martins and great crested flycatchers liked them fine!) All that need be said about these box and shelf dimensions is that they provide adequate room for the species in question, while avoiding an excess of waste space. This news will be welcome to the amateur woodworker. If your early boxes turn out ½ inch short here and 1 inch long there, not to worry. The birds will do quite well in them.

Entrance-hole dimensions, on the other hand, should be taken fairly seriously. The holes are designed to be barely adequate for the particular species. If you make most of these holes ¼ inch smaller (even ⅛ inch smaller in some cases), the birds can't get in. The birds won't care if you make the holes bigger than called for, but then you may be inviting trouble. The 1⅛-inch chickadee hole, for example, excludes house sparrows, but only by ⅛ inch. Similarly, the bluebird box entrance barely excludes starlings, while the wood duck box hole is kept barely adequate to deter raccoon predation.

It will come as no surprise that cavity nesters, like other birds, nest at a variety of heights. If your sample is large enough, you can document an astonishing height range for some species. A bluebird nesting study conducted in two areas of Michigan located ninety-eight nests; they varied in height from under two feet to fifty-five feet! The figures in the box-placement column represent average (or, in the case of the higher-nesting species, low-average) values, heights at which the birds will be comfortable. Obviously there is nothing magical about these numbers; deviating from any of them up to 20 percent lower or 30 percent higher should not affect your chances of attracting the particular species.

■ Multiple-Species Birdhouses ■

MANY PEOPLE DO NOT INSIST upon attracting a particular species, but would like to attract *something*. With minimal compromising in dimensions, and with middle-of-the-road placement, it is possible to increase your chances of doing so by suiting several species with a single birdhouse. Indeed, the following five houses will satisfy the nesting requirements of most of our popular birdhouse species.

1. A box 4 x 4 x 8 inches with a 1¼-inch hole 6 inches above the floor will attract both chickadees, tufted titmouse, both nuthatches, all three wrens, and downy woodpecker.

2. A box 5 x 5 x 8 inches with a 1½-inch hole 6 inches above the floor will attract eastern bluebird, mountain bluebird, and tree swallow.

3. A box 6 x 6 x 12 inches with a 2½-inch hole 9 inches above the floor will attract great crested flycatcher, red-headed, red-bellied, and hairy woodpeckers, and saw-whet owl. (If you have no hope for a saw-whet, reduce the entrance to 2 inches.)

4. A box 8 x 8 x 16 inches with a 3-inch hole 13 inches above the floor will attract northern flicker, screech-owl, and American kestrel.

5. A shelf 7 x 7 x 7 inches with three sides open will suit American robin, eastern phoebe, and barn swallow.

■ Notes on the Birds ■

BEFORE BUILDING A PARTICULAR BIRDHOUSE, check the account of that species below to make certain you have proper habitat available. Be sure also to check any unfamiliar bird's range in a recent field guide before setting to work. It won't do any good to erect a box for Bewick's wren or red-bellied woodpecker in Manitoba or the Maritimes; nor will you have any luck attracting breeding red-breasted nuthatches in Missouri.

WRENS

Wrens, and especially house and Bewick's wrens, are famous for their bizarre nest locations — in discarded tin cans, cow skulls, the pockets of clothesline garments, under the hood (or in the upholstery) of junked cars. Male house wrens are also notorious for building "dummy" nests in hopeful locations within their small (about an acre) breeding territories. If the female chooses a site other than your birdbox, dump out any dummy nest and relocate your house well away from the active nest. You may well attract another pair of wrens.

Wren boxes are often made with horizontal slot entrances (about 2½ inches long) rather than circular ones. This facilitates the nest-building process, which involves maneuvering outrageously long sticks into the small box. A circular hole presents more of a challenge to the wren, but it is one that it meets with characteristic vigor and success. Wrens typically hunt in low, woody cover, and their boxes should be located near brushy areas, thickets, hedgerows, and so on. Boxes for house and Bewick's wrens will do best in the open, in good sun; a thicket-edge location, with partial sun, is ideal for Carolina wren.

SWALLOWS

The best way to attract barn swallows is to buy a farm and open the doors of all the outbuildings. A search of some 5,000 Canadian barn swallow nest records showed that 99 percent were located on man-made structures. The remaining 1 percent were found on cliffs and in caves, presumably the species' original nesting locations. If you live in an area where horizontal supports are not readily available, barn swallows can be attracted to shelves erected on garage, shed, barn, or porch walls. Barn swallows are semicolonial; a half-dozen shelves on one garage may all accommodate tenants.

Just about everyone loves tree swallows, although the proprietors of bluebird trails,* which often fledge twice as many swallows as bluebirds, might demur. A recently published book says: "Any backyard with a large pond or lake, located in the northern third of the U.S., has a better than even chance of attracting tree swallows to a birdhouse." That's true. So does any suburban or rural backyard without a large pond or lake. Tree swallows congregate on the drowned snags often found in standing water, but it is quite wrong to conclude that they require water in order to breed. Many a dry farmyard and village property offers evidence to the contrary.

House wrens occupy backyard nestboxes—and deliver their rollicking, bubbly song—from the Atlantic to the Pacific.

A bluebird trail is simply a string of bluebird houses — numbering from several to several thousand — usually erected and maintained by a particular individual or club.

Before the invention of mailboxes and birdhouses, tree swallows were dependent on old woodpecker holes and natural cavities. They continue to use those sites, but are delighted to use nesting boxes wherever they find them. Put up a couple along an open fencerow, and divert your family with an old rural custom. Tree swallows line their nests with great numbers of feathers, and farm children have long gathered chicken feathers to release from upstairs windows on breezy spring days when nest building is well along. The tree swallows quickly learn to chase down and capture the feathers in midair, and will even approach the windows in hopes of more.

The purple martin is the ultimate birdhouse bird. A check of nearly 3,000 nest-record cards from eastern Canada and the Prairie Provinces turned up exactly two nests in natural cavities. The far western martin population is still largely dependent on natural sites, but the much larger eastern population is almost entirely dependent on nest boxes. This doesn't mean martins are easy to attract. They are not. Time and again one sees people put up a $150 martin house that will never attract anything but starlings and house sparrows. To have a decent chance at starting a colony of martins you need two things: (1) one or several thriving colonies somewhere in your area to provide "seed" birds for your own; and (2), more important, an open site for your box(es) which faces directly on a broad open feeding area (water or meadow, most likely). Anyone who has seen and heard the scores of crowded, gurgling martin houses on the broad lawns fronting gigantic Mille Lacs Lake in Minnesota will know what constitutes an ideal purple martin nesting situation.

The building of a multi-apartment martin house is a considerable feat, expensive both in time and money; experience in carpentry and blueprint reading would also be a help. (Building and "planting" a ground-support device on which to raise, lower, and support your fifteen-foot pole and house is no small engineering feat either.) Since in most areas martin attracting is a chancy business anyway, I think it makes sense to start small. Hang up three or four hollowed-out gourds, as certain southeastern Indian tribes were doing when the colonists arrived. (Apparently the Indians were less interested in the martins' diet than in their predator-mobbing behavior, which would alert the village to animals raiding the corn patch.) Or erect three or four individual boxes in a group, or a single — but relatively simple — house divided into four compartments. Starting small doesn't mean you have to end small. Ray Denning started with six individual boxes outside his gas station in Princeton, Indiana. Martins took to the houses and Denning obviously took to the martins, for eight years and $4,000 later he had 400 occupied apartments.

The dimensions given for an individual martin house (or apartment) in the chart are the conventional ones. The author of a book on the purple martin objects to the notion of forcing a seven-inch bird to nest in a 6 x 6 x 6-inch compartment, and recommends one 8 x 8 x 8 inches instead. But this is to introduce the irrelevant human value of living-space comfort. Secondary cavity nesters do not require, and primary cavity nesters do not make provision for, stretch-out space. Cavity nesters typically incubate with their tails up the cavity wall; indeed, the tropical cavity-nesting quetzal incubates with half its famous tail extending out the hole! Martins will make do with entrance holes down to 2 inches in diameter; but, since starlings can still enter, there seems little point in reducing the conventional hole size.

Before you buy or build one of those three- or four-decker martin houses, make sure that it provides for adequate in-house ventilation. Martin houses are erected in full sun, and living quarters are tight and close. This is reason enough, also, to break the no-paint rule; colonial martin houses are traditionally painted white to reflect heat. You may also want to violate the box clean-out rule. A martin study based on information from the entire East suggests that these birds prefer to reuse old nests. The two ornithologists conducting this ongoing study suggest that you dump any starling or house sparrow nests, and dust the martin nests with a short-life miticide. Most people don't put their martin houses up in the spring until a day or two before the birds are due back from the South; starlings and house sparrows will be problem enough without giving them a head start on the martins.

NUTHATCHES

White-breasted and red-breasted nuthatches ordinarily nest in natural tree cavities or abandoned woodpecker holes; the red-breasted, at least, sometimes excavates its own cavity in rotten wood. Both nuthatches are basically woodland nesters, but the white-breasted will nest in tree-mounted boxes in orchards or suburban locations as well. Red-breasted nuthatches are difficult to attract to birdboxes, and it is virtually impossible unless they are placed in coniferous or mixed woods. It is no mistake that the dimensions chart indicates a larger entrance hole for the smaller nuthatch. The red-breasted invariably smears its entrance with pitch, which makes entering the nest cavity — usually accomplished in full flight — a delicate and potentially dangerous business. (This resin-smearing may serve to discourage squirrels from enlarging the hole to get at eggs or young.)

TITS

Black-capped chickadee, Carolina chickadee, and tufted titmouse — all members of the *Paridae,* the tit(mouse) family — are basically woodland nesters. All three utilize woodpecker holes and natural cavities. In addition, the chickadees will excavate their own cavities in rotten stubs. So if you come upon a nervous chickadee with a beakful of mysterious light-colored stuff early in the breeding season, sit down and watch; the bird will soon calm down, spit out the sawdust, and go back to work at the nearby nest site.

Some people recommend "rustic" houses for these species. This means hollowing out a length of log, or building a box of slab wood (which, of course, is rustic on the outside only). Chickadees and titmice will utilize such houses, as well as those built of conventional lumber; it would be difficult to ascertain their preference, if indeed they have one. Whatever sort of box you build should be erected on a post or tree trunk in or near a woods. You may also attract a pair of chickadees or titmice to your backyard apple tree, provided your neighborhood is not overly urbanized and is at least amply blessed with shade trees.

WOODPECKERS

The good news about woodpeckers is that there are lots of them; the bad news is that all except one are difficult to attract to nesting boxes. The exception is the northern flicker, which ordinarily drills its cavity in the trunk or a major branch of a dead tree in open farm country, open woods, or suburban habitat. Hammer your box well up on a snag in full sun, and you may have flickers at your anthills all summer.

One might expect downy and hairy woodpeckers, common at suet feeders in the winter, to nest in boxes more often than they do — especially the hairy, which usually drills its cavity in a live tree, taking as long as three weeks to finish a nest hole in sound hardwood. With luck you may attract a pair of downies to a tree-mounted box in village, park, or open woodland habitat. The hairy is the most retiring breeder of the five woodpeckers considered here; a box for this species should be placed in or very near an extensive woods or wooded swamp.

Red-headed and red-bellied woodpeckers have much in common. Unlike the

Carolina and black-capped chickadees are familiar feeder birds; both species will use birdhouses as well.

basically insectivorous downy and hairy, they are generalist feeders, taking quantities of nuts, seeds, and berries as well as insects. (Both get into trouble with fruit growers; formerly, red-heads were regularly shot in cherry trees, red-bellies in southern orange groves.) Both store winter food, cramming acorn pieces and beechnuts into cracks and crannies. And both have adapted quite nicely to inhabited areas, nesting and wintering in towns and villages. The red-headed woodpecker, in fact, followed civilizing man's march into the prairie states, drilling its nesting cavities in telephone, telegraph, and electric streetcar poles. (This did not endear the bird to communications- and transportation-minded man; Kansas City shortly appointed an official Woodpecker Exterminator in defense of its streetcar system.)

The red-head remains a controversial bird. Its aggressiveness is applauded when directed at the starling (which few other cavity nesters will even attempt to fight), but condemned when directed at the eggs and young of other birds, which it sometimes eats. Red-headed woodpeckers like any kind of open habitat with standing snags, whether pasture, old burn, flooded river plain, or lake margin; it both nests in and fly-catches from those snags. The bird also thrives, again, in park and town environments. You can't do better than a utility pole for box placement; the trunk of a dead tree will also do. Unlike the red-headed woodpecker, which is in trouble in much of its range, the red-bellied woodpecker is extending its range to the north and east. A less aggressive bird than the red-head, the red-belly nests in open woods, orchards, and suburban situations. A box on a pole or tree in a semi-open environment may attract this species.

Again, it is often claimed that woodpeckers prefer hollowed-out logs or slab-wood boxes to those made of conventional lumber. Certainly woodpeckers have used all three types, but, except for flickers, none regularly. Whatever sort of box you build, remember that, unlike many cavity and niche nesters, woodpeckers don't build nests. They lay their eggs on the sawdust and wood chips left over from excavation, and you'll want to add an inch or two of this material before erecting your box.

FLYCATCHERS

The eastern phoebe builds its bulky, moss-covered nest on ledges of cliff faces and, more often, on horizontal surfaces of man-made structures — beams of outbuildings, bridge girders, and the like. If such sites are scarce in your neighborhood, the phoebe may well nest on a shelf tacked up on your porch or woodshed.

A more exciting possibility is the cavity-nesting great crested flycatcher. Normally a bird of the woods, and especially wet woods, the great crested sometimes frequents wooded inhabited areas. If the species breeds in your area you'll know it; its loud *wheeep! wheeep!* call is unmistakable. Put your log, slab-wood, or conventional box up on the trunk of a live tree, and you may attract this colorful flycatcher. If you are successful, you may be in for a start when you clean out the box; this species has the curious habit of decorating its bulky junk nest with a cast-off snake skin.

THRUSHES

The inclusion of the American robin on the dimensions chart is more a nod to tradition than anything else. Robins do sometimes utilize nesting shelves, but no species is less in need of nest-site help. By all means put a robin shelf up on your grape arbor, but don't make any bets with skeptics. Your robins will probably nest in the lilac bush or apple tree, as usual.

Our cavity-nesting thrush, on the other hand, is in desperate need of nesting help. Lawrence Zeleny, founder of the North American Bluebird Society, says that "today, few people under thirty years of age have ever seen" our once-common eastern bluebird. This is something of an overstatement, but the bluebird has certainly come out of the last several decades with the short end of the stick, facing as it has chain saws, steel posts, house sparrows, starlings, and periodic severe winters. A measure of the present scarcity of nesting sites is the fact that bluebirds are now nesting in forest clear-cuts, provided snags are left standing. Forest is not natural bluebird habitat, but it does have a singular advantage: the house sparrow will be absent, the starling present in very small numbers, if at all.

Now that house sparrows and starlings have driven the species out of towns and villages, prime bluebird habitat is open rural country, from meadow and woodlot farm country to golf courses and cemeteries. It is in country of this sort that people are running their bluebird trails along fencerows and back roads; and bluebirds readily accept these boxes. The world's longest bluebird trail runs, counting numerous offshoots, some 2,000 miles from Winnipeg, Manitoba, to Denholm, Saskatchewan. This trail, now two generations old, consists of something like 7,000 nesting boxes, from which, in a recent year, an estimated 8,000 bluebirds and 15,000 tree swallows fledged!

Whether you are building houses for mountain bluebirds in Saskatchewan and the western Great Plains, or for eastern bluebirds across most of the East, build them carefully to size. Bluebirds will nest quite contentedly in many sizes of cavi-

**Hawks typically build open tree or cliff-ledge nests;
only the American kestrel will use a nest box.**

ties, both open and with restrictive entrance holes; they choose flicker and hairy woodpecker cavities as frequently as they do those of the downy woodpecker. The advantage of the bluebird box is that it can minimize the starling menace. The 1½-inch hole is critical — over ⅟16 inch smaller, the bluebirds can't get in; over ⅟16 inch larger, the starlings can. Most plans call for an 8-inch cavity depth. I have followed Zeleny in calling for a deeper box; this makes it more difficult for the starling, which can get its head and neck into the house, to prey on bluebird young.

Conventional wisdom calls for hundred-yard spacing of boxes, to provide for the bluebird's territorial requirements. If you try this, and get all tree swallows, try spacing boxes in pairs, eight or ten yards apart. This should prove too close for two pairs of tree swallows, and the empty box may be claimed by bluebirds. Post your boxes low, in the open, and away from houses and barns, to discourage house sparrow competition. Bluebirds are normally double-brooded, and they will want to build a new nest before laying the second clutch. So clean out your boxes as soon as all first-brood young have fledged.

HOUSE FINCH

It has now been a half century since a group of house finches, illegally shipped from California to New York for the cage-bird trade, were released ahead of the long arm of the law. This opportunistic western finch has now spread widely in the mid-Atlantic region, well into northern New England and southern Canada, and west into the prairies. Where the bird is scarce people may want to attract it as an exotic; and it will readily nest in a birdbox and may accept a shelf. Where the species is common, however, some people will have second thoughts. These finches tend to congregate and chatter about town and city buildings, so that some consider them nothing more than house sparrows with red heads. Indeed, French speakers, who know the house sparrow as the "domestic sparrow" *(moineau domestique),* call the house finch the "familiar finch" *(roselin familier).*

AMERICAN KESTREL

Almost everybody — even those people who still think dark thoughts about the larger hawks and owls — likes this lovely and delicate falcon, the familiar utility-pole sitter and wind-hoverer breeding in open country straight across North America. Long called the sparrow hawk (a misnomer with which the bird was saddled by early settlers, who apparently thought it resembled a common Old World accipiter of the same name), the kestrel nests in tree hollows, woodpecker cavities, and cliff niches. It also occasionally nests in other birds' open nests, which fact, together with that of its pigmented eggs (cavity nesters eggs need no camouflage, of course, and the rule is pure white), leads ornithologists to suspect the kestrel may only recently have evolved the cavity-nesting habit. It will readily accept a nest box, preferably mounted well up on a pole or dead tree in fairly open country. A few wood chips or shavings will not be amiss, but the birds don't seem to appreciate a full layer.

You may not want to attract a pair of kestrels if you have a thriving purple martin or cliff swallow colony on your property. Ordinarily kestrels take mostly insects, mice, voles, and snakes during the summer. All those martin or swallow young represent a considerable temptation, however, and if a kestrel once begins to extract young from box, gourd, or jug, it will probably end up taking them all.

OWLS

The northern saw-whet owl breeds virtually throughout the extended Northeast; it is a retiring and strictly nocturnal woodland species, however, and relatively few people have even seen one. This diminutive mouser nests in abandoned flicker and pileated woodpecker cavities, and is famous for poking its head out the hole when its nest tree is thumped. You might attract this owl to a box mounted on a stub in a woodlot, but your chances would be better locating it in a damp mixed or coniferous woods.

The eastern screech-owl is a fringe bird in Canada, but it breeds — and probably winters — in every one of the United States. It makes itself at home in desert, savannah, farm, and open wooded country; it also breeds and winters in parks, orchards, and towns, whence, to the puzzlement and consternation of local inhabitants, it issues its whinnying wail. (No, it doesn't screech.) The screech-owl looks rather like a small great horned owl, and it shares with that species a reputation for fierceness. (The French names for the two are *grand duc* and *petit duc!*) The stories illustrating the screech-owl's toughness and aggressiveness are legion — one bird, entering a house via the chimney, discovered, extracted, and consumed the family's caged canary — but those who have seen its courtship and bathing antics also consider it a clown.

**Close quarters are the general rule for cavity nesters,
but this eastern screech-owl has appropriated palatial digs.**

The screech-owl is almost everyone's best chance for attracting an owl. Mount your box on a tree at the edge of a woodlot or in an unsprayed orchard. If you don't happen to have one of those handy, erect it almost anywhere else; screech-owls are obligingly unparticular. They are also unparticular about diet, feeding on mice, voles, small (and some not-so-small) birds, shrews, insects, even fish and worms. Fair numbers of both young and adult songbirds are taken during the nesting season, and this is another species you may not want to encourage near a martin or cliff swallow colony.

The French call the valentine-faced owl the *effraie* (from the verb *effrayer,* "to frighten"); perhaps American culture is not the only one for which the barn owl has become a standard gothic prop for the films and fiction of the haunted house. Barn owls are big and they are white (very ghostly in the moonlight); and they long ago gave up looking for hollow trees and cliff niches for roosting and nesting in favor of eerie places like abandoned towers and church steeples.

And, of course, barns. These owls are completely beneficial around the farm —

their diet consists of rodents and more rodents — and European farmers have long cut special owl windows high up on barn gables to admit the birds. But in many areas, abandoned buildings, open church steeples, and open barns are few, and barn owls are, as a consequence, scarce. Three biologists recently noticed, for example, that only a few barn owls were nesting in a region of northern Utah, and those in sub-optimal locations (haystacks, mostly). Suspecting that the species' problem was simply a lack of nest sites, they set to work building nesting boxes, which they placed near the top of unused, roofless concrete silos. A check during the second summer showed barn owls nesting in twenty-four of thirty boxes.

You may be able to attract barn owls whether you live in an urban or a rural area. The key is a nearby open area — field, meadow, pasture, golf course, airport, even a dump — harboring mice, voles, or rats (or, in the midwestern and prairie regions, gophers or ground squirrels). Suggested dimensions for a box, somewhat longer than high and wide, are given on the chart; but almost anything large enough — a nail keg, for example — will do. Mount your house well up on a pole or the side of a building. (A couple of inches of wood chips and shavings, the older the better, will be welcome in boxes for all three species of owls.) Of course, if you happen to own a nice barn or tower of some sort, you can dispense with all that building and erecting. Simply make access over any horizontal structure available, and the barn owls will take it from there.

DUCKS

If you have access to water — whether river, pond, slough, lake, or reservoir — with a wooded margin, you may want to try your luck at attracting wood ducks. Put several inches of old sawdust or wood shavings in the box, and mount it either over water or on a mature tree within a hundred yards or so of the water. If raccoons are numerous in the area, it's probably a good idea to make your house 24 inches long with a 3 x 4-inch slot hole well up toward the top. This should slow down raccoon predation, but it won't make your box any more selective. Everything from flying squirrels to screech-owls to grackles to Carolina wrens makes itself at home in wood duck boxes; where common, starlings are likely to be the biggest competitor.

There is a possibility of other ducks, too. The elegant hooded merganser is most likely, as it shares with the wood duck a wide common range as well as habitat preferences; in the northern part of our region, common goldeneye is a possibility. But wood duck is your best bet; this species, like the bluebird, seems actually to prefer a birdbox to a natural cavity, given the choice. Whatever duck you get, you won't see much activity around the box. The males of most species — the wood duck is an exception — desert the nest area shortly after the eggs are laid, and the females leave the wood-chip-and-down nest infrequently once incubation begins. What many would give a week's pay to see happens a month later. On the morning after the eggs hatch, the female calls from outside the box, and one at a time the ten or a dozen ducklings pop out the entrance hole and plop into the water or onto the ground, whence, in the latter event, the hen leads the collective fluff on a march to the water.

Oh, yes. Your wood duck habitat should be just right for what many consider our most spectacular box-nesting bird. If you are willing to play a long shot, mount a downy woodpecker or white-breasted nuthatch box four or five feet up on a stub over (or very near) standing or moving water along a wooded slough or river, and you just might attract a pair of our only cavity-nesting warbler, the beautiful and elusive prothonotary.

A pair of wood ducks — one of several cavity-nesting ducks — checks out prospective housing.

Watering Holes and Hummingbirds

In March the door of the seasons first stands ajar a little; in April it is opened much wider; in May the windows go up also; and in June the walls are fairly taken down and the genial currents have free play everywhere.

— JOHN BURROUGHS, ***Leaf and Tendril*** (1908)

JUNE 19TH, 4 TO 6½ P.M. [CAMDEN COUNTY, NEW JERSEY]— *Sitting alone by the creek — solitude here, but the scene bright and vivid enough — the sun shining, and quite a fresh wind blowing . . . the wild flageolet-note of a quail near by — the just-heard fretting of some hylas down there in the pond —crows cawing in the distance. . . . And still the clear notes of the quail . . . the swift darting of many sand-swallows coming and going, their holes in a neighboring marlbank — the odor of the cedar and oak, so palpable, as evening approaches — perfume, color, the bronze-and-gold of nearly ripen'd wheat — clover-fields, with honey-scent — the well-up maize,*

with long and rustling leaves — the great patches of thriving potatoes, dusky green, fleck'd all over with white blossoms. . . .

The pond itself, with the sword-shaped calamus; the water snakes — occasionally a flitting blackbird, with red dabs on his shoulders, as he darts slantingly by — the sounds that bring out the solitude, warmth, light and shade — the quawk of some pond duck — (the crickets and grasshoppers are mute . . . but I hear the song of the first cicadas;) — then at some distance the rattle and whirr of a reaping machine as the horses draw it on a rapid walk through a rye field on the opposite side of the creek — (what was the yellow or light-brown bird, large as a young hen, with short neck and long-stretch'd legs I just saw, in flapping and awkward flight over there through the trees?) —the prevailing delicate, yet palpable, spicy, grassy, clovery perfume to my nostrils; and over all . . . the free space of the sky, transparent and blue. . . .

—WALT WHITMAN, *Specimen Days* (1882)

AH, SPRING! The feeders are down, the birdhouses are up. Burroughs was right. The walls are coming down. Whitman had the right attitude. Time to relax and enjoy. Sit down by the pond, watch the red-wings, listen to the cicadas, smell the perfume of the new grass. Time to take a gin and tonic out on the patio, watch the robins and barn swallows gather mud, make sure the house sparrows don't get into the bluebird house. Courtship displays are in full swing. Probably you are already tired of the male grackles' swell-and-shriek act. The cowbirds are at it, too, and at least they are more inventive than the grackles. The male swells up toward the female, then simultaneously lifts and spreads his wings, elevates his tail, and ducks his head to the ground. If, as is usually the case, the female pays no attention, a short run at her may precede the main act, the general effect of the whole suggesting some sort of mechanical contrivance of wonderful execution but of doubtful purpose, misprogrammed perhaps.

Spring is a glorious time merely to sit and absorb. But before you progress from repose to languor and from there into outright stupor, it may be well to remember

---

Flowers such as bee-balm (page 192) and cardinal-flower
(page 193) attract ruby-throated hummingbirds. *Right:* Come spring,
a suet feeder becomes a handy container for dispensing
nesting materials for orioles and other birds.

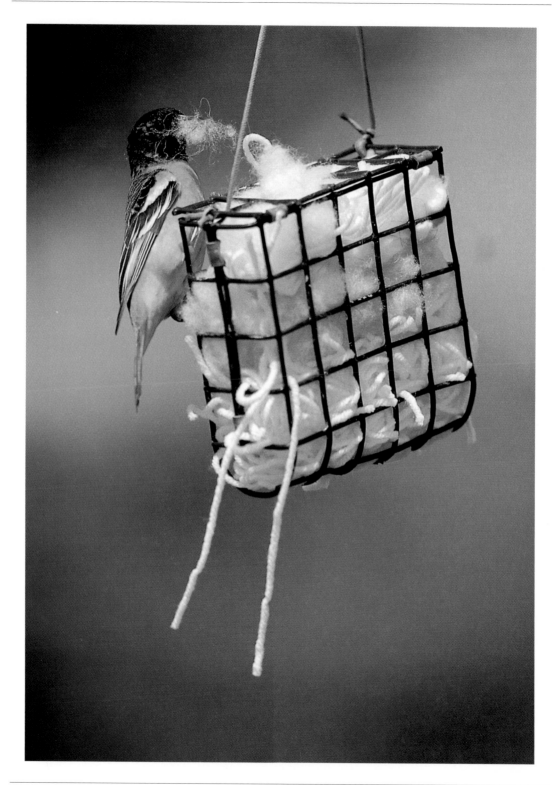

that there are a few things to do in spring besides cut the grass, even if you cannot or will not undertake the rigors of breeding-bird census work (see Chapter 8). One such task usually escapes the attention until one late-spring day. You pop around the corner of the house and surprise a female oriole trying to dismantle the clothesline or tugging at the drawstring of the pajamas hanging thereon. That's when you remember you had meant to put out some nesting material for the benefit of the local breeding birds. Of course, litterbugging mankind has been generous about scattering a wide variety of materials and objects around the landscape; and, although many of these items seem unpromising as nesting materials, most of them — including coins, nails, diaper pins, bottle caps, and the like — do in fact turn up in nests. Indeed, the great crested flycatcher has taken to substituting cellophane cigar wrappers for the traditional shed snake skin.

There are better nesting materials, however — soft, weaveable, insulative — some of which may be readily available around the house. I like the list in Thomas McElroy's *The New Handbook of Attracting Birds* (2nd edition, 1960):

• string	• bristles from old	• horsehair
• excelsior	paint brush	• stuffing from old
• knitting yarn	• thread	furniture
• kapok	• dried sphagnum	• dried grass
• shoemakers' flax	moss	• bits of fur
• cotton	• pieces of soft cloth	• dental floss
• raveled rope	• feathers	• wool
	• raveled burlap	• Spanish moss

Spanish moss is in short supply in the Northeast, of course, and most of us wouldn't recognize shoemakers' flax if we stepped on it; but used dental floss — now *there's* an idea!

McElroy anticipates a mistake that hadn't occurred to me. It might seem reasonable to poke some of these materials into your birdboxes — to give prospective tenants a start on a nest, as it were. Don't. This will only lead them to believe the box is occupied, sending them elsewhere. Put your materials out in some sort of open container — most suet feeders are ideal — where birds will see them, and let them do their own picking and choosing. However you choose to issue your materials, be sure any string, yarn, floss, or the like is cut into short lengths and dispensed individually. Nobody who has ever found a half-starved bird hung up in shrubbery, so tangled in string that it required surgical scissors to free it, will ever put out such materials in a mass or in lengths over eight inches.

E ARLY SPRING IS ALSO THE TIME to scrub up and fill your birdbath(s). Not all birds will drink or bathe in a birdbath (indeed, some species don't appear to bathe at all, preferring to dust or "ant"*), but many will; and it is not surprising that John K. Terres was able, after some years of observation, to record sixty-five species using birdbaths on his Long Island property. Of course, many of these birds were migrants, and baths are likely to draw the best variety of species in spring and fall. But water, both for bathing and drinking, is especially important during mid- and late summer, when days are hot and seasonal ponds and streams have dried up.

Few people have a reliable natural source of water on their property; for those who don't, a birdbath (or two) is a helpful alternative. The term "birdbath" immediately brings to mind an image of the conventional saucer-on-a-pedestal item sold by hardware stores and dealers in lawn paraphernalia. It needn't, however, as anything from a salad bowl or a flowerpot saucer to a garbage-can lid or the shell of a giant clam will do. Or a boulder with a depression in its upper surface, which can be enlarged and shaped with a stone chisel. Geodes, if available, will do nicely. Any of these — or any other basin-shaped object† — can be situated in your rock garden or sunk into the ground. (You can even dispense with the basin altogether, and simply line a depression in the ground with plastic or concrete.)

Ground baths are easy to install, but they have two major disadvantages. They act as catch-basins for whatever flotsam happens to be drifting about the neighborhood; and birds using them are vulnerable to ground predators, especially cats. A pedestal bath — or your boulder or garbage-can lid perched on a stump — will collect less refuse, be easier to clean out, and afford its users a better vantage point from which to watch for danger. Conventional birdbaths are available in a variety of materials. The cheapest is of plastic — you fill the hollow pedestal with sand for stability — and sells for under $10. From plastic one moves up by stages from clay

---

* Anting is the process by which birds dress their feathers with bill-held ants (or other acidic substances such as cigarette butts or moth balls), apparently benefiting from the ants' formic acid for purposes of parasite control, feather maintenance, or, during molt, the alleviation of skin irritation.

† A neighbor of ours complains that the birds ignore his conventional birdbath; what they prefer is the spare hubcap he keeps filled under a front-yard maple tree.

to concrete, each lasting longer and costing more. The most elegant baths are sculpted from marble, and are much appreciated by a very exclusive clientele. (The people who buy them, that is; the birds don't make the distinction.)

It has long been recognized that birds are especially attracted to moving water — water they can *hear*. So people install jet fountain systems in their baths, or

build a stone-and-cement edifice featuring a series of descending basins, each positioned to catch the miniature waterfall issuing from the one above. Obviously these systems require power to move the water, whether it recirculates through the agency of a built-in pump or merely runs off. The poor man's answer to jet sprays and waterfalls is the old bucket trick. Drill a tiny hole low down on the side of a bucket (holes through the bottom tend to clog), suspend it a couple of feet over the birdbath, fill it with water, and sit back to enjoy the *drip-drip* and the birds. Then you get up to enjoy the exercise of refilling the bucket.

Birds don't much care, then, of what material your birdbath is made; nor will they mind whether you mount it in the ground, on the ground, or above the ground. Size doesn't much matter either, though obviously the bigger the saucer, the more drinkers and bathers it can accommodate simultaneously. But *shape* does matter. Backyards are full of objects sold as, or intended for, birdbaths that never bathe a bird, simply because it never occurred to their

**Birds will use both in-ground and raised watering facilities;
the former is more natural, of course, but the latter provides
some protection from ground predators.**

owners that songbirds and people have diametrically opposed notions about what constitutes a desirable bathing facility. The bathtub is like a miniature swimming pool — deep, steep-sided, smooth-bottomed. Now, virtually all songbirds (dippers are the remarkable exception) are petrified of deep water. They require not a tub but a saucer, one which is shallow (no more than two and a half inches at the deep-

est point), gradually sloped right from the lip, and rough-bottomed. If what you are using for a birdbath is too deep, try putting a flat rock in the saucer and filling it to a level about two inches over the rock's surface. A layer of coarse sand on the bottom of a properly shaped but smooth-bottomed bath should help. Something of contrasting color may have to be added to a white saucer before many birds will use it; a birdbath isn't perceived as shallow unless the bird can *see* the bottom through the water.

Finally, the question of birdbath placement relative to accessible cover deserves consideration. Birds don't fly well with water-loaded plumage, and they appreciate preening perches near the bath. But low, heavy cover near birdbaths is an open invitation to cats, which soon learn to take birds directly from the bath. I think it makes sense, then, to have some kind of high cover (tree limbs, for example) or spare cover (your garden bean poles, for example) within, say, twelve feet of your bath, but to have no hedge or heavy bush cover within, say, twenty feet of it.

VARIOUS STRUCTURES ON YOUR PROPERTY may house the nests of species the bird-attracting books don't talk about, and spring is the season to watch for them. Of course, people are accustomed to house sparrows and starlings wedging their nests into gutters and under chimney flashing, and rock doves making themselves at home in barns. But relatively few people are aware of two other, highly attractive, species making use of their engineering enterprise. The rough-winged swallow, relatively quiet and noncolonial, is almost certainly the least-known of our six eastern swallows. Basically a burrow nester, the rough-wing has taken to nesting in pipes, especially drainage pipes. Where common, it moves into hill towns to nest in the pipes installed every few yards in the retaining walls holding earth on the uphill sides of streets and alleys. These nests can use some watching. There isn't much you can do about washouts, but schoolboys are wont to help themselves to nests and eggs once they notice the adult birds entering the drainpipes. (The boys' parents, of course, don't *know* birds are nesting in their drainpipes; if they notice the rough-wings at all, they write them off as odd-looking tree swallows.)

The other inadvertent "birdhouse" species I have in mind is more generally known, despite the fact that, being our most exclusively aerial bird, it is almost never seen close up.* A fellow clergyman related to Gilbert White a story about this bird's European counterpart; about how, when he was a schoolboy, "some workmen, in pulling down the battlements of a church tower early in the spring, found two or three swifts . . . among the rubbish, which were, at first appearance, dead, but, on being carried toward the fire, revived. He told me that, out of his great care to preserve them, he put them in a paper bag, and hung them by the kitchen fire, where they were suffocated."† This miscarriage occurred two and a half centuries ago, and swifts have been coming to grief at the hands of kitchen (and other) fires ever since.

The only eastern North American swift, the chimney swift has pretty much given up nesting in caves and hollow trees in favor of chimneys, to whose vertical inside walls it cements its half-a-cup twig nest with its gluey saliva. (Incidentally, the celebrated bird's-nest soup, valued in the Orient as an aphrodisiac, is made from the nests — constructed almost entirely of saliva — of several Asian relatives called swiftlets; you boil the whole nest in water, remove any feathers and vegetable impu-

---

*So totally divorced from the world of terrestrial man is this bird that, on the rare occasions when they meet face to face, they do so on unique terms. Unlike other birds, this one manifests, in the hand of the birdbander, no fear, no recognition, nothing. Released on the bander's arm, other birds flee; this species may well burrow up a sleeve or into an armpit and fall asleep!

† White relates this incident in Letter X to Thomas Pennant, dated August 4, 1767, in The Natural History and Antiquities of Selbourne.

rities, and eat what remains, a sort of glue stew.) Probably you will know it if you have a pair of swifts nesting in your chimney. The unique chippering note calls attention to them overhead, and they are quite noticeable as they circle and dive over a house in late spring, checking out a chimney, and later on as they dive into it with twigs and, eventually, with food for the young. Often, from inside the house, the adults' wing flutter can be heard descending the chimney, followed, as the nestlings mature, by their cheeping at feeding time.

Swift young are fed regurgitated insects, then straight insects, while they remain in the nest through at least midsummer. But even after fledging they may return to sleep and rest in the chimney until shortly before migrating. Thus swifts populate northern chimneys even into September, making those early-fall fireplace blazes a major cause of chimney swift mortality.* Before you start a fire to take an early-summer or early-fall chill off home or cabin, be sure you aren't destroying nests or killing birds in the process. If you want to be free to use a fireplace any time of the year, screen off the appropriate chimney entrance to prevent swifts' nesting and roosting there in the first place.

SWIFTS ARE SPECIAL. So are hummingbirds. Indeed, no other bird was greeted with the surprise and fascination directed at the ruby-throated hummingbird by the early European immigrants to our Atlantic shores — in part, no doubt, due to the fact that no hummingbird is indigenous to the Old World. Colonist William Wood wrote, in *New Englands Prospect* (1634): "The humbird is one of the wonders of the Countrey, being no bigger than a Hornet, yet hath all the demensions of a Bird, as bill, and wings, with quills, spider-like legges, small clawes: For colour, she is as glorious as the Raine-bow; as she flies, she makes a little humming noise

---

* *Autumn fires may kill more than a family of swifts, as the species flocks up prior to migration and roosts communally. Audubon writes in the* Ornithological Biography *about a remarkable roost tree — a giant hollow sycamore — he was shown outside Louisville, Kentucky. He stationed himself at the tree before dawn, hoping to witness the birds' exit. "All was silent within when I placed my head to the tree, which I did for about twenty minutes. Suddenly I thought the great sycamore was giving way and about to come down on me. Instinctively I sprang from it. I looked up and to my astonishment saw the Swifts pouring out in a black continued stream and the tree standing firm as ever. Again I ran back to my listening post; I can only compare the noise within to the sound of a large wheel revolving under a powerful mill stream." It took the flock a half hour to leave the roost tree, and Audubon estimated its numbers at 9,000 birds.*

like a Humble-bee: wherefore shee is called the Humbird."

The colonists would have been astonished to learn that the hummingbird family is a huge one: something like 320 species have been identified, and new species are still coming out of the mahogany woodwork of northern South America. (Koepcke's hermit, for example, was collected and named from eastern and northern Peru in 1969, while the royal sunangel — the fork-tailed male is entirely deep violet-blue — was discovered in northern Peru in 1975.) Nor would the colonists have credited descriptions of many of these birds, whose irradiant colors, rococo feather adornments, and bizarre bill shapes match (and are often described by) their exotic names — lazuline sabrewing, sparkling violetear, buff-tailed sicklebill, peacock coquette, glittering-bellied emerald, red-billed azurecrown, marvelous spatuletail, empress brilliant, fiery topaz, shining sunbeam, bearded mountaineer, hyacinth visorbearer, magenta-throated woodstar, and on and on.

The hummingbird tribe, undoubtedly of tropical origin, largely remains a tropical and subtropical one, with but a handful of species ranging more than 30 degrees north or south of the equator. In North America, only eight species are extensive breeders north of the Mexican border. Seven have followed the Central American mountain chains into the American West, of which one — the rufous hummingbird — breeds as far north as southeastern Alaska. Only one species has so far exploited eastern North America for breeding purposes. The ruby-throated hummingbird nests across the entire eastern half of the U.S., and across southern Canada from Nova Scotia to Alberta.

Our ruby-throat, though plain by comparison with many of its tropical relatives, exemplifies the intriguing hummer traits: the diminutive dimensions, the blur-winged flight, the unique feeding habit, the fearlessness and curiosity. If few birds have so stirred human interest, few have been subject to so many misconceptions. Take flight speed. Ordinary birds "fly," but hummingbirds "zip" or "dart," and great speeds have been attributed to them. Mostly their apparent speed is an optical illusion, based upon the fact that the smaller of two objects traveling the same speed will appear to be going faster, and upon our tendency to translate wing-flap speed into flight speed. Hence, on both counts, ducks seem to fly faster than geese, and hummers appear positively jet-propelled. But experiments in a wind tunnel

Twin ruby-throated hummingbird nestlings are a tight fit in their quarter-size, lichen-camouflaged nest.

suggest that ordinary hummingbird flight speed is about 25 mph, little faster than that of most songbirds.

Many early observers thought hummingbirds were attracted to flowers not for their nectar, but for the insects attracted by the nectar; this is not surprising, since north-latitude Europeans and Americans had much experience with insectivorous birds but none at all with nectivorous ones. Audubon was one of these, writing in the *Ornithological Biography* that the "nectar which they sip from flowers is less to support them than to allay their thirst." But for those few species for which controlled diet studies have been made, nectar constitutes the bulk of the diet whenever it is available, with insects added for protein. (Relative to other birds, hummers have small stomachs and large livers, which is what one would expect for an animal subsisting on a high-carbohydrate diet.) Those observers who recognized that hummingbirds were after nectar assumed the birds sucked it up. But a hummer tongue is no straw. The part of the organ that can be extended beyond the bill tip is split into two thin membranes, each of which curls to form a kind of trough. These troughs apparently take up the nectar through capillary action, whence it is transferred by the retracted tongue to the throat for swallowing.

Finally, Audubon, among others, believed the male ruby-throat to be a model of conjugal affection and paternal attention, the former notion probably deriving from the courtship display, during which the male repeatedly swings in pendulum arcs over the perched female. But, after the manner of the polygynous hummingbird tribe generally, the male ruby-throat's part in family life typically ends with copulation, after which he goes his own way, never even knowing the location of the resulting nest(s).

THE SMALLEST BIRDS IN THE WORLD, of course, are hummingbirds,* and their size is no small part of their fascination. This applies not only to the birds themselves, but to their tiny, exquisitely structured and decorated nests, their pea-sized eggs, and their newly hatched young, which the noted Central American naturalist Alexander F. Skutch has described as "ugly, unpromising little grubs." But these homely hatchlings soon grow into resplendent adults, whose iridescent

---

Not all hummingbirds are tiny. The appropriately named giant hummingbird of western South America is nearly as long as a robin, and the bill of northern South America's sword-billed hummingbird is longer than our ruby-throat lock, stock, and bill.

plumage and delicate proportions drew the attention of the early-nineteenth-century European fashion industry. Although many people know of the infamous egret-plume trade in the American Southeast, few realize that hummingbirds were shipped by the *millions* from the American tropics across the Atlantic to be plunked whole on women's hats. Skutch, in *The Life of the Hummingbird* (1973), claims that "a single London dealer imported more than 400,000 [hummingbird] skins from the West Indies" in one year alone. He continues: "Keeping a keen eye on this vast flow of desiccated birds from little-known lands, the cabinet naturalists of Europe detected and described many hitherto unknown species, often naming them for men or women whom they admired or wished to flatter. In this way, many birds of the republican Americas came to bear the names of European princes and noblemen."

The rapacious eye of female fashion no longer turns the hummingbirds' way, but diminutive size poses other problems. Energetics is very dicey for a tiny, high-metabolism animal. Some ornithologists believe a hummer ends a feeding bout before its crop is full simply because the energy that would have to be expended to carry the extra weight would make a full meal counterproductive. Many hummingbirds become torpid during cold nights (this has been called "noctivation") to avoid burning themselves out of fuel before morning. And, although their marvelous maneuverability on the wing makes them largely immune to ordinary bird predators, hummers are subject by virtue of their size to unexpected kinds of predation. They get trapped in spider webs and are occasionally captured by fish and frogs while hovering about ponds. Even insects have been known to prey on them; there are records of both dragonflies and praying mantises seizing ruby-throats.

THE STORY OF HUMMINGBIRDS is, more than anything else, the story of flowers. The first stop for migratory hummers in North America in early spring is the citrus groves of California and Florida, whence they drift north following the early blossoms. (Often they overrun their flowers in the last migratory push, ruby-throats, for example, arriving on their northernmost Canadian breeding range in late May, where they subsist on sap and insects at sapsucker feeding holes while waiting for the season to catch up.) It is natural that we think of the hummers as exploiting the flowers; this was Audubon's perception when he expressed the hope that the flowers would forgive the "theft" of nectar in light of the hummingbirds' service in relieving the plants of injurious insects. But, of course, the plant isn't saving the nectar for dessert; the nectar is a lure, designed to attract hummingbirds as an agent of cross-pollination to ensure the vitality of the plant's progeny. So it is the plant that exploits the bird, really, rather than the other way around. (Exploitation need not imply that one party is disadvantaged, and in the case of flower and hummer the exploited party is perfectly content with the arrangement.)*

Most plants that attract pollination help with the lure of nectar utilize insects rather than birds, and presumably plants were doing so long before there *were* any hummingbirds. There has been a great deal of interest recently in the question of the origin and subsequent evolution of this wonderfully co-adapted system of hummingbird/flower mutualism. The following scenario, based on both research and guesswork, suggests how it may have happened.† An ancestor of the hummingbird tribe (swift-like? honeycreeper-like?) took to sampling nectar while picking insects out of flowers, liked it, and began to visit flowers regularly. One or more nectar-producing plant species now saw a good thing developing, and took a chance by opting out of the competition for insect pollinators to go exclusively for bird pollinators. To this end, a typical flower probably dropped its blue coloration, which is well seen by bees, in favor of red, which is well seen by birds but not by bees. It may at the same time have given over producing perfume, which is attractive to insects but not to birds.

Meanwhile, the floral parts were undergoing changes. The flower's reproductive

---

**Hummingbirds are known and much appreciated
for their aerial acrobatics.**

A similar strategy is employed by berry-producing plants, for which the pulp surrounding the seed(s) is merely a lure to attract eaters as a help to dispersal. These plants, called "zoochores," make their berries attractive, accessible, and adequately nutritious all in hopes of drawing consumers. A distinguished British ornithologist has even suggested that the sliding north-to-south timetable for the ripening of these fruits may not be the result of climatic pressures, but rather a tactic employed to take advantage of the north-to-south movement of fall-migrating birds. See D. W. Snow's article "Evolutionary Aspects of Fruit-Eating by Birds," in The Ibis *(1971).*

† This discussion is particularly indebted to Karen A. Grant and Verne Grant's Hummingbirds and Their Flowers *(1968). Although I treat this co-evolutionary development in terms of boardroom decision-making, the reader will appreciate that the developments described, or something like them, were the result of natural selection operating with random aberrations over many generations.*

organs migrated to positions assuring contact with the bird's feathers. (Typically anthers and stigma are stalked above or below the corolla entrance, so that hummers pick up pollen with, and deposit it from, crown or chin feathers.) Floral tubes, like the new hummingbird's bill and tongue, lengthened, and landing platforms — which the new "hover-bird" didn't need — disappeared, both to discourage visits from insects. (Insects weren't likely to pick up pollen from the repositioned anthers, so it no longer made sense to grant them access to the nectar.) The flower's ovary got a protective cover or migrated away from the nectary, in order to protect it from the jabbing bill of the new pollinator. Finally, a given area's bird-flowers arranged to stagger their peak blooming periods, both to reduce competition among themselves for pollination service and to assure that nectar would be available to their pollinators throughout as much of the tropical year as the rains allow.

In the temperate zone, hummingbird plants may even want to settle on a common flower color. It was long ago noticed that most bird-pollinated flowers in the American West, for example, were red, and observers plausibly concluded that hummingbirds preferred red to other colors. But controlled experiments have shown that hummers show no such preference. The Grants theorize that the plants have "decided" on a single color — it might just as well have been yellow — as a form of advertisement, a strategy advantageous to both plants and hummers, especially in the North, where the birds are both few and migratory. As the migrating ruby-throats and calliopes and broad-tails move up and down the North American continent, they don't have to waste time searching for good nectar-producing flowers in strange territory: they merely head for red. The situation is different in the American tropics, where both hummingbirds and their flowers are far more plentiful and various. Here most hummers are year-round residents, and hence they have the opportunity to learn and utilize a much wider variety of plants featuring a wide variety of flower colors.

THE HUMMINGBIRD ATTRACTION CENTER of North America is, of course, the American Southwest. Mile Hi Ranch in Arizona's Ramsey Canyon — now owned and protected by The Nature Conservancy — is particularly famous for its hummers, with more than a dozen species, including occasional visitants from Mexico, turning up more or less regularly. With only one species to hope for, attracting hummingbirds is a low-key business in the Northeast; but ruby-throats are wonderfully appealing birds, and it is not difficult to attract them. First of all, grit your teeth and bear it if a pair of yellow-bellied sapsuckers decides to drill one of your apple or birch trees. Ruby-throats will feed at sapsucker drills all through the breeding season. (A study in Michigan recorded twenty species of birds feeding at seven sapsucker trees; of these, ruby-throated hummingbirds visited most frequently — more often than the sapsuckers themselves!)

Next, establish a variety of plants whose flowers are known to attract hummers. Some of these — a good clue is a trumpet-shaped blossom — are plants specifically adapted to bird pollination ("ornithophilous plants" is the fancy name), while others are also pollinated by insects; many are common garden flowers. Among hummingbird favorites are: various lilies, including the tiger-lily *(Lilium tigrinum)* and day-lily *(Hemerocallis fulva)*; painted-cups *(Castilleja)*; azaleas *(Rhododendron)*; sages *(Salvia)*; currants and gooseberries *(Ribes)*; fuchsias *(Fuchsia)*; the horsemints bee-balm *(Monarda didyma)* and wild bergamot *(M. fistulosa)*; clematis *(Clematis)*; the purple loosestrifes *(Lythrum)*; foxgloves *(Digitalis)*; larkspurs *(Delphinium)*; petunias *(Petunia)*; gas plant *(Dictamnus albus)*; phlox *(Phlox)*; pinks *(Dianthus)*; bleeding heart *(Dicentra spectabilis)*; snapdragons *(Antirrhinum)*; gladioli *(Gladiolus)*; penstemons *(Penstemon)*; and scarlet runnerbean *(Phaseolus coccineus)*. Favored trees are black locust *(Robinia pseudo-acacia)* and, in the southern part of the region, the mimosa or silk-tree *(Albizzia julibrissin)*.

The above species of hummingbird plants have something else in common — they bloom, for the most part, in summer. But ruby-throats arrive in St. Louis and Washington, D.C., in mid-April, and hit the Canadian border in mid-May. If you want hummers to stay in your neighborhood to breed, you'll want some spring-blooming plants waiting for them. Among the best are: lilacs *(Syringa)*; honeysuckles *(Lonicera)*; columbines *(Aquilegia)*; coral bells *(Heuchera saguinea)*; and, in addition, the early pinks, azaleas, larkspurs, and sages. Hummers also feed at several early-blooming trees, including, along with fruit trees, the common horse-chestnut *(Aesculus hippocastanum)* and the early hawthorns (among those occurring widely in the Northeast are *Crataegus chrysocarpa, C. crus-galli, C. intricata, C. macrosperma, C. margaretta,* and *C. roanensis).*

Then you'll want to have autumn-blooming hummingbird plants as well, to which female ruby-throats breeding in the area can bring their young, and where migrating birds can spend a few days feeding along the way. The best of these plants include: trumpet creeper *(Campsis radicans)*; jewelweed *(Impatiens capensis* and *I. pallida)*; cardinal-flower *(Lobelia cardinalis)*; morning-glories *(Ipomoea)*; hollyhock

(Althaea rosea); petunias *(Petunia);* and the late sages (especially pineapple sage, *Salvia rutilans).**

Finally, you can, like most hummingbird fanciers, supplement nectar-producing plants with a hanging or staked hummingbird feeder or two. Simple test tubes or small beakers will suffice, although the commercially available feeders, which dispense the syrup from the bottom, are more efficient and are not expensive. (These are available from bird-feeder manufacturers and from garden centers.) What you feed in a hummingbird feeder is a sugarwater solution; but which sugar? If honey has at least a few nutritionally redeeming qualities while white sugar has none, oughtn't honey be used for hummers, too? The people at Arizona's Mile Hi Ranch, who feed as much as four gallons of syrup a day through twenty feeders, say no. They maintain that birds find ordinary sugar more easily digestible than honey. Additionally, honey is subject to fermentation during hot weather, and fermentation produces alcohol, which kills beneficial microorganisms in the birds' digestive tracts. While many people feed a three-to-one mix, the Mile Hi formula is four parts water to one part sugar — the former boiled to kill bacteria and ensure a good mix. Excess syrup can be refrigerated for later use. Red food coloring is often suggested as a syrup additive, but it is neither beneficial (and may be harmful) nor necessary. It is, after all, the flower that's brightly colored, not the nectar. Color the feeder if you wish, but leave the syrup clear. Most commercial feeders feature red plastic parts — often in the form of rosettes (simulating flowers) around the feeding hole(s). The test-tube feeder can achieve the same effect with the addition of a red ribbon or a piece of taped red plastic. Once hummers have discovered a feeder, they remember its location; for them, the color attractant serves no further purpose.

Northeastern gardens, no matter how rich in blossoms and syrup, are not going to attract black-chinned or Rivoli's or white-eared or Lucifer or berylline hummingbirds. For those you'll have to visit Ramsey Canyon, perhaps spend a week at Mile Hi Ranch. But you should attract ruby-throated hummingbirds, which will animate your flower beds and may even appear at garden watering sessions to sport in the spray. For bonuses, sphinx moths and butterflies will visit your flowers, while orioles and the odd warbler will probably partake of your syrup. Other, less appreci-

---

* In the Northeast, a southern plant like pineapple sage will need to be overwintered indoors in the form of rooted cuttings taken before frost; these can then be planted in the garden the following spring.

ated creatures are fond of sugarwater, too. Bees will come, and some of William Wood's "humble-bees" will dominate the hummers! And then there are the ants, which are to hummingbird feeders what squirrels are to sunflower feeders. If all else fails, the gooey commercial stuff called Tanglefoot will stop ants; but first try tansy *(Tanacetum vulgare),* the traditional anti-ant herb.

CHAPTER VIII

Mapping the Birds of Summer

Our amusements on Saturday afternoons and vacations depended mostly on getting away from home into the country, especially in the spring when the birds were calling loudest . . . . Like devout martyrs of wildness, we stole away to the seashore or the green, sunny fields . . . to join our companions, oftenest to hear the birds sing and hunt their nests, glorying in the number we had discovered and called our own. A sample of our nest chatter was something like this: Willie Chisholm would proudly exclaim — "I ken (know) seventeen nests, and you, Johnnie, ken only fifteen."

"But I wouldna gie my fifteen for your seventeen, for five of mine are larks and mavises. You ken only three o' the best singers."

"Yes, Johnnie, but I ken six goldies and you ken only one. Maist of yours are only sparrows and linties and robin-redbreasts."

. . . One night, when David and I were at grandfather's fireside solemnly learning our lessons as usual, my father came in with news, the most wonderful, most glorious, that wild boys ever heard. "Bairns," he said, "you needna learn

your lessons the nicht, for we're gan to America the morn!" No more grammar,
but boundless woods full of mysterious good things; trees full of sugar, growing in
ground full of gold; hawks, eagles, pigeons, filling the sky; millions of birds' nests,
and no gamekeepers to stop us in all the wild, happy land.

— JOHN MUIR, *The Story of My Boyhood and Youth* (1913)

I N THOSE AREAS OF THE TROPICS with minimal climatic variation, there is no breeding "season." Populations of various species breed the year round, and individual birds may shorten their breeding cycle from the temperate zone's standard twelve months.* Since breeding need not be synchronized with a favorable weather season, it can be timed to coincide with other sorts of seasons. A particular species may nest when its prey is most abundant, when its predators are scarcest, or when its preferred nesting sites are most numerous. (The least popular period for breeding among Central American resident birds corresponds with North American winter, presumably because of increased competition for food from our migrant flycatchers, swallows, thrushes, vireos, warblers, and tanagers.) Many species inhabiting the arid interior of Australia are opportunistic breeders; they nest after a good rain, no matter what the time of year.

If it is fair enough, in contrast, to call our North American breeding season a restricted, annual affair, it is nevertheless a surprisingly prolonged one. Indeed, it never quite ends in the Deep South and on the west coast, where there are breeding records for several species of birds for every month of the year. Even at the latitude of the Canadian border the breeding season extends from February, when the big owls commence nesting, through September, when a few late-clutch songbird young are still being fed. Owls aren't the only birds getting an early start in the North. House sparrows begin to cart nesting material around during late February, and March finds them courting just when the local starlings begin to show green in the head. Spring hawk migration watchers in April discover incubating birds of several species well north into Canada.

More often heard than seen, the prothonotary warbler
(page 213) is a denizen of shadowy swamps and sloughs.

* *A pair may, for example, initiate nesting at intervals of eleven months; hence the birds will —*
if they live long enough — eventually nest in every month of the year.

June and July, however, are the heart of our songbird breeding season; and they have traditionally been considered, along with August, the dead part of the birding year: a hiatus between the excitement of spring and fall migrations. The passage birds are gone, and resident species fade into the bush, increasingly quiet, to get on with the business of breeding. Hunting birds' nests was all very well for schoolboys like John Muir, but the passion, alas, soon fades. High summer, most birders agreed, was Dullsville, and they cased their binoculars, folded their tents, and stole away. That was before Atlas.

Three books, each bearing a 1976 copyright date, published the results of an idea that would quickly change the summer habits of birders on several continents. They are titled *The Atlas of Breeding Birds in Britain and Ireland, Atlas des Oiseaux Nicheurs de France,* and *De danske ynglefugles udbredelse.* What the British Isles, France, and Denmark had done was nothing less than organize and carry out a breeding-bird census of every square (or rectangle) of their respective national grids, in order to map, by presence or absence, the breeding status of every summer resident in every part of the countries involved.

The British were first in the field, and their experience is instructive. Leading British ornithologists had spent the mid-1960s debating the possibility and merit of a Great Britain — or even British Isles — bird Atlas. They had for a model the 1962 *Atlas of the British Flora,* which mapped the distribution of some 2,000 plant species within each 10-km square (100 square kilometers) of the national grid. It had taken 1,500 botanists over a decade to complete that census. Ornithological optimists pointed out that there were a lot more birders than botanists in the British Isles, and that there were only 200-plus species of nesting birds to chase down. Pessimists objected that, since birds move around, you cannot afford to spend ten years censusing them; doubters also pointed out that, while you have only to *find* a plant, you have to *prove* a bird is breeding. Even the optimists believed that coverage would prove uneven — good in England, mediocre in Wales, poor in Scotland, and in Ireland (if included) a total disaster.

The optimists finally prevailed — impetus was provided by the successful completion of a regional bird Atlas in the British West Midlands — and the project was launched in 1968 under the sponsorship of the British Trust for Ornithology and the Irish Wildbird Conservancy. It would encompass the whole of the British Isles. It must be completed in five years, "a short enough time to freeze distributions, but long enough to ensure an adequate sample of remote areas." The British Isles' 3,862

Brown thrashers, like their mimic relatives, tend to nest in thick cover, preferably viny and spiny.

10-km squares were divided into 121 regions, each of which became the assigned responsibility of one or several regional organizers. A special annual supplement to the British Trust's *BTO News,* devoted to the Atlas project, was distributed through regional organizers to participating birders. By the end of the project, over 21,000 copies of the supplement were being printed.

J.T.R. Sharrock, the national organizer, and David Scott led mobile units summer after summer through the remote areas of Scotland and Ireland. When it became clear after several years of fieldwork that certain species were being underreported, the *BTO News* published articles detailing how and where to find them, and finally pleas for help were directed to the general public through several appropriate journals and over the BBC. In the final year, squares with inadequate coverage were assigned to at least two independent observers; if all else failed, "squares were given emergency coverage by a flying squad of special experts."

When it was all over, some 12,000 birders had filled in 95,000 record cards while atlasing those nearly 4,000 10-km squares. Master cards were checked and rechecked; they were then passed to a commercial firm for computer punching, after which the data traveled to the Biological Records Centre at Monks Wood for mapmaking. The ensuing volume, which proudly refers to the Atlas as "the most comprehensive co-operative ornithological project ever undertaken in Britain and Ireland, and probably anywhere in the world," transfers over 285,000 breeding records onto 218 species-distribution maps. Virtually blank maps mean rare breeders: one Temminck's stint (a small shorebird) confirmed; a single snowy owl confirmed on the northernmost islands; two confirmations of the elusive spotted crake; two hoopoes (an exotic Mediterranean bird) breeding on the southern coast of England. The most common species produced nearly solid-red maps, and it is a pleasure to learn that skylark, noted in 98 percent of the blocks, and wren (our winter wren), found in 97 percent, beat out both starling (96 percent) and house sparrow (94 percent) in terms of general distribution. A supplementary series of twelve transparent overlay maps of environmental factors (altitude, mean January and July temperatures, rainfall) and special habitat types (lowland heath, moorland, chalk and limestone — whose well-drained soils are "particularly attractive to some ground-nesting species") was made available, with which one can seek for particular correlations among the maps.

Opposite each distribution map is a page of text, a wonderfully interesting essay treating the bird's present and past breeding status and something of its breeding biology. A black-and-white sketch of the species and an educated guess as to numbers of breeding pairs in the British Isles complete the attractive package. *The Atlas of Breeding Birds in Britain and Ireland* remains the class of the field, a model for Atlases since published and yet to come.

The English, Welsh, Scots, and Irish were still in the midst of their five-year program when New Zealand, France, and Denmark undertook Atlases of their own. When it became clear that national Atlases were possible, nearly the whole of Europe got into the act. West Germany, Belgium, Finland, Italy, the Netherlands, Norway, Portugal, Spain, Sweden, and Switzerland started to atlas in the West. In the East, Bulgaria, Czechoslovakia, Estonian SSR, Poland, Turkey, and Yugoslavia undertook Atlas projects. Malta, the Mediterranean island country the size of three British Atlas squares, was atlased. In Australia, birders set out to atlas an entire continent.

The Atlas germ had crossed the Atlantic by 1971, where it found a foothold in Montgomery County, Maryland, just northwest of Washington, D.C. Organized by the county chapter of the Maryland Ornithological Society, the Montgomery County project took three years to atlas sixty blocks, each representing one-sixth of a standard 7½-minute U.S. Geological Survey topographic map. Each such block represents approximately 10 square miles. Because the blocks are about five kilometers on a side, they are also called 5-km squares, of which four approximate the area of a single British Isles 10-km square.

While Montgomery County was finishing up in 1973, neighboring Howard County started a three-year program atlasing on a still finer scale, dividing the 7½-minute topographic maps into twenty-four 2½-km squares. Chandler S. Robbins, research biologist with the U.S. Fish and Wildlife Service, senior author of a popular field guide to birds, and an authority on North American bird distribution, was a leading force behind the Maryland (and subsequent U.S.) Atlas projects. He says the Maryland people were sold on the smaller 2½-km squares, feeling that they require little extra work and provide a better sense of detail: "In Howard County we've been able to address questions like how extensive a piece of habitat is required to support nesting in a particular species."

Obviously the smaller the census unit the more particular and useful the information. The smaller the square, however, the more time and effort required, the more map copying and administrative work, and the more onerous the record-keeping burden on the birders involved. The 5-km, 10-square-mile block has become the standard North American Atlas unit, one providing good geographical detail and requiring as much fieldwork as the traffic is likely to bear.

The 5-km unit was chosen by the first organizations to undertake statewide Atlases. The Commonwealth of Massachusetts took the plunge first, in 1974, hoping to census the state's 989 blocks in five years. The Massachusetts program, sponsored by the Massachusetts Audubon Society and the Massachusetts Division of Fish and Wildlife, was well organized and well manned. Some 1,200 birders profited from a series of newsletters explaining the program, offering advice on how best to confirm breeding for difficult species (owls, hawks, hole nesters, vireos), and noting problems and field triumphs along the way. Still, the end of the five years came and a number of blocks were insufficiently covered. Undaunted, Mass Audubon dug up $4,000 to hire three full-time fieldworkers, and threw everything they had into a sixth and final year. Atlas coordinator Richard A. Forster believes that, given the scope of the project, the results have been satisfactory. He puts the number of uncovered blocks at fewer than ten, and believes that something like half the state's blocks were well covered. An early newsletter predicted that 180-plus species would be found nesting in the state; in the event, 192 were confirmed during the program, with seven additional species recorded but unconfirmed.

Meanwhile, in 1976, Vermont became the first rural state to take on the challenge of Atlas. Deborah Howard, then coordinating the Massachusetts effort, spoke at the 1975 Vermont Institute of Natural Science's annual statewide bird conference. She pointed out that atlasers in her state were finding the U.S. Geological Survey topo-map marshes metamorphosed to parking lots and shopping centers, and urged Vermont to get going while the state was still relatively undeveloped. Most of the state's active birders were enthusiastic, and a trial-year project was set up by the Vermont Institute of Nature Science (VINS) and the state Audubon Council, a loose federation of seven Audubon chapters plus VINS. But the trial year showed the predictable difficulty with atlasing rural areas: lack of personnel. Vermont is twenty times the size of Montgomery County, Maryland, but has many fewer people. Metropolitan Boston alone has eight times the population of Vermont, and presumably eight times as many birders. VINS and the Audubon Council then set up a program to atlas one of the six 5-km squares from each 7½-minute topo map, the priority blocks to be randomly selected to ensure statistically valid results. In addition to these 179 priority blocks, some sixty additional blocks were chosen as "UFAs" (containing, that is, unique and fragile areas). Vermont commenced its five-year program in 1977.

When the calendar turned 1980, then, only Massachusetts had completed a statewide Atlas in North America. But Maryland was working its way through its counties, Vermont was well along on its program, and now other states were atlasing. Illinois, Maine, Wyoming, and New York had begun statewide Atlases; California and Michigan had undertaken to atlas selected counties. Other projects were in the planning stages, and then, in the late fall of 1980, a North American Ornithological Atlas Committee was established at the Symposium on Estimating the Numbers of Terrestrial Birds being held at Asilomar, California. Chaired by California State University (Sacramento) ornithologist Miklos D. F. Udvardy, NAOAC is comprised of delegates from Canada, the U.S., and Mexico; it works to encourage and coordinate regional Atlas programs, and hopes to "promote, at an appropriate time, a North American Breeding Bird Atlas Project." The 1970s had been the decade of the breeding-bird Atlas in Europe; the 1980s and 1990s would prove to be the Atlas decades in North America.

I spent much too much time — glorious time — during the summers of the late '70s and early '80s tracking down breeding birds in Vermont and upstate New York. What follows is a journal remembrance of one of those summers, devoted to Atlas block No. 5135. (The first two numbers represent north-south and east-west coordinates on the 15-minute topo map; the third number locates the proper 7½-minute quarter of that map, and the final number identifies the position of the block within the quarter.) While block No. 5135 is in fact a scruffy, hilly lowland piece of Champlain Valley farm country in west-central Vermont, it could pretty well pass for 10 square miles of field-and-woodlot back country anywhere in northeastern or north-central America.

May 27 You get up and look out the window and it strikes you that spring is over. Spring migration has been petering out, of course, but mostly it's the look of the open spaces. The dandelions have blown in the pastures, and quite suddenly the world is a duller place. Clover, daisies, cow vetch, and birdsfoot trefoil are putting on their modest show, but the great glorious waves of yellow are gone. The spirea is fading around the farmhouses, and the peonies, after all that ant-foot stimulation, are finally beginning to bloom. (This likely forecasts two days of wind and rain.) The early nesters — robin, grackle, starling, song sparrow — are already feeding young. Time to start atlasing.

PAST TIME, ACTUALLY. One of the most difficult tasks Atlas coordinators and area organizers face is getting birders into their blocks in late winter and through the spring. February and March may seem implausible months to be worrying about breeding birds, but great horned and barred owls are incubating, red-tailed and red-shouldered hawks are courting, and woodcock are back and *peent*-ing on the strutting grounds. Then, too, late winter and early spring constitute the best season to locate avian predators' nests, before the deciduous trees leaf out to make nest hunting difficult. At least one Massachusetts atlaser wasn't content to mark the location of winter-discovered bulky stick nests on his map; he also marked each tree with special short-lived fluorescent paint. He then checked each nest in early spring, hoping to find a nesting crow, hawk, or owl. (You pretty much take potluck at these nests; this year's crow nest may be next year's long-eared owl nest, while this year's red-tailed hawk nest may be tenanted next year by a great horned owl.)

Most songbird atlasing, however, is done in June and July, when all birds present can be assumed to be residents rather than migrants. And what residents are doing in June and July is breeding, if only you can catch them at it.

June 7 Singing cuckoos (mostly black-billed) seem to be everywhere in the Champlain Valley this year, due perhaps to the good tent caterpillar crop. A black-billed skulks about a hedgerow down a farm road. I stoop down and look up into the tangle, and shortly spot a nest of about the right size. It takes ten minutes to climb to a nest a mere eight feet off the ground in the dogwood and grape tangle. The nest proves not only empty but too well-made for cuckoo. The gray-stemmed dogwood and prickly ash hedgerow, undercarpeted with poison ivy, stretches a couple of miles along the road. There may well be a cuckoo nest in that hedgerow, but clearly nobody is going to find it before the leaves come down.

Something big lands in the tree row down the road. It proves to be a female pileated woodpecker. She's working a branch on a dead elm for under-bark insects, her feet clasped around the sides of the limb while she probes with the bill behind a section of bark, then whacks it off. Then the probe (probably securing insects with the tongue), then the whack. Pileateds are funny birds. The big, floppy black-and-white body topped by an enormous bill with an insufficient head attached is supposed to belong to a wary deep-woods bird that gets a living by excavating for carpenter ants, producing those great oblong holes that leave a tree looking as if someone had meant to turn it into bread-pan molds. But this bird is foraging down a sparsely treed road between open fields, bark-whacking like an overgrown hairy woodpecker,* and paying no attention to the man standing on the road wondering in which woods this bird is nesting, remembering how difficult it has proved in the past to find the pileated's dome-shaped nest hole. Mark black-billed cuckoo and pileated woodpecker down as Possibles.

A stop at the cliff along the glorified drainage ditch called the Lemon Fair River pays off. A quick scan of the cliff face reveals a phoebe sitting on one of those beautiful big mossy nests, perched on a tiny ledge well up the face. (Phoebe nests are of-

---

* A four-year study of woodpecker foraging strategies conducted in Virginia's Jefferson National Forest suggests that bark-scaling, a fairly common winter tactic among hairy woodpeckers, is seldom used by pileated woodpeckers during summer or winter, but is occasionally employed during the fall months. See Richard N. Conner's "Seasonal Changes in Woodpecker Foraging Methods: Strategies for Winter Survival," in The Role of Insectivorous Birds in Forest Ecosystems, edited by J. G. Dickson et al. (1979).

ten picturesquely located. A week later I find one with eggs inside a two-holer behind a long-closed one-room stone schoolhouse.) Phoebes are a dime a dozen, but we'll take every confirmation we can get: mark NE for eastern phoebe.

A quick stop down Doolittle Road, where a kestrel had perched on a likely-looking snag in the middle of a pasture a week before. I watch the huge dead elm, but there is no kestrel activity. Then, as I'm leaving, I hear young birds hollering at the approach of a parent. *Loud* hollering. Twenty yards down the road I put the binoculars on a large hole in a dead elm trunk. Two fuzzy kestrel heads are peering out. I back off and watch. After five minutes the male parent streaks in, drops off prey, and is gone before I can get the glasses up. I'm ready the next time, but the transfer is so fast I still can't identify the prey. Kestrel is the easiest predator to confirm, but *any* predator is a good bird. Mark it down: NY on American kestrel.

AMERICAN ATLAS RECORD CARDS (or sheets) are very like those used in the British Isles. Basically, the card is a list of all breeding species likely to be encountered in the state, followed by three columns labeled Possible, Probable, and Confirmed. A check in the Possible column indicates that the bird has been discovered during the breeding season in proper nesting habitat, without further evidence of breeding. Five kinds of evidence indicate that a species is *probably* breeding, and the appropriate single-letter code is entered in the Probable column:

S   Singing male present at the same location on at least two dates during breeding season.

T   Bird (or pair) apparently holding territory. (In addition to singing, chasing of other individuals of the same species is good evidence.)

D   Courtship and display, or agitated behavior or anxiety calls from adults, suggesting the probable presence of nearby nest or young. (For banders, the presence of a brood patch or cloacal protuberance on a trapped bird is also code **D**.)

N   Bird visiting probable nest site.

B   Nest building by wrens and woodpeckers. (Since wrens build dummy nests and woodpeckers drill roosting cavities, nest building or excavating does not constitute proof of breeding in these species.)

Several varieties of evidence are considered *proof* of nesting; the appropriate double-letter code is entered in the Confirmed column:

DD Distraction display or injury feigning (the broken-wing act perpetrated by shorebirds and a few other species). Copulation is also entered as **DD**.

NB Nest building in species other than wrens and woodpeckers.

UN Used nest found. Caution: these must be carefully identified; a few nests (e.g., those of Baltimore oriole) are easy to identify, but most are difficult.

FE Road-killed or bander-caught female with egg in the oviduct.

FL *Recently* fledged young (including downy young of precocial species). Caution: some species (e.g., swallows) may move some distance soon after fledging. Recently fledged songbirds are dependent on, and fed by, their parents.

FS Adult carrying fecal sac.

FY Adult(s) with food for young. Caution: some species (gulls, terns, birds of prey) continue to feed their young long after they've fledged, by which time they may have moved considerable distances. Also, some species (e.g., terns) may carry food considerable distances; be careful, especially near the edges of blocks. Care should be taken to avoid confusion with courtship feeding (code **D**).

ON Adult(s) entering or leaving nest site in circumstances indicating occupied nest. *Not* generally used for open-nesting birds. This code is used for hole nesters when a bird enters an appropriate hole and remains inside or leaves a hole after having been inside for some time, or when birds change over at a hole.

NE Nest with eggs, or bird incubating on nest, or eggshells found below nest. (A cowbird egg in a nest is coded **NE** for both cowbird and host species.)

NY Nest with young. (A nest containing a young cowbird is coded **NY** for both cowbird and host species.)

THE FEAR HAS BEEN EXPRESSED that any project seeking to confirm nesting will, whatever the intentions, adversely affect the birds by causing nest desertions. But Atlas workers seldom disturb nests; indeed, of all the codes listed above, only the last two usually require a close approach to an active nest. When you do find an active nest, the simple rule is to get in and get out in a hurry, disturbing the veg-

**Widespread in open habitats, including golf courses and airports,
the killdeer is our best-known upland shorebird.**

etation as little as possible. Undoubtedly some nests are abandoned because of nest visitation (especially if it occurs early in the incubation period), but the greater danger is subsequent predation. When predators — domestic or wild — come across a human trail while hunting, they will likely fall in and follow. The successful human nest searcher tends to retrace his steps after a discovery, so that his trail leads a dog or a skunk directly to a nest and stops. Result, predated nest. After you have located your song sparrow nest on the ground or your field sparrow nest in a small bush, backtrack a short distance and turn away from the direction of your approach, returning to the road or wherever in a circle. But tramp the trail several times where the spur leads off to the nest; the predator will probably pause at the junction and follow the heavier trail.

In the case of rare birds, human predators sometimes have to be misled as well. During the five years' fieldwork for the British/Irish Atlas, some 1,800 breeding records were submitted on special secret cards, provided with the understanding that they would be seen by no one but the national organizer. At the end of the project, where the observers felt secrecy was still warranted, symbols representing those records were either misplaced on or omitted from the distribution maps, each map so indicating. The system was designed to produce maps as accurate as possible while minimizing "direct threats to rare birds, from egg-collectors, falconers and over-enthusiastic birdwatchers and photographers."

June 13 The season progresses. Color comes to the roadsides. The hedgerows of dogwood are in full bloom. The giant matured heads of yellow goatsbeard nod from the road shoulders, which are turning a soft coral as the heads of the reed canary grasses color up. The first chicory blossoms are opening, and early monarch butterflies are arriving, reminding one to notice that the milkweed is coming on.

The breeding season progresses also. There is less singing now, and more feeding of young. The first phalanxes of brown starlings, young of the year, are patrolling the pastures. I kill the engine on my moped (the *Atlas Express*) and ease down a long, gradual hill running between a hayfield and a field of new corn. A pause to watch the killdeer, than which there is no easier bird to get for code D. Killdeer are always upset with people, flying and calling, running along through the young corn and abruptly stopping to squat on imaginary eggs. It would be a waste of time to hunt for a killdeer nest, or for that of the vesper sparrow singing across the road; you just come back and back, hoping eventually to catch them with food or young.

Killdeer is not the only upland shorebird in this block. Two miles north on the same farm road an upland sandpiper, a scarce and local breeder, sits on a fence post and gurgles. Standing, head up, it is the classic upland sandpiper; then it tucks its head down on its back and looks like an absurd, long-legged meadowlark. From a cornfield beyond the highway comes the wolf-whistle call of another upland. There are a couple of pairs on territory here, but don't hold your breath waiting for confirmation of breeding. Uplands, like most ground nesters, are secretive around the nest for obvious reasons, and I'm not about to tramp around in this farmer's hayfield in any case.

Riding through hilly pastureland in the southwest corner of the block, I stop to watch a kingbird. If you can't confirm eastern kingbird, you may as well give it up. They nest in open country, usually in trees where there are few to choose among. They are arrogant, belligerent birds, quite disdaining secretiveness around the nest. I remember, as a boy, listening to my grandfather tell about kingbirds he had seen harrying bald eagles in the Quetico country of Ontario, and checking out a kingbird nest in a hawthorn tree in another Atlas block two years before had cost me the hassle of my life. The only unpredictable thing about kingbird nests is elevation. Many aboveground-nesting species tend to nest in a limited range of elevation: one looks for cuckoo or Swainson's thrush nests from five to ten feet up, for blackburnian or pine warbler nests well up in the canopy. Not so the eastern kingbird. I have found active nests ranging from sixty-five feet up in a giant dead elm to one horizontally espaliered on the top of a three-foot-high ground juniper. The bird I'm watching eats two captured insects, but flies with the third directly to the nest, well up in a dying elm. FY plus NY for kingbird.

A quick stop back at the prickly ash/dogwood hedge to check on the black-billed cuckoo. I park the moped and walk down the road. I'm hanging about watching for activity when I get the oddest feeling I'm being watched. An uneasy glance about reveals a woodchuck, flattened on a roadside elm branch ten feet off the ground, perfectly still. I address some remarks to the woodchuck, wondering how he'll respond. He doesn't. He pretends I don't exist. If I don't exist, I'm obviously no threat. A pickup stops, ending the one-way conversation. The farmer wonders what the hell I'm doing standing around in the middle of nowhere, but he doesn't ask. Typically laconic, he merely nods, waiting for me to begin. Does he own the woodlot beyond the hayfield? He nods. Does he mind if I spend a couple of hours looking around his woodlot? "What for?" he asks. I explain that I'm censusing birds, hoping to prove breeding for every resident species in the area. His face registers neither understanding nor surprise. "What for?" he asks.

WHAT FOR, INDEED? Why should some tens of thousands of people spend a considerable part of five summers of their lives tracking down breeding birds? Surely we know already what birds breed where; the field guides *tell* us as much. In a general way, of course, breeding-bird distribution has been "mapped," but as often as not the boundaries are inferred or extrapolated from scattered reports or isolated studies. And the fact that your state shows up entirely red on the field guide's distribution map is no guarantee the species has ever nested in your county, or even in your half of the state. For species with currently expanding or shrinking breeding ranges, no published source can possibly be accurate.

Atlas is after what scientists call "baseline data," a solid base of detailed information systematically gathered throughout a county, state, or country, which, when published, will provide an accurate, dated picture of breeding-bird distribution against which subsequent change can be measured. In countries or states with a long history of serious field ornithology — England and Massachusetts would be examples — much of the information provided by Atlas will merely clarify or adjust previously published range information. Even so, Atlas workers in Massachusetts confirmed breeding for three species for the first time in this century, and for eight species for which there was no single previous nesting record, including two (least sandpiper and Wilson's phalarope) that were totally unexpected.

In rural states, such as Vermont, breeding-bird distribution is likely to be very nearly virgin territory. Sarah Laughlin, then director of the Vermont Institute of Natural Science, and Annette Gosnell, then VINS research assistant in charge of Atlas fieldwork, wax eloquent on the subject: "There are no data whatsoever. There's nothing to support a list of proposed threatened or endangered species in the state. There are no comparative data for developers to use or for [Vermont's Environmental] Act 250 Commissions to review with regard to species' status in the state." Atlas data are producing "revolutionary distribution maps" for some species. "Yellow-throated vireo is listed as rare in the only previous publications, but we've found you have to kick them out of the way in the river valleys of the Connecticut watershed."

Robert Spencer, of the Ringing [banding] and Migration Section of the British Trust for Ornithology and a member of the Atlas Working Group, writes me as follows about the British/Irish Atlas: "Our conviction was that the value of the work would grow as the years passed. Already, in the seven years which have elapsed since the completion of fieldwork, we have seen that certain species are increasing (in some cases reducing) their range at a surprising speed. Had we had the kind of documentation which the Atlas affords some thirty or fifty years ago we would be very much more aware than we are now of the pattern of change." How was the British/Irish *Atlas* received, I asked, and was it being put to good use? "I can only record that the *Atlas* has been the subject of uniformly good reviews. For example our governmental body responsible for conservation — the Nature Conservancy Council — immediately ordered copies of the *Atlas* for all its regional offices throughout the country." Sarah Laughlin echoes Robert Spencer: "We expect that the results of our Atlas will be extremely valuable for land-use planning immediately in Vermont, not to mention its value in the future for measuring increases or declines in particular species."

June 26 The dogwood hedgerows are done blooming, and the back roads are duller now. The milkweed is heading up, and Queen Anne's lace is beginning to bloom. The first patches of brilliant-orange day-lilies are showing in the roadside ditches, escapees from farmhouses past and present. Farmers are hard at work making hay. Down the road, a wagonload of hay bales is being run up an elevated conveyer through the gable "window" into a barn's upper loft. This "window" is also the only entrance for several pairs of barn swallows with young to feed. They panic momentarily, but soon learn to time their entrance flights to coincide with spaces between moving bales. The Atlas worker, who should also be hard at work, is sidetracked by red raspberries.

Newly fledged swallows line the wires, looking sad with the soft, white "clown" mouths of baby birds. This week and the next are the height of the breeding season in the North, the period when the begging calls of young and the food carrying of adults make confirmation easiest; and Atlas workers are off to the woods and fields for FYs and FLs. A stop at the upland sandpiper cornfield, and an upland obligingly appears, flying circles while uttering the bouncing ball *tu-tu-tu* call. The bird then drops straight out of the sky, switching to the wolf-whistle call, whose prolonged descending whistle accompanies the bird's own descent. Once on the ground, it sneaks along among the corn plants as if espionage were afoot. I stare through binoculars until my arms ache, but if there are downy young out there, I can't locate them.

There have been a couple of pairs of horned larks in this same field since March, when their wind-chime tinkling song could be heard from the fence posts. Horned lark is another ground nester difficult to confirm. The nest isn't hidden in vegetation, like that of the upland sandpiper, but rather plunked down on nearly bare ground, waste or cultivated. The nest should be easy to find by flushing the sitting bird; except that the adult leaves the nest at first sight of a distant intruder, sitting on a fence post to watch while you hunt the whole field in vain. The strategy is called "nest concealment by abandonment," and it's so effective that there is no confirmation for the species in the state after two years of atlasing.

The lark I'm watching picks about in the carefully harrowed field, starts up, flies a short distance, sets down and picks some more, in the typically nervous manner of the species. It chases an intruding lark across the road, returns to walk and pick. Then I get lucky. Like most birds that are primarily seed eaters as adults, larks feed

**Two summer tanager nestlings look on as their father feeds
an interloping young brown-headed cowbird .**

their young soft animal prey. I happen to have my glasses on the bird when it finds
what looks like a cutworm. It is immediately up and winging toward the center of the
huge field, prey dangling. Bravo! FY on horned lark.

On to the thickest woods in block No. 5135, up a class-four road that rises steeply
over the shoulder of a ridge featuring some fairly sizable hemlock. I park the moped
and walk, listening. From off-left comes a chorus of begging cries, loud but muf-
fled, which probably means hole nester. Twenty yards off the road I locate the nest
hole, small and fairly high up in a white birch. I have arrived at downy woodpecker
by a process of elimination when a female downy flies in with food, spots me, and
goes berserk. I get out of there in a hurry. NY and FY for downy woodpecker.

On up the hill I am greeted by the distinctive nasal alarm call *(whit-whaaaaaang)*
of the scarlet tanager. It proves to be a female, who sits overhead in the canopy and
complains. I go through the motions of looking for a nest when, to my amazement, I spot one, well out on a maple branch, twenty feet directly above the road.
Binoculars show the tops of several fuzzy heads, and a closer look from underneath

reveals a typically flat, flimsy nest. Most people are disappointed upon finding a tanager nest, expecting better workmanship from such elegantly lovely birds; but I'm ecstatic. Three species confirmed in an hour — this is how atlasing should go, and seldom does.

I'm stopped at the base of the hill road hoping to upgrade from Probable a territorial pair of brown thrashers when two schoolboys from the next farm roar up on their dirt bikes. First they want to know about the moped — how many horsepower and how fast will it go? One horse and 21 mph. They are visibly disappointed. Then they want to know what I'm doing, and I tell them I'm censusing breeding birds. "How much do you get paid for that?" one wants to know. The boys are disappointed in that answer, too.

VIRTUALLY ALL ATLAS WORK IS VOLUNTARY. Who could afford to bankroll the thousands of hours required to atlas a county, the tens of thousands of hours required to atlas a state, or the 100,000 hours required to atlas a small country? Even so, Atlas projects aren't free. Sponsoring organizations have to have, or find, funds to cover inevitable costs. The British Isles Atlas cost £30,000. Richard Forster puts the cost of the Massachusetts program at about $750 a year for the first five years. This expense, borne by the Massachusetts Audubon Society, covered printing and mailing the newsletter as well as a mileage rebate for headquarters staff and a very few field workers.

The VINS general budget carried the Vermont Atlas program on a shoestring, and Sarah Laughlin is bitter about the treatment she's received in search of supporting grant money. "The big foundations turn up their noses," she says, "because the fieldwork is being done by amateur birders." Apparently the foundations don't realize there aren't enough academic and governmental ornithologists in the whole Northeast to atlas one state; and even if there were, they wouldn't be available to work five summers, nor would they be affordable if they were. Chan Robbins points out that granting institutions deal almost exclusively with requests coming down the academic and governmental pipelines; they apparently don't know what to think about a project like Atlas. Robbins adds that serious amateurs are better at field identification than most professional avian biologists, whose work — whether in the lab or with game species — neither necessitates nor encourages birding expertise.

■ BBC and BBS ■

ATLAS IS NOT THE ONLY KIND of breeding-bird census carried out in North America. If you hear biologists or birders deep in conversation about the BBC or the BBS, they are referring not to the communications industry, but to the Breeding Bird Census and the Breeding Bird Survey.

The Breeding Bird Census, sponsored by the National Audubon Society, has over a half century of experience behind it. The BBC monitors the density of breeding populations of various species of birds within particular habitats. A study plot is carefully measured (the base unit is the hectare, or 2.471 acres), after which a detailed quantitative vegetational analysis describes the plot's trees, both by species and size, in terms of density, "basal area" (a measure of breast-height cross-sectional area), and evenness of distribution. Further analysis determines the density of shrub cover, the percentage of ground and canopy cover, and the average canopy height.

The variety of habitat types studied for the BBC is astonishing. A sample of the 200-plus surveys from a recent year includes: a "selectively logged mature tuliptree/oak forest" in Maryland, a "wooded city ravine" in Ontario, a "black oak/sassafras woods" in Indiana, a "virgin scrub oak foothill" in Oklahoma, an "upland scotch pine plantation" in New York, a "Kentucky blue grass prairie" in North Dakota, an "aspen clearcut" in Minnesota, a "ponderosa pine/scrub oak/mahogany woodland" in Colorado, a "silver buffaloberry/silver sagebrush coulee" in Montana, a "creosotebush wash" in Texas, a "disturbed coastal salt marsh" in California, and a "wet coastal plain tundra" in Alaska.

The BBC worker visits his plot — sizes vary from less than the recommended minimum 15 acres to over 200, but most are in the 25-to-50-acre range — repeatedly during the breeding season, mapping encounters with singing males. By comparing the locations of singing birds from all visits, individual territories can be fairly well determined. The published report indicates the number of territorial males of each species found in the plot, as well as those numbers adjusted to reflect the same densities for 100-hectare and 100-acre plots, so that one can easily compare population densities for particular species from different plots, regardless of plot-size differences.

Some BBC plots have been studied for a number of consecutive years, a situation which provides an opportunity to examine the changing breeding status of birds in light of plot vegetational changes — whether catastrophic (fire, storm damage) or gradual (normal plant maturation and succession). Hence, for example, an anbandoned pasture gradually transforming itself into woods, or a mature forest broken by a transmission-line corridor, will show significant changes in the makeup of its bird community.

The Breeding Bird Survey, sponsored by the U.S. Fish and Wildlife Service and the Canadian Wildlife Service, is a younger and quite different program. Starting in 1965 as a sixty-route pilot project in Maryland and Delaware, and quickly becoming a continentwide operation involving over 1,800 routes, the BBS is a road survey whose idea dates back to the mourning dove bag-limit surveys of the 1950s. It works this way. Each volunteer picks a nice day in June to run his route, which was randomly located and plotted on secondary roads back at headquarters. He starts his survey at precisely thirty minutes before local sunrise, noting all birds seen or heard for three minutes. He then drives half a mile, stops, and records again for three minutes. The procedure is repeated until all birds have been recorded during fifty three-minute stops. Then home for lunch, an afternoon of filling out forms, and the BBS volunteer is through for the year.

Now the computers go to work on the mountain of data, eventually producing population indices by species at four levels: continental, regional, state/province, and physiographic (or "ecoregional," the continent having been divided into sixty-some areas, each having a particular topographical/vegetational identity). Many things cannot be learned from BBS data. You cannot, for example, compare numbers for different species, either from a single route or several, simply because species differ widely in their detectability from roadside stops. And you cannot adequately judge state distribution for a particular species from the inevitably scattered sample. What you *can* detect from these data is year-to-year variation, regionally and continentally, in the populations of many species of North American birds. And these year-to-year variations, graphed over a period of time, may show upward or downward trends of great interest to biologists and conservationists.

Of course, all animal populations fluctuate; some up-and-down movement on the graph is normal. But drastic changes or persistent movement in one direction may be cause for alarm, and the BBS seeks to quantify those changes so that explanations can be sought. Yellow warbler, it has been found, has been declining at the rate of 11 percent per year in the Central region (the Midwest and middle Canadian provinces) since the late 1960s. Is this decline explained by the increase in cowbird numbers in that region during the same years? Flicker and red-headed woodpecker are declining at the rate of 3 percent per year in the East. Is this explicable in terms of competition for nesting holes from starlings, which are increasingly spreading away from their traditional urban breeding haunts? In June of 1972, Hurricane Agnes brought five days of heavy rain to the Appalachian states, depriving nesting purple martins of flying insect food. BBS data show that, while purple martin numbers rose slightly in the East as a whole from 1972, the species crashed in the Appalachian region, a crash from which the population failed to recover until 1975.

I asked Chan Robbins, who directs the BBS and has a hand in Atlas and the BBC as well, whether we really need three major breeding-bird census programs, and whether, given the limited personnel available, we can *afford* them. Robbins points out that each of the three projects produces information the others cannot provide. Only Atlas can accurately determine breeding distribution over wide geographical areas. Only the BBC correlates population densities with particular habitats. And only the BBS can determine year-to-year population trends based on a widely distributed survey sample. Then, too, as Robbins notes, people willing to do one sort of census may be unwilling or unable to do another. Atlas and the BBC require a great deal of field time; the BBS does not. Those who, like the British, favor a qualitative approach to biological investigation, will prefer the straightforward mapping of Atlas. Those who, following the American academic establishment, prefer a quantitative approach, will be happier with the vegetational analyses of the BBC, and with the "weighted means" and "regression analyses" of the BBS.

July 2 It should be a super honey year; the long spikes on five-foot-high yellow and white sweet clover are beginning to blossom, and the plants (especially the white clover), are flourishing on the roadsides this year. The wild parsnip umbels are yellow-greening on the road shoulders, too, and the hydrangeas are starting to bloom around the farmhouses. The delicate pink blossoms are showing in the leaf axils of the motherwort, and a flannel-covered common mullein found on a logging road measures an inch under seven feet tall. Summer is coming along.

The ringing alarm note of a wood thrush issues from a woods off Doolittle Road, and I catch a glimpse of her with a beakful. (You want to get on alarmed birds fast in the event they're carrying food; some will quickly swallow the food once they've detected the intruder.) From farther along comes the distinctively harsh begging call of a fledged cowbird. Cowbird young, whatever you think of the

**Scarce over much of its range, the yellow-billed cuckoo
is a seldom-seen skulker in dark riverside cover.**

species, are pure gold to the atlaser; they mean two birds for the price of one if you can stick with them until the foster parent shows up. This one flies, lands, and begs; flies, lands, and begs. Finally a female rose-breasted grosbeak slips in with food. FY on grosbeak; FL on cowbird. (On a later trip I find a wood thrush feeding a cowbird in the same area. At least in these cases the host was not, as is usually the case, dwarfed by the beggar.)

Down the road a mile, near the privy with the phoebe's nest, a black-billed cuckoo flies across the road carrying a caterpillar. Groan. All that stalking on the other road for naught. (Not really; I got FY on yellow warbler there as well as FL on Baltimore oriole and T on red-tailed hawk.) Thirty yards farther down the road I am attracted to an odd commotion well up in a live elm. Binocular inspection reveals a pair of cedar waxwings systematically dismantling an oriole nest, which requires a considerable amount of flapping and tugging. The birds are carting the hard-won materials two elms down the road, where they are starting a nest of their own — recycling, as it were, pendant bag into bulky basket. NB for cedar waxwing.

(It deserves an NB! really, but that would only confuse the computer puncher.)

July 6 Heading for Mutton Hill, hoping for warblers. Mutton Hill shows on the topo map as a mile-long ridge running north and south in the southwest corner of block No. 5135. A lowland block such as this will inevitably be warbler-poor, but you head for the highest part of the block and hope. The crest of Mutton Hill shows an elevation of 566 feet, probably too low to be of much help. It looks pretty well timbered from the distant road, however; there ought to be *something* on that ridge.

I hike in off the road, sticking to tree lines to avoid corn and hay and the attention of landowners. (I have permission from the nearest house, but I'll undoubtedly cross other properties, and you can't spend *all* your time knocking on doors.) I'm crossing a corner of a white pine pasture heading down toward a stream when a bunch of cows spot me. They tramp right up and stand all around staring. I wave them off; they stand and stare. I swing a sizable stick at them; they stand and stare. Cows can give you the jeebies with their know-nothing look. They don't look angry, they don't look curious, they don't look playful; they don't look *anything*. You stand and they stare, heads down, dumbly attentive.

I decide the hell with it. I'm not going to stand here until I starve to death. I start off in my intended direction, and *here come the cows*. I walk faster; the cows speed up. Now I've got thirty black-and-whites hustling along back, front, and both sides. The cows are flowing around the pines, cutting me off at the pass as I duck here and there through the passageways. They crowd in, and I'm wondering how much a Holstein weighs, feeling like the movie cowboy who wakes up at midnight with the stampede bearing down and wishes he had his pants on but wishes even more that his horse hadn't headed for Cheyenne when the rumble began. We're charging between pine trees when the Holstein on my immediate right steps on my foot, and I believe the end is near. (The headline won't even read LONE AT-LASER MEETS TRAGIC END; it will say TRESPASSING BIRD-WATCHER TRAMPLED BY COWS.) Somehow I ride out the storm and splash across a stream. The cows lose interest and drift away, leaving me to climb the ridge.

What Mutton Hill proves to have the most of is begging oriole young and singing red-eyed vireos and wood-pewees. As persistent singers, the latter two species are among the easiest of birds to record as probable breeders, yet I've found them among the most difficult of common woodland birds to *confirm*. Single adults sing and forage, sing and forage, all day long. You can follow them about week after week and never confirm breeding. If a vireo song doesn't *move,* however, it's worth checking out. Unlike species where bright plumage rules out male incubation, dull-plumaged male vireos not only incubate but sing while sitting! Tracing a lazy, repetitive warble from medium-high up in a shade tree may net NE for warbling vireo, while an endless, short-phrased monologue ten or fifteen feet up in small timber may lead to a red-eyed nest. I'm not having any luck today, however; I'll have to come back after the leaves are down to get vireo (and possibly pewee) for UN.

It turns out that a logging road runs along the crest of Mutton Hill, which is typically timbered with maple, beech, hardhack, elm, and white birch. Someone logged the ridge two or three years ago, and there are enough maple and beech tops on the ground to heat half the county. The butt end of a maple top measures twenty-five inches across. I walk down off the hill, depressed by the wasteful logging and at having found nothing of note except a singing black-and-white warbler, when a movement in the margin of the wet woods brings the binoculars up to reveal a long tail attached to a white belly with cuckoo written all over it. And there's lots of pattern under that tail — *yellow-billed!* Come on, show your head. After a bit he does, and the yellow lower mandible makes it certain. Black-billed cuckoos are nice; yellow-billed are three times as good. A very scarce breeder in the state, its skulking habits and fondness for wet woods make it difficult to find and extremely difficult to confirm. Lucking out with a confirmation of a pair of yellow-bills in another block is one of my happiest Atlas memories. I was searching a wooded swamp margin for the bird, which I had heard calling on several occasions, and was sitting tight when a pair flew in and landed right over me. The male presented the female with a large green insect (it looked like a lacewing), which she held in her bill while he mounted her. After a pause, they mated a second time, and I had the best DD I'm ever likely to record on an Atlas sheet.

This particular cuckoo is jump-hunting through the foliage at head level, apparently for moths. It hops this way and that, one wing occasionally opening for balance, reminding me of crows hunting grasshoppers on short-cut late-summer hayfields. This is typical yellow-billed cuckoo habitat, which means I've got miserable visibility and two inches of water underfoot. The bird seems to be eating whatever it is it's catching, and then, after the manner of cuckoos, it is simply gone. (I return a week later in hopes of upgrading the bird to Probable or Confirmed, but it is nowhere to be found.)

I move on to the east to track down a calling towhee. A lovely male. He doesn't sound particularly upset, but there's probably a nest close by. The bird isn't doing anything promising, however, so I wander away to check a nearby area. When I return, the towhee is calling from back in the bush. I want to be getting on, and decide to see what "shushing" might do. The male comes up and calls, then another call from deeper in the bush. I "shush" again, and the female flies in with a billful of food. Hallelujah! That's the way "shushing" is supposed to work! FY on rufous-sided towhee, which is scarce in this block, and can be a tough bird to confirm even when more widely distributed. Mutton Hill hasn't been a complete bust after all.

IT'S NICE TO SPEND A SUMMER atlasing a single block, to become familiar with every meadow and woodlot and hedgerow, to learn what birds breed where and when; to watch the turning of the season from a particular piece of geography. While that's an attractive style of atlasing, it is not always possible. Probably every Atlas project (except perhaps on tiny Malta) has had to rely on storm troops to census remote areas, people willing and able to get into outlying blocks and hit them fast and hard. The businesslike British call it "square-a-day surveying." Americans favor a more dramatic idiom. Massachusetts birders call it "square-creaming"; Vermonters call it "block-busting."

Block-busting works this way. The individual (or team) first drives through the blocks to be censused (assuming there are roads present, which is not always the case), checking out access and habitats. Then the topo maps are double-checked for missed habitat possibilities. When the preliminary work is completed, you get down to business, which means climbing out of the sleeping bag about 3:00 a.m. and heading for a predetermined block, to spend the day checking the most accessible samples of each available habitat. Block-busters will pause to try to confirm "good" species, but mostly they keep moving, ticking off birds as they come. Along about 4:00 p.m. you head back for camp, fix something to eat, and thence to bed. Tomorrow means another day and another block.

Most block-busting goes forward during late June and early July, when the FLs and FYs make it possible to confirm a fair number of species while censusing on the run. Expert birders can be surprisingly successful with this method. A team may record fifty species with twenty confirmed during a single day in a fairly good block. A super day in a great block may produce even more, but I'd like to see a block-busting team turn fifty species out of my present block, with no waterbird habitat and insufficient elevation for warblers. A patient summer's work will, as usual,

**During high summer, eastern bluebirds frequently
call and hunt from farm-country fences.**

produce a high proportion (about 60 percent) of species confirmed; but clearly it's going to be a chore to get the total recorded-species list into the seventies.* (By way of contrast, my two earlier blocks — one of which had enough elevation for warblers, the other an extensive marsh — produced over ninety species each.)

July 12 What summer in the East is striving for is green, and by mid-July it has pretty well succeeded. The landscape is so uniformly green that the eye hunts for other colors. Here and there it discovers some, mostly in very small doses. There is the amazing blue (shading toward pink or lavender, depending on distance and the light) of the chicory, and the brilliant yellow of trefoil. For white we have Queen Anne's lace and the tiny, daisylike blossoms of mayweed, flourishing along road shoulders under the mower's blade. We have the mustard charlock for yellow. Milk-

---

A fair amount of work through the following summer did boost block No. 5135 into the seventies, but barely.

weed adds a subtle pink. Early morning-glories and hollyhocks are showing about the farmhouses.

Meanwhile, the vegetable world is quietly going about the business of fruiting. The clusters of light-green samaras show up against the darker-green foliage of the boxelders. The hop-hornbearn seed-pod clusters hang like full stringers of semi-inflated miniature footballs. (My wife objects to the inelegance of that image; the proper metaphor, she says, is Japanese paper lanterns.) The staghorn sumac is at its most thrifty, the fat velvety heads fully developed. Berries are coming, too, on prickly ash (crush one for the most outrageous citrus flavor imaginable), grape, dogwood, buckthorn, and woodbine. And all, in keeping with the dominant mood, are green.

I stop the *Atlas Express* on a hot, dusty farm road to follow what will prove the year's last cuckoo up into an isolated roadside elm. To my surprise, a binocular glimpse reveals a yellow-billed. Can this be the bird that belongs over a mile west-southwest off the north end of Mutton Hill? And what is it doing out here in dry, open country? I intend to watch that elm all afternoon if necessary, but a bluebird has been calling from somewhere behind me, and now a family (or two) sweep by to perch down the fencerow. I give up on the cuckoo and put the glasses on the nearest young bluebird. It is spot-breasted and dull-backed, but the wings and tail are already that electric bluebird blue, a color so strong and pure it seems to have come straight from the palette of the Nazarene School. The birds are hunting now, and through the rising heat waves of a binocular-foreshortened half mile of country road, one adult and six young bluebirds sweep back and forth from fence to road and back, fluttering after insects and calling softly. An exquisite tableau of high summer, and probably the image I'll remember longest from Atlas block No. 5135.

THEN, A FEW DAYS LATER, something happens that will ring down the curtain on all this. You are birding in your favorite marsh, hoping for rails, when the eye registers something delicate and elongated poised along the edge of a pool well out in the marsh and a voice (which is not a voice) in your head says *shorebird,* and it will take a second and a half to get the binoculars up and focused while the voice says *don't fly dammit don't fly,* and then, almost anticipating the eyes, the voice says *yellowlegs* and then (after an instant's bill-check) *lesser yellowlegs,* and while the binoculars search for downy young and the mind races with dates and questions, the voice is already claiming *first United States breeding record.*

But, of course, there are no downy young; there is no breeding record. The

mind has straightened it out, and you remind yourself that it's mid-July, and the first of the tundra-nesting shorebirds have abandoned the breeding grounds and started south. And suddenly, before the pulse has begun to slow — for the adrenaline responds to the voice, and not to the mind — elation passes into something like sadness. It doesn't matter that the garden is just starting to produce. It doesn't matter that a number of local songbirds are incubating second clutches, or that many goldfinches have yet to begin nest building. It doesn't matter that the first of the goldenrod has yet to bloom, or that grasshopper and cricket numbers are just beginning to build in the farmhouse dooryards. The first of the shorebirds has come, and from this day forward, whatever the appearances, summer is only marking time. (Where was it among those fourteen volumes of journals that Thoreau wrote: "How early in the year it begins to be late!"?) *Scolopacidae fugiunt. Tempus fugit.*

And so it happens that the Atlas worker stands in his Maine or Michigan marsh in mid-July, with the hottest weather of the summer ahead, watching a yellowlegs or a dowitcher, thinking through the rest of summer and into fall. Thinking through August, when a wandering southern heron or egret may appear in this same marsh, and when the flocks of fall-plumaged bobolinks descend on the cornfields. Thinking through September, when the broad-wings and warblers fly, when the asters transform the pastures while the maples and ashes and sumac transform the hills and fencerows, and the yellow-rumps move into the valley farms and villages to feast on the myriad flies buzzing about sun-warmed silos and houses. Thinking through October, when the accipiters move down the ridges over the fading color, and the first snow flurries and rough-legged hawks are in the wings.

Notoriously late breeders, American goldfinches while away
most of the summer feeding amongst the flowers.

CHAPTER IX

The Appointed Time of Their Coming

"I'm going to fly to the moon," said Little Bear.
"Fly!" said Mother Bear. "You can't fly."
"Birds fly," said Little Bear.
  "Oh, yes," said Mother Bear. "Birds fly, but they don't fly to the moon.
And you are not a bird."
  "Maybe some birds fly to the moon, I don't know. And maybe I can fly like
a bird," said Little Bear. . . . "I'm going now. Just look for me up in the sky."
  "Be back for lunch," said Mother.
              — ELSE HOLMELUND MINARIK, *Little Bear* (1957)

WE MODERNS HEAR IN THIS DIALOGUE a common-sense mother and a cutely credulous cub. But during most of the history of civilization this could have been a serious debate, for neither mother bears nor anyone else knew where birds fly and where they don't. Indeed, in an eighteenth-century British pamphlet called "An Essay Toward the Probable Solution of this Ques-

tion: Whence come the Stork and the Turtle, the Crane, and the Swallow, when they Know and Observe the Appointed Time of their Coming," the author, a "Person of Learning and Piety," argued, in support of Little Bear, that the disappearing hordes of autumn birds fly to and winter on the moon.

That author may well have possessed more piety than learning, but his predecessors, contemporaries, and followers did little better. Much the most impressive thing about the study of bird migration until very recent times is the name someone coined for it: ornithophaenology. The results of that study were a collection of fantastic myths and old wives' tales. Aristotle subscribed to the notion that swallows hibernate through the winter. The hibernation theory — one scenario depicted flocks of birds diving into ponds and marshes, where they overwintered in the mud along with the turtles and the frogs — remained well into the nineteenth century a viable explanation for the fall disappearance of birds.* The notion that small overwater migrants hitch rides on the backs of stronger birds is said to persist to this day in some Latin countries.

World War II radar operators in England were mystified by weak "blips," barely standing out from background "noise," which tended to concentrate at certain altitudes and moved in repetitive patterns. They weren't aircraft; they didn't seem to be meteorological phenomena. What could they be? The radar people dubbed them "angels." The military classified them top-secret. The angels were eventually identified as birds. Many of them were migrants, observing the "time of their coming," as the author of Jeremiah had put it a couple of thousand years before.

The honking of geese (page 242) and the bugling of sandhill cranes (page 243): primordial music out of migratory skies.

---

* *The great eighteenth-century Swedish naturalist Linnaeus believed that swallows hibernated; and the careful field observer Gilbert White, Linnaeus's British contemporary, struggled with the notion throughout his life, finally concluding that "at least many individuals" of two species of swallows "do never leave this island at all, but partake of the same benumbed state [one finds in] torpid insects, reptiles, and quadrupeds." White even hired men to search the "shrubs and cavities" of a hillside outside his native village of Selborne where he believed the local swallows' "secret dormitories" were located. The reader will find a record of White's debate with himself among the letters making up* The Natural History and Antiquities of Selborne *(1788–89), more particularly in Letters X, XII, and XXXVIII to Thomas Pennant; and in Letters IX, XII, XXXVI, LI, LV, and LVII to Daines Barrington. (White's classic Selborne remains in print in several editions.)*

R ADAR DID NOT DISCOVER BIRD MIGRATION, of course, but it has helped clear up a number of questions about it. Some early ornithophaenologists argued, for example, that birds must migrate at tremendous heights, so that they could see their distant destinations. Migration actually proceeds at a wide variety of altitudes. Some pelagic species make their great looping migrations around the world's oceans just above wave-top. At the other extreme are the bar-headed geese, whose ancient route between India and Tibet was complicated millions of years ago by the upthrust of the Himalayas. But the bar-heads have remained faithful to their traditional route, honking today over Makalu and Everest, flying at nearly 30,000 feet in air whose oxygen content would not support human life.

Most migration, however, takes place at intermediate heights. Diurnal songbird migrants — blue jays,* for example — tend to fly low: from treetop level to several hundred feet. Strong-flying nocturnal migrants — geese and shorebirds, for example — often fly at several thousand feet, even as high as two miles. But the bulk of migration takes place at moderate heights of 1,000 feet or so. When waterfowl and migration researcher Frank C. Bellrose flew a spotlight-equipped small plane back and forth over a set midwestern route at 500-foot intervals of altitude, he found well over half of all nocturnal songbird migration taking place between 500 and 1,500 feet above ground level.

Radar and plane observation work have also cleared up the matter of the airborne speed of migrating birds. Some early theorists had, on the basis of several faulty assumptions, posited extraordinary flight speeds. But birds migrate at their ordinary flight speeds. Most songbirds average 20 to 30 mph. Medium-speed migrants — some hawks and shorebirds — fly perhaps 45 mph. High-speed migrants, such as geese, falcons, some shorebirds, and swifts, typically top off at about 55 mph. Winds aloft will, of course, materially affect actual flight speed, and all these birds are capable, under duress, of attaining higher speeds for brief periods.

Doubtless my generation grew up as ignorant about migration as any other. But

---

* Blue jays are conventionally classed as permanent residents rather than migrants, and it is true that some jays winter almost to the northern extremity of the Canadian breeding grounds. But blue jays are highly migratory throughout the Northeast, where fall hawk watches often record more passing jays than hawks. What the casual backyard observer fails to realize is that his summer jays and winter jays are probably not the same birds. Most of his Connecticut or Nebraska breeding jays drift south for the winter, to be replaced by breeders out of Maine and the Maritimes or the Dakotas and the Prairie Provinces.

A small dabbling duck, the blue-winged teal migrates to the southern United States, and well beyond, for the winter.

the geography of bird migration across North America we knew — or thought we knew — indelibly, thanks to the large colored maps that hung in countless elementary schools in the United States and Canada. These maps showed the four great migratory flyways, "discovered" by a U.S. Fish and Wildlife Service biologist in 1935, called Atlantic, Mississippi, Central, and Pacific. The flyways looked like those time-exposure photos of nighttime California, the great bright trunks of light identifying freeways, the thin bright lines locating feeder routes. The implication was that northeastern birds headed from the nesting grounds over to, and then flew down, the Atlantic Coast; that north-central birds headed down either the Mississippi Valley or the Great Plains; and that northwestern birds gathered to fly down the Pacific Coast. It never occurred to us to wonder why, if all those billions of birds flew up and down those four flyways spring and fall, the discovery of that fact should have had to wait until 1935. Why would not those four corridors have mapped themselves in permanent whitewash?

We might well have profited from European experience in this matter, for or-

nithologists across the Atlantic had debated the geography of migration for generations. The "fly-line" advocates in Europe were contested by the "broad-front" school,
which argued that migrants fly along a broad front in favorable weather; so that the
appropriate aquatic metaphor is not the river, but the wave. It had long been assumed
that the Nile Valley served as a concentrating migration route. When observers
happened to check the desert east and west of the Nile, they found migration proceeding there as well. It had been the naturalists, not the birds, who were restricted
to the river valley. A couple of years ago someone got hold of the New England
hawk migration data, and published a magazine article which purported to describe the major hawk migration route through the region. The author merely
noted active hawk-watch sites on a map, connected them from north to south, and
pretended that the resulting line was a path followed by hawks! (The hawks were
plotted leaving my own watch headed southeast, while in fact the great majority of
them left headed southwest.) Without some way of identifying individual birds
(various forms of color marking are now being used to track the movements of particular populations of some species), one simply cannot conclude that the flock of
hawks or mixed warblers observed flying past Point A is the same flock subsequently
observed at Point B.

THE FOUR GREAT NORTH AMERICAN FLYWAYS were originally posited on the
basis of banding data for waterfowl. Ducks and geese breed, in greatest concentration, in the north-central part of the continent, while most of them winter
on (or near) the Atlantic, Gulf, and Pacific coasts. Waterfowl are extremely faithful
to their breeding and wintering grounds, and also to traditional migratory stopover
areas. They do not, however, lend much support to the notion of four great north-
south migratory routes. F. C. Lincoln, the inventor of those flyways, claimed that the
canvasbacks, redheads, and scaup that leave their central Canadian prairie breeding
grounds and fly cross-country to winter on Chesapeake Bay are part of the Atlantic
Flyway. But the Atlantic in this case is not a flyway, but a fly-goal. White-winged
scoters breeding in the Canadian interior head almost due east for the Great Lakes
and the North Atlantic Coast. These ducks too were said to migrate the Atlantic
Flyway.

Several thousand blue-winged teal captured and banded in fall migration in Illinois ought to have been heading down the Mississippi Flyway for the Gulf Coast,
where many teal winter. Returns showed that a few did so. A few also ended up in

Texas, on the Central Flyway. A few headed northwest, north, and northeast. But the majority of those teal were recovered (a euphemism for shot) along a line southeast from Illinois through Georgia and Florida to Cuba, and beyond Cuba into South America, following what we may as well call the Urbana-Havana Flyway.

The great majority of our songbirds are nocturnal migrants, and the major flyway hypothesis stands up even less well for them. Bellrose's small-plane transects over western Illinois, for example, showed that the greatest flight density often occurred over flat agricultural land *between* the Illinois and Mississippi valleys. And a transect from Decatur, Illinois, to Daytona Beach, Florida, revealed peak songbird flight not along the Appalachian ridges or over the Wabash River, but over topographically undistinguished country between Evansville, Indiana, and Nashville, Tennessee.

Songbirds are no more restricted to north-south migration than are waterfowl. The Connecticut warbler, for example, breeds from the Great Lakes northwest well into the western interior of Canada. The closely related mourning warbler breeds in the same territory, but also east through the Maritimes and Newfoundland. The Connecticut warblers ought to migrate down the Mississippi Valley to Central America; the mourning warbler ought to split into two populations, the western accompanying the Connecticuts, the eastern flying down the Atlantic Coast. In fact, the Connecticut warblers head southeast cross-country and jump off the Atlantic Coast for South America. Mourning warblers, including those from the far northeast, converge on Mexico and continue on for Central America.

The point of all this is not to argue that birds migrate randomly. Most birds are faithful to traditional wintering grounds as well as breeding grounds, and it makes sense to believe that they have more or less traditional ways of getting back and forth. The point is that the thousands of populations of our several hundred species of migrating birds are heading from innumerable breeding areas of various sizes in the North directly or indirectly for innumerable wintering areas of various sizes in the East, West, and South. They fly at various altitudes, handling various weather patterns in various ways, covering various distances (from tens to thousands of miles) at various times of the day and night, alone or in the company of other birds. For the majority of these birds, the four popularized flyways are neither handy nor (as we shall see) necessary, and it should not be surprising that if you hung a tiny flashlight on every migrating North American bird through the month of September and assembled a composite time-exposure photograph of the continent, the light streams would be found to crisscross the whole continent (the Rocky Mountain chain would likely remain fairly dark), with considerable tracery evident over both oceans as well.* If this comes as a surprise, it ought to be a pleasant one, for it means that the migratory show is not restricted to hypothetical major flyways. Wherever you live, migration flows, twice a year, *over your house.*

But if migration flows over my house, you may object, why haven't I seen it? Most migration, remember, is nocturnal. But *some* migration you must have seen. Everyone is familiar with Vs of Canada geese; and everybody living from the North Atlantic coast to the northern Great Plains must have seen passing flocks of blue jays above late September's treetops, or the broken lines of crows rowing along through October's skies. Surely everyone is familiar with the great troops of red-winged blackbirds hurrying north in February and March, or the tree swallow flights of April and May.† Coastal residents have the best opportunity to watch migrating loons, gulls, and many waterfowl and shorebirds (which migrate both by night and day). Anybody, with luck, may come upon one of those great concentrated swarms of migrating chimney swifts or common nighthawks. And, of course, even the occa-

---

The notion of four major flyways is stubbornly entrenched in both official and popular ornithological literature, in no small part, I suspect, because the Fish and Wildlife Service long ago divided the United States, for purposes of waterfowl management, into four administrative units based on (and named after) those flyways. However, an interesting way has been found to circumvent the fiction while pretending to honor it: simply enlarge the flyways. A current hunters' duck-identification guide, for example, prints maps of those four flyways, each on a separate page. Anyone going to the trouble of putting the four maps together discovers that with the exception of a narrow north-south strip of land cutting through Ohio, Kentucky, Tennessee, and Alabama, the four flyways cover every square foot of the continental United States! Indeed, in a small book on migration published in 1950, the "discoverer" of those flyways blandly announced that the "four great flyways . . . cover practically the entire width of the North American Continent and extend from the Arctic coast to South America," apparently oblivious to the fact that the statement invalidates the whole concept.

†*Red-wings and tree swallows are social, diurnal migrants, and as such are highly visible in spring. In general, however, fall migration is easier to "see" than spring migration, both because many more birds are involved (many young of the year complete a first southerly migration but don't survive their first winter) and because spring migration tends to be more diffuse than fall migration. This explains why most migration watching — spring warbler freaks notwithstanding — concentrates on the autumn flights.*

sional spring or fall birder is familiar with the "fallout" from nocturnal songbird migration, from those special days when his park, woodlot, or backyard is suddenly alive with a newly arrived flock of warblers, vireos, kinglets, tanagers, thrushes, grosbeaks, and others, feeding and loafing after the previous night's flight.

THE CLASS OF THE DIURNAL MIGRATORY SHOW is fall hawk migration, a spectacle that attracts casual and serious hawk watchers from Maine to Texas. Serious watchers staff lookouts on a regular basis and fill out data forms for the Hawk Migration Association of North America, an organization founded in hopes of answering the what, where, when, and how of continental hawk migration. Some species concentrate on the coast, and the mid-Atlantic coastal sites log them in amazing numbers. In a recent autumn the Cape May, New Jersey, watch had 47,790 sharp-shinned hawks, 1,172 ospreys, and 766 merlins. Assateague Island, Maryland, recorded 150 peregrine falcons the same season.

The majority of hawks identified at most eastern watches are broad-winged hawks, the lovely small buteo that breeds throughout the eastern U.S. (except peninsular Florida) and across southern Canada. Like other soaring hawks, the broad-wings characteristically seek migratory aid in the form of rising air currents. These may be slope updrafts (wind deflected upward by an obstacle such as a mountain) or thermal updrafts (warm air rising from a sun-heated area of high heat capacity). Unlike other soaring hawks, broad-wings have the delightful habit of migrating in groups of from several birds to hundreds (exceptionally even thousands) of birds, the compact flock called a "kettle." The kettle locates a thermal or deflection current and spirals up the aerial elevator, the hawks funneling up one over the other in widening circles, like bubbles rising out of the steaming vortex of a stirred kettle. Then, having gained sufficient altitude, the birds peel off the top one by one and set their wings in a long glide south.

The broad-wings begin to drift out of Canada in late August, and the flights move through the U.S. in September. Geography and topography combine to assure spectacular broad-wing flights at several favored locations. The westward slant of the North American east coast helps funnel hawks out of Quebec, the Maritimes, and New England down the mountain ridges of eastern Pennsylvania, and especially to famous Kittatinny Ridge, where gunners gathered until the 1930s at Hawk Mountain and Bake Oven Knob to blaze away at migrating hawks, taking a terrific toll, especially of low-flying accipiters. Now thousands of people bring binoculars to those same lookouts every September and October to enjoy the passage hawks — goshawks, Cooper's, and sharpies; red-tails and red-shoulders, and broad-wings in the thousands; kestrels and merlins and turkey vultures; ospreys and harriers; and a sprinkling of eagles and peregrines, to make things interesting.

Less widely known, but even more productive of broad-wings, is the Hawk Ridge site on the bluffs overlooking the western tip of Lake Superior outside Duluth, Minnesota. Broad-wings are reluctant to cross wide bodies of water, so a fair number of Ontario's breeders turn southwest along the top of Superior, swinging south around Duluth. This suits northern Minnesota hawk watchers just fine; and in one memorable fall they tallied 44,220 broad-wings during 788 hours of hawk watching. In case you're counting, that's just about one broad-wing per daytime minute over the course of a migratory season.

Chances are you live neither on the Kittatinny Ridge nor in Duluth. Don't despair. Your particular location probably doesn't concentrate hawks in that spectacular fashion, but hawk migration undoubtedly proceeds. Pick a fine sunny day with light northerly breezes (preferably following a stretch of inclement weather, which may have bottled up birds to the north) in early or mid-September, and head for an open area where you can see lots of sky, especially northern sky. (A woman I know has good luck from her front yard; she believes a nearby village asphalt parking lot creates a reliable thermal.) If a ridge, hill, or mountain is handy, climb it and search for a good lookout point. Your hill or ridge may produce updrafts, which ought to attract hawks. Even if it does not, however, it is an advantage to gain some elevation. If the hawks happen to be flying at 5,000 or 8,000 feet, the higher your lookout the better.

All you really need to hawk-watch is a pair of binoculars and patience. At most locations, hawk flights are on-again off-again affairs. If you have an unproductive watch, it's a bad *day*, not necessarily a bad *location*. Go back the next favorable day. If the hawks are flying high, you'll have to do a lot of staring into space, and you'll throw your binoculars up on a lot of airplanes and migrating monarch butterflies over the course of a watch. But sooner or later you'll put them up and find migrating hawks — a sharp-shin flying low along the ridge, a red-tail soaring south, a kestrel winging out of the north like a giant swallow.

And if the broad-wings are flying, you're in for a special treat. Mostly the kettles will seem too far or too high, but eventually a flock will kettle up right in front of you, and you'll be looking not at distant flying objects but at identifiable *hawks,* the

adults complete with silver wing linings, red breast and belly barring, and black-and-white-banded tails, just like the illustrations in the field guides. Look for different shapes and sizes in broad-wing kettles. Accipiters, falcons, harriers, ospreys, TVs (as birders call turkey vultures), and other buteos are temporarily attracted to, and thermal with, broad-wing kettles.

Most of the time, hawks will be few and far between at most locations. But occasionally special meteorological circumstances can produce a massive flight anywhere. Northern New England is not known for hawk concentrations, but you wouldn't have known that on Wednesday, September 13, 1978. Most hawk watching takes place on weekends, when more people are free, but some of the popular sites are manned daily. Not many watchers were out on the 13th, but what a show they had!

Synoptic weather maps for the period suggest what happened. Two large low-pressure systems, one centered over Newfoundland, the second over Montana, dominated the North during the 10th and 11th, shrouding most of southern Canada and the northern U.S. in clouds. Then, on the afternoon of the 12th, a high-pressure cell building off Hudson Bay suddenly shot south, bisecting the two low-pressure systems and producing a narrow, north-south isthmus of open sky in a sea of overcast. Veteran Massachusetts hawk watcher Paul M. Roberts, who with physicist-astronomer Leif Robinson has carefully studied the situation, believes that during the next day the "eastern low and the intervening high functioned like two electric beaters, churning counterclockwise and clockwise, respectively, literally funneling birds into that corridor of clear skies over New England."

Diann MacRae, then northern New England regional representative for the Hawk Migration Association of North America, knew nothing of these unusual meteorological circumstances when she climbed to the fire tower atop lowly (606-foot) Warner Hill in southeastern New Hampshire on the morning of September 13. She only knew it was a glorious day following a period of clouds and rain, a day of surreal blue skies and breezes out of the northwest. It was one of those days that make you feel alive, she remembers, and she had a hunch the hawks would be flying. Alone on the tower, MacRae spent a pleasant morning, but with disappointingly few hawks. She was just breaking out lunch when, at two minutes past noon, she caught

---

Sharp-shinned hawks pause to hunt during migration.
This one perches on a porch railing.

three broad-wings on a "glide path from directly over the tower heading southwest. I went to the opposite (east) window to see if more were coming and from there I could see tiny pinpoints everywhere from NNE to SSE," pinpoints that resolved themselves into a kettle of 346 broad-wings.

She remembers those first minutes, dashing from one to another of the tower's twelve windows and five stair landings, seeking desperately for the best angle of visibility, trying eyes, binoculars, and scope, finding hawks everywhere. She shook herself mentally, she recalls, settled at the top southwest stair landing, and started counting. But the next two hours were an exercise in frustration, with the hawks flying by to the west, to the east, and directly overhead, many out of range of the unaided eye, many blocked from her view by the tower above her. When the flight ended shortly before 2:00 p.m., MacRae's broad-wing count stood at 2,010, and she believes she missed as many hawks as she recorded.

Mt. Wachusett, to the southwest, was luckier on the 13th. For one thing, the Massachusetts mountain is 1,400 feet higher than Warner Hill, and its lookout offers an unobstructed view of the sky. For another, there were four pairs of eyes on Wachusett that day, belonging to Nancy Clayton, Paul Roberts, Leif Robinson, and Michael Sporer. The watch had recorded only a sprinkling of hawks when, at 11:52 a.m., Sporer, on his first hawk watch, called a small kettle thermaling to the northeast. Looking above those birds to see if others had left the kettle, he was astonished to discover several hundred broad-wings rising in a tight ball. Roberts remembers the surge of adrenaline when, on glassing past the top of that kettle, he found the sky "littered with broad-wings from horizon to horizon. We can't know how many birds had already passed from view, but within fifteen minutes we had 2,387 hawks, almost invisible to the naked eye, pass directly overhead." Broad-wings were washing over the mountain like a tidal wave, reminding him of the Flying Fortresses over Germany in World War II films.

The crew divided up the sky and went to work with scopes. Each major kettle was counted by two observers, the lower figure being recorded. Broad-wings were flying as far as the scopes could reach. Robinson located a prime thermal far to the north of the mountain, utilized by flock after flock through the afternoon, the kettles looking through the 20-power scope like distant swarms of midges. The flight ended about 4:00 p.m., and the four watchers left Wachusett an hour later both exhilarated and exhausted, having recorded 10,086 broad-wings, forty-six ospreys, thirty-nine sharp-shins, eighteen red-tails, two kestrels, two red-shoulders, one each turkey vulture and merlin, and eighteen unidentified hawks. The euphoria, Roberts recalls, lasted three days, during which time his wife found him insufferably effusive. What would she have had to endure had he been able to recover in time to get down to Pennsylvania the next morning? For that remarkable flight hit Hawk Mountain on the 14th, and when the air had cleared an unprecedented 21,000 broad-winged hawks had been logged.

DON'T EXPECT FLIGHTS LIKE THAT EVERY YEAR, or even every decade. What hurts is that most of us miss those flights when they do occur, no matter how much weather watching goes on. "What were *you* doing on the 13th?" New England hawk watchers subsequently asked one another. Carpentering, lawyering, teaching, traveling, punching computers, selling hardware. That's bad enough. I stayed home and cleaned out the garage.

Of course, if you're really into the numbers game, there's not much point in waiting around for big flights in the North. Hie yourself to south Texas about September 25, and plan to spend ten days. Most of the continent's broad-wings end up coasting down around the western end of the Gulf of Mexico, heading for wintering grounds in Central and South America. The result is that the Corpus Christi area boasts the ultimate in American broad-wing concentrations. During a recent twenty-four-hour period in early October, hawk watchers on the Nueces River estimated a flight of three-quarters of a million broad-wings heading for the Rio Grande. Now that's hawk watching!

But hawks, remember, are atypical migrants. The majority of birds, including most songbirds, migrate at night. Nocturnal migration is a tougher proposition, but it has two signal advantages. It reserves the daylight hours for foraging in unfamiliar territory, and it enables songbirds to avoid day-flying hawks. Nocturnal migration is both mysterious and affecting; probably nobody can listen indifferently on a calm October midnight to the mile-high crescendo-decrescendo honking which alone in the immensity of empty sky marks the passing of a flock of geese. One can also hear, on a still night, the call notes of shorebirds and songbirds on their semiannual journeys. Obviously it is difficult to see night migration; but it is not impossible. One simply moon-watches. This is done with an ordinary birding scope, utilizing a 20- or 30-power eyepiece. You pick a clear, windless night with a full moon in May or September; you point your scope at the moon; and you watch.

It will take a while for the watching eye to become accustomed to that astonishingly bright disk of light; and then you'll want to shop around the lunar topography for a time. To see migrants, however, it's best to stare fixedly at a central point on the moon. The moon is merely your backdrop; what you are interested in is the first mile of the narrow cone of light extending from your eye to the moon. Sooner or later, depending on the flight density in your area that particular night, a migrating bird will intersect that cone. You will have no way of knowing whether it's a hermit thrush at 2,000 feet or a goose at 4,000 feet. It will look like neither. Unless the bird is flying very high, it will look like a dark, wingless object, moving with mechanical directness, furious speed, and absolute silence across the brilliant disk of the moon. You will see the object for about one second, and unless your concentration is fixed, you may not be certain you've seen anything at all. The scope finds nocturnal migration as mysterious as did World War II radar, and it pleases me to see those dark, anonymous silhouettes crossing the face of the moon, visual analogues of those enigmatic blips the radar men called angels.

IT IS DIFFICULT NOT TO ROMANTICIZE MIGRATION on a calm, clear September night. How grand it must be, winging south in the starry deeps, watching the terrestrial constellations slip by. ("There's Indianapolis; Louisville coming up.") Yet whenever nocturnal migration makes the news, it is in the form of a disaster report, with dead birds littering the ground. And the Victorian poets, fond of the epic simile and the melancholic mode, found a perfect subject in the long-distance migrant. Here are some typical lines from Tennyson:

> *Faint as a climate-changing bird*
> *That flies all night across the dark,*
> *And on the threshold of the land*
> *Sinks to the earth and can no more.*

Yet John Janovy, in *Keith County Journal* (1978), says this is mere sentimentalism, that migration must seem a joy after the rigors of the breeding season. "We . . . romanticize migration: in fall they assume this metabolic and physical burden, during which all these beautiful birds lose their colors and undertake this trek through untold dangers to a miserable and undeveloped place called South America. . . . The cliff swallow must be telling us this is all bull. . . ."

So which is fall migration — post-breeding lark or perilous journey? Of course, migration is relatively undemanding for the birds the Germans call *Wettervögel* ("weather birds"). These species leave the northern climes late in the fall, and return early in spring; they tarry during mild early winters, and press the weather and food supplies back north. Typically these are short-distance migrants, mostly wintering in the southern states; many of them, like blue jays and red-wings, are diurnal, social migrants. The population of Ohio song sparrows studied by Margaret M. Nice in the '30s proved partly migratory, partly resident; and a few individuals migrated in the face of hard winters, but stayed put during open winters. Ordinarily, migration is not terribly arduous for these weather birds, requiring perhaps a few easy day or night flights to attain the wintering territories.

It's different for the *Instinktvögel,* mostly long-distance, largely nocturnal migrants that move independently of weather and food supplies. They come and go on schedule (and are often called "calendar birds"), leaving early in the autumn and arriving late on the breeding grounds. Now, Janovy's Keith County, Nebraska, cliff swallows are *Instinktvögel,* all right, but not really typical ones. Swallows and swifts are diurnal migrants, presumably because, being strong fliers, they are relatively immune from predation. They are also social migrants, and, as aerial insect eaters, have the additional advantage of being able to feed while migrating. So if any calendar bird finds migration fun, it ought to be the cliff swallow, drifting the days south for Argentina, flying in good weather with friends and family, snacking on the way.

It's a tougher row for the blackpoll warbler, a typical calendar migrant. Blackpolls breed straight across the northern boreal forest from Alaska to Newfoundland. Some blackpolls funnel toward the Florida peninsula, whence they jump off for Cuba and the wintering grounds in northern South America, a distance of more than 5,000 miles for northwesterly breeding birds. Moon watches, radar, and plane transects have shown that most nocturnal songbird migration is a pretty lonely business. The majority of these birds travel alone or in loose aggregations of three or four birds. Migration starts shortly after sunset, and will be heaviest ahead of a high-pressure cell after the passage of a cold front, which promises the best chance of favorable autumn flying weather.

Our blackpoll, having fed up the previous day, will climb rapidly to altitude and, ignoring topography, head for Florida. Things will likely go well unless the weather turns sour. While night migrants are reluctant to initiate flight under unfa-

Mourning doves may not look particularly hardy,
but they overwinter north to the Great Lakes.

vorable weather conditions, they may well persist under those conditions once a flight has begun. The worst possible weather is of the sort responsible for the disaster of early October 1954. A cold front, accompanied by wind, decreasing temperatures, drizzle, and low cloud ceilings, moved from the northern states straight down to the Gulf. The front overran a heavy migratory flight, and the birds, moving down under the cloud ceiling, began to run into everything from tall buildings to radio and television transmission towers. Other migrants were attracted to and disoriented by strong ceilometer lights,* dashing themselves to death just as migrants did under similar meteorological conditions at nineteenth-century lighthouses and lightships. From Hempstead, New York, to Topeka, Kansas, south through Alabama and Georgia, everything from rails to cuckoos to sparrows was killed. Over

A ceilometer is a ground-based photoelectric instrument that beams a powerful ray of light skyward. Ceilometers are used at airports to measure cloud ceilings, and have been common instruments of nighttime attraction utilized by county fairs and used-car lots.

100,000 birds, probably a fraction of the actual toll, were counted. Of these, some 9,136 individuals were identified to eighty-six species. As usual, the warblers were especially hard hit. Leading the body-count list were ovenbird (1,172), magnolia warbler (995), red-eyed vireo (821), and chestnut-sided warbler (703). Blackpolls were relatively lucky; 203 were counted among the victims of that cold front.

The best way to avoid ceilometers and TV transmitting towers (the latter alone kill over a million migrating birds annually) is to take an over-water route to South America, and this is exactly what many blackpolls do. It has long been known that some songbirds accompany the strong fliers (mostly shorebirds) that regularly overfly the Atlantic, as on occasion numbers of them land exhausted on ships at sea. These birds, however, were generally considered victims of wind-drift, east coast migrants blown out to sea. Recent radar studies in New England, the Antilles, and on strategically placed ships suggest that a few species of songbirds — most notably the blackpoll warbler — regularly fly the Sargasso loop.

A Quebec-nesting blackpoll will move southeast toward the coast. After a week of heavy feeding, its ordinary lipid (fat) content of perhaps 5 percent of body weight has increased to about 40 percent. (The great advantage of fat is that it contains twice the energy value per unit of weight of carbohydrate or protein.) The blackpoll will jump off behind the Nova Scotia or New England coast along with the lesser yellowlegs and short-billed dowitchers following the passage of a cold front and in the vanguard of the northwesterlies and favorable weather of an advancing high-pressure system, and head south*east* into the empty immensity of the Atlantic — empty, that is, except for the speck called Bermuda. If all goes well, somewhere in the vicinity of the Sargasso Sea the northeasterly trade winds will overcome the continental westerlies, and our blackpoll (cruising at an astonishing shorebird altitude of two or even four miles), perhaps without even changing its heading, will be turned back south-southwest to overfly the Antilles for landfall in South America after a nonstop flight of eighty hours.

Of course, all does not always go well, and the blackpoll, unlike the shorebirds, can neither outfly nor outlast storms or adverse winds. The bird jumps off the North American coast with a third of an ounce of fat reserves to fuel a trip of 2,000 miles over open ocean. That supply is adequate, provided the weather and the westerlies hold on the trip out, provided the front that preceded the flight doesn't stall and block it, provided the trade winds appear on schedule, and provided the bird is not met on the leg in by a storm out of the Caribbean. Sometimes the blackpolls and other birds run out of luck over the Bermuda Triangle. Sadder still are the wandering mid-Atlantic blips sometimes picked up on radar. These belong to other songbirds, many of them native sparrows such as white-throats and juncos, birds programmed for short overland migration to the middle and southern states. Victimized by faulty orientation or offshore drift beyond the point of return, these birds waste their reserves on aimless, disoriented flight. A few happen onto Bermuda; a few find haven on passing ships. Most, like bad-luck migrants over all the world's oceans, sink unrecorded into the rolling sea.

S O MUCH WE KNOW ABOUT BIRD MIGRATION, and on these matters we can afford to patronize the ornithophaenologists of yesteryear. But mostly we have looked at fairly simple questions, or have satisfied ourselves with broad outlines. We are left with two complex problems, both of which continue to resist scientific assault. What triggers and controls migration? How do birds navigate? (Or do they?)

If birds moved north and south in random fashion, breeding and wintering wherever the season happened to find them, we wouldn't need to ask the navigation question. But they do not. Banding and other sorts of marking have demonstrated that adults typically show a remarkable fidelity to the first breeding location. Northern shoveler hen No. 47-604004 returned four consecutive years (a long life for a game duck) to Lyle K. Sowls's Delta marsh study area in south-central Manitoba. Her four nests were all within a few hundred yards of one another. Nest placement among colonial-nesting seabirds may vary by only a foot or so from year to year.

Of course, waterfowl and pelagic birds are restricted in terms of breeding habitat, but the same fidelity to previous breeding territory obtains for the songbirds in your garden. Four out of five mourning doves and house wrens will return to nest in the same immediate neighborhood as long as they live. (Occasionally this fidelity can be proved without recourse to artificial marking. A song sparrow outlasted us at one house; he was easily recognized from spring to spring on the basis of his idiosyncratic song, the first five notes of which were the beginning of the title refrain from the song "La Cucaracha!" Among the population of grackles at our next place was an easily identified male with a white tail feather.) Interestingly, young birds do not characteristically return to the immediate area of their hatching. The young of most songbirds apparently imprint on the last area visited during their first autumn's premigratory wanderings, a habit which assures healthy dispersion over the breeding range.

The return of adult birds to the same nesting area is well documented; evidence grows that they are similarly faithful to a particular wintering area. How do these birds find their way from the one to the other? Students of migration differentiate among three possible strategies for getting from Point A to Point B. *Pilotage* means proceeding from known landmark to known landmark, the way your child learns to get from home to school and back. *Orientation* is the ability to determine and maintain directional flight, regardless of landmarks. *Navigation* is more demanding yet; it means the ability to get to a specific goal from unfamiliar areas.

Simple pilotage could account for much migratory homing. A flock of blue jays might well work its way south from somewhere in Ontario, say, to somewhere in Kentucky on the basis of landmarks known to older, experienced members of the flock; younger birds could learn the route while accompanying adults. The early German researcher Ernst Schüz's experiments with white storks show that there is, in fact, a large learning component involved in migration. European-nesting white storks are divided into two populations. Those nesting east of central Germany migrate southeast around the eastern end of the Mediterranean, while the storks nesting west of central Germany head southwest around the western end of the Mediterranean, both heading for Africa. Young storks from the eastern population were raised in western Europe, and were released at the normal migratory period. The young birds migrated southwest with the local birds. Young mallards taken from a nonmigratory English population were released in Finland, whose mallards do migrate. The English birds migrated with the latter.

But pilotage obviously cannot explain all migration. What about the young of those shorebird species whose adults depart the breeding grounds before the young can fly, leaving them to migrate independently later on? And how about nocturnal migration, which often proceeds when most terrestrial landmarks are invisible at flight altitudes? Schüz did a clever thing. He took more young eastern storks, raised them in the west, and released them as before, except that they were detained until all local storks had migrated. The color-marked young were subsequently plotted on a south*east* track for the Adriatic, a track which, from their original home territory, would have taken them on their population's traditional route through the Bosporus and around the eastern end of the Mediterranean for Africa.

Other displacement experiments, with European hooded crows and starlings and with American herring gulls and blue-winged teal, confirmed what the storks had suggested: that the young of migratory species have an inherited directional ten-

**Spotted sandpipers nesting in the South are short-distance
migrants, while tundra nesters are long-haul travelers.**

dency. That is, they migrate in a predetermined compass direction which they
maintain when displaced from the breeding grounds or along the migratory route,
even if this takes them to an inappropriate wintering area. That this ability is in fact
innate has been proved by hand-raising birds from the egg, completely shielded from
ordinary environmental information. These birds readily orient in the direction appropriate to their particular population.

How is this compass orientation managed? G.V.T. Matthews, working in England in the early 1950s, noticed that homing pigeons' initial homeward orientation
after release was better under sun than under clouds. Then came the German researcher Gustav Kramer's classic experiments utilizing orientation cages. Birds in a
migratory state show a characteristic restlessness, usually known by its German name,
Zugunruhe. Placed in an orientation cage, the bird jumps and flutters in the direction
of its intended migration. These movements are recorded, using sophisticated electronic equipment. (Originally the recorder was the researcher, who lay on the floor
underneath the cage, watching the bird through a transparent floor!) Kramer's tame

starling oriented northwest, and continued to do so when everything but the sun was blocked from view. Jumps were random under cloud cover. When mirrors were installed outside the cage's windows, deflecting the sunlight 90 degrees from its actual direction, the starling changed its orientation accordingly, heading for an apparent northwest but an actual southwest.

Kramer thus demonstrated what biologists now call sun-compass orientation: the ability to determine a compass direction on the basis of sun position. This ability has since been experimentally demonstrated for many other bird species, and appears to account for most short-range diurnal migration. The sun, however, because of its apparent movement during the course of the day, is useless as a compass without a clock. Birds' "biological clock," presumably either neural or hormonal in nature, operates automatically in roughly twenty-four-hour cycles (biologists call this cycle the "circadian rhythm," "circadian" meaning "approximately daily"). It is apparently fine-tuned by environmental pacemakers, of which photoperiod — the seasonally variable relative duration of daily light and darkness — seems to be most important. Indeed, the clock can be reset by exposing the bird to artificial light schedules; this clock skewing (like Kramer's mirrors) results in predictable orientation errors in orientation cages or in actual releases.

THE COMBINATION OF ORIENTATION CAGES AND PLANETARIA soon brought a breakthrough in the area of nocturnal migratory orientation. The German team of Franz and Eleonore Sauer showed that certain Old World warblers oriented properly when shown replicas of real skies, but could not orient when the simulated stars were obscured. German researcher Hans G. Wallraff discovered that ducks could orient when only parts of the sky were visible, and that they had the ability to memorize incredibly complex star patterns. Cornell's Stephen T. Emlen, testing hand-raised indigo buntings, found that young birds failed to orient well if denied visual experience of the sky until fall. Apparently, young buntings "learn" the sky during their first summer, and particularly the part of the sky which shows least rotational movement — i.e., the circumpolar sky. Clock-shifted birds of other species, which misorient predictably during the day, orient properly at night, suggesting that they, too, are cuing on the North Star (or nearby stars), whose apparent lack of movement renders their clocks superfluous. Emlen got some young buntings to treat Betelgeuse as if it were Polaris, simply by rotating the planetarium sky around that star.

Sun-compass and star-compass orientation can be made to explain most migration. A bird starting with an inborn directional tendency and the ability to choose and maintain a compass direction might well make its way back and forth from summer to winter territory, perhaps using landmark recognition near both ends of the trip. But neither sun compass nor star compass can explain homing, or true navigation — that ability to locate a goal from an unknown location.

Navigation has been demonstrated unequivocally for a relatively few species. Homing pigeons are famous for the ability, but then they are bred and trained for it. Among wild birds pelagic species seem most adept. One dramatic experiment involved eighteen adult Laysan albatrosses, removed from their nests on the Midway Islands in mid-Pacific and flown all over the Pacific. Released, among other places, on Oahu and Guam, from Honshu (Japan) and Luzon (Philippines), and on the coast of Washington State — places none had ever been — fourteen birds returned to their nests. A Washington coast bird covered the 3,200 miles back to Midway in ten days. A Philippines albatross negotiated 4,100 miles in a month.*

Petrels, shearwaters, gulls, terns, swifts, and swallows have all proved capable of homing. Displaced Adelie penguins have navigated distances of over 1,000 miles, walking, of course, every step of the way. Dutch biologist A.C. Perdeck's classic displacement experiments showed something very interesting about European starlings. Thousands of the birds were trapped and banded as they passed through the Netherlands on their fall migration west to wintering quarters in northern France and England. The starlings were released nearly 400 miles south-southeast in Switzerland. When recoveries from later in the fall were plotted, Perdeck discovered that young birds, on their first migration, continued west, as they would have done from the Netherlands, and set up new wintering grounds in southern France and northern Spain. Adult starlings, however, were mostly heading northwest, in a line pointing toward the traditional wintering grounds. The immature birds, which either did not recognize the displacement or could not compensate for it, were orienting. The

---

* *The extraordinary nesting-site tenacity of these birds got them into trouble with the U.S. government during and after World War II when the Navy controlled Midway. For the "gooney bird" — the servicemen adopted the traditional seamen's name, which attributes to stupidity the albatrosses' fearlessness of man and, perhaps, their awkward antics on land — continued to nest about the runways, colliding with aircraft and being sucked into jet intakes. The Navy tried relocating nesting birds, but, like MacArthur, they returned, prompting the Navy to take the drastic steps of slaughtering birds and bulldozing updraft-producing dunes.*

adults (like the Midway albatrosses, though in less impressive fashion) were navigating.

To navigate, to get "home" from an unfamiliar place, a bird (or person) needs either an inertial system or a bicoordinate mapping system for guidance. An inertial system assumes some sort of motion-sensitive organ to "record" the displacement trip, whether initiated by adverse winds or an experimenting biologist. Movie kidnappers are notorious believers in inertial systems: the victim is always blindfolded, driven a labyrinthine course, even spun around like a pin-the-tail-on-the-donkey candidate, all in order to make it difficult for him to locate the hideout after his release. The exact same things have been done to homing pigeons, and for the same reason. The birds are taken to release points in sealed boxes and driven complicated routes. They have been tumbled in drums and rotated on turntables during the trip out, all in hopes of confusing a presumed recording instrument; they have been transported heavily anesthetized, in hopes of deadening it. Various inner-ear organs, thought to be possible sites of directional recording, have been snipped, punctured, and cauterized. The birds homed anyway. (Why, in the latter case, they would want to is a question science isn't prepared to ask. Homing pigeons have many abilities; the ability to choose a reasonable course of action, which we sometimes define as intelligence, isn't one of them.)

A contemporary Italian school, under the leadership of Floriano Papi, believes olfaction is the key. (Salmon fry imprint on the odor of their hatching stream, to which they return, through the agency of olfaction, years later as breeding adults returning from the sea. Why not birds?) They argue that young pigeons map their loft area in terms of characteristic odors borne on winds from various directions. Detour experiments (in which the bird is expected to leave the release area in a direction opposite to the initial leg of a circuitous journey to the site) and nasal-pouch experiments (in which a pouch containing a strong-smelling substance is applied to the bill just prior to release) have proved ambiguous. Detoured pigeons expected to deflect clockwise often did so; those which ought to have deflected counterclockwise did not! Some birds flew off in a direction intermediate between expected and home directions. Nasal pouches result in more initial scatter at release, but homing success is not impaired. A German team completely deadened birds' olfactory nerves with xylocain. Results were ambiguous, but largely negative.

Most current research seeks the key to homing in terms of bicoordinate navigation. This would require, in addition to the compass and clock needed for orientation, a map. With these aids, a bird could determine the direction of its displacement in terms of both latitude and longitude, and then navigate home. But how is this system supposed to operate? The British ornithologist Matthews has vigorously defended the sun-arc theory which he propounded in the early 1950s. Matthews argues that the sun alone can provide the necessary bicoordinate information. It would work this way. Upon finding itself in a strange location, the bird observes the sun, measuring a short part of its movement along its arc. It then extrapolates from that segment to determine the sun's highest position. (At noon, of course, extrapolation would be unnecessary; simple observation would do.) Then, using its internal clock, the bird determines the sun's progress along its arc. Now the bird need only compare those two values (noon altitude and progress position) with remembered home values to determine its present location. If the sun's noon altitude is too high, the bird is south of home; if the sun is too far along on its arc, it is also east of home. It is now a simple matter to fly northwest. When sun values are correct, the bird is home.

Birds could, by the same token, navigate at night by the stars. They would determine the coordinates of an unfamiliar location by gauging the altitude of Polaris above the horizon, and the degree of westward rotation of the star field. These values would be compared with remembered home values, and a homeward direction could be deduced.

There is no question that sun-arc (or star-arc) theory *could* account for homing, but few students of migration have been convinced. Skeptics doubt that birds are capable of the fine measurements of sun movement and time required, or of the process of extrapolation. Among these critics are State University of New York (Stony Brook) biologist Charles Walcott and members of the Frankfurt school, whose work with pigeons and Old World robins and warblers, respectively, suggests that birds can orient by exploiting a sensitivity to earth's magnetic field; might they not navigate by it as well? The magnetic field theory, a century old now, holds that birds can detect varying inclination and/or declination intensities forming a grid over the earth. Until recently, most biologists believed this theory absurd, for there was no evidence that birds were sensitive to the low order of force involved. Experiments carried out in the 1970s, however, have given the notion new life.

Pigeons have now been taught, for example, to detect earth-strength magnetic fields in the laboratory, and pigeons released at locations known to represent magnetic-field anomalies have shown reduced orientation ability. Birds transported to release sites in altered magnetic fields have sometimes been affected, sometimes not. Wolfgang and Roswitha Wiltschko, prominent members of the Frankfurt school, spent a year with the Cornell group working with indigo buntings. Tests seemed to show that the birds were sensitive to the horizontal component of the magnetic field, but some kinds of orientation cages showed better results than others.

Cornell's William T. Keeton attached magnets to pigeons' heads to see how the birds would perform when ordinary magnetic information was interrupted. The results are very interesting. Released under clear skies, experienced adult homers — both controls and experimentals — oriented well. Under overcast skies, controls oriented homeward, while experimental birds mostly scattered. Young, inexperienced homers, furthermore, scattered under sunny or overcast skies with magnets attached. Do young pigeons, then, as well as adults under overcast, utilize magnetic information? Or did the magnets somehow block the reception of other information? In either case, all the experimental birds eventually homed; somehow they solved whatever problem the magnets presented.

IN 1926 ABERDEEN PROFESSOR J. ARTHUR THOMSON published a three-volume work called *The New Natural History,* which fairly represents our knowledge in that area from the post-World War I period. With regard to the question of how birds navigate, Thomson fell back on "the interesting old view that birds have in a high degree . . . *a sense of direction."* That is, of course, a non-answer, and it would be worth the job of any academic researcher who uttered it today. But the question itself remains unanswered. Thomson pointed out that experiments with pelagics prove they do home, but the tests "do not throw any light on the problem of where the sense of direction has its seat." A great deal of time and money spent in modern laboratories hasn't pinned down that "seat" either. Possibilities we have. There's the pecten, for example, a curious structure in the avian eye, which presumably casts a straightedge shadow on the retina, such that horizon and sun image could be viewed simultaneously. The pec-ten could function as a compass, a sundial, even a sextant; so that it could, conceivably, make sun-arc navigation work. Then there are the rhodopsin molecules in the retina, and, recently discovered between brain and skull, specialized cells rich in magnetite crystals, both of which have been proposed as possible centers of perception of magnetic-field forces.

But we simply don't know. Part of the problem is that birds obviously have ac-

A northern breeder, the American tree sparrow is a short-range migrant; for it, Maine and Montana *are* the South.

cess to redundant cues.* When you block one sort of input, and the bird performs successfully, you have not proved that it cannot or does not use that information, but only that, under the particular set of circumstances, it did not *require* that input. And it is very difficult to design experiments that control several sources of potential information simultaneously. Then, too, different species test differently, making it difficult to generalize from necessarily limited experiments. Even within a given species, individuals show a frustrating variability of performance. (Charles Walcott's wonderful homing pigeon B38 was a fine navigator but a lousy pilot. She would fly unerringly for home, then shoot right past, failing to utilize landmarks near the loft. Five or ten miles down the road she seemed to realize her mistake, and a surprised homeowner would subsequently discover on his front porch an odd-looking pigeon, harnessed into a radio transmitter, patiently awaiting assistance. He would find the loft's telephone number on the transmitter, and B38 would soon arrive home in a taxi.) And a final, nagging doubt remains.

* And new potential cues are complicating the situation. Pigeons have recently been shown to be sensitive to both ultraviolet and polarized light, and to be able to make fine discriminations of barometric pressure differences. There is also experimental proof that pigeons can hear low-frequency sounds over great distances, leading to speculation that a flock of migrating geese cruising high over the Midwest may be able to hear storms over the Rockies and the crashing Atlantic surf simultaneously. Any or all of these talents might help a bird navigate.

Most navigation research utilizes pigeons, which are readily available from established lofts and are accustomed to human handling. But how much have homing pigeons, generations of directed inbreeding removed from wild stock, to tell us about the migratory behavior of wild birds? It is possible that we may figure out pigeon homing and still not know much more than we do now about warblers and shearwaters.

This is not to suggest that recent work has been in vain. Much has been learned by the way — about the hierarchy of cues used for orientation by night-migrating songbirds, for example. Stephen Emlen and Natalie J. Demong released white-throated sparrows at migrating altitude through the agency of a trap-doored box carried aloft by helium-filled balloons under different weather conditions. State University of New York (Albany) ornithologist Kenneth P. Able tracked migrants under similar circumstances with radar and portable ceilometers. Both studies, carried on in the northeastern U.S., found visual cues to be most important. Birds oriented best with a view of the stars, whatever the wind conditions. They also oriented successfully under overcast skies if post-sunset glow was visible before overcast set in. If neither stars nor sunset were available, Able found birds simply flew downwind. The white-throats, however, hovered or circled, apparently attempting to get a fix; they then oriented fairly accurately, but flew at subnormal speed, and often in a zigzag pattern.

These observations suggest that stellar cues are more important than wind, and wind — at least in Able's study — seems more important than landmarks or, in the short run at least, magnetic information. (Results of some research by the Wiltschkos suggest that birds may consult a magnetic compass only occasionally, on the order of once a day or every other day.) Visual cues, then, seem most important under ordinary circumstances, at least for nocturnal songbird migrants. But it has been proved that visual information can be dispensed with entirely in some cases. Homing pigeons blinded by the attachment of opaque glasses have homed successfully. And the European robin has been shown to be capable of orientation in a totally dark room. The mystery remains.

It may be less immediately evident that migratory birds face a temporal as well as a spatial problem. In addition to the problems involved in getting from Point A to Point B is the problem of when to leave A, and how to know when B has been reached. For fall migration the plausible answer to the first would be that the bird leaves the North when cold weather and dwindling food supplies begin to make life uncomfortable. Weather migrants, as we have seen, generally do operate this way. But not the calendar migrants, many of which abandon even temperate zones long before weather or food shortage becomes a factor. Birds vacate the far North wholesale in August, just when the seed, berry, and insect crops are reaching a peak. (This works out very neatly on the tundra, where much of this food is preserved flash-frozen over the winter; the spring melt then makes it available to the returning birds, which otherwise would face a food shortage.)

The author of Jeremiah, in the passage quoted by our eighteenth-century pamphleteer, seems to have sensed that typical long-distance migrants migrate on schedule rather than in response to environmental exigencies: "Yea, the stork in the heaven knoweth her appointed times; and the turtle and the crane and the swallow observe the time of their coming." The turtle dove and the swallow "know" their appointed times not in the brain, but in the blood. They initiate the repetitive events of their lives in response to an inborn annual (circannual) rhythm analogous to the daily (circadian) rhythm mentioned earlier.

BIRDS ARE PROGRAMMED, through changing blood chemistry, to take life one thing at a time. The sequence, one biologist has written, is "rigid and inexorable." When baby house sparrows were introduced to adult house sparrows at the nest-building stage of breeding, the adults either tossed them out or used them for nesting material. A couple of weeks later, when they were physiologically prepared for attachment to young, the same house sparrows accepted and raised introduced young. This is not, obviously, an "intelligent" way to order life; indeed, it is a system which *substitutes* order for intelligence. The system works well enough, but it tolerates no deviation. This is especially evident in the far North, where the breeding season is short and timing is critical. Well-grown young redpolls have been found frozen in their nests by fall wanderers on the Alaska tundra. Probably the adults had, for one reason or another, laid the clutch of eggs late. Birds are famous for selfless dedication to their young. But only in season. The redpoll young matured on schedule, but high summer passes quickly on the tundra, and blood chemistry changes with the seasons. Area redpolls began to flock up, to experience migratory restlessness. Then, one day, the birds were up and away, and our pair with them, leaving a nest of hopeful young perhaps only days away from fledging.

The circannual rhythm, which controls and times these events, is automatic, at least to a point. Birds — including hand-raised young — will exhibit molt, *Zugun-*

ruhe, and so on in the proper sequence even if denied normal environmental stimuli. Apparently those glands (especially the pituitary and hypothalamus) whose secretions stimulate migration-related processes such as fat deposition and gonad development will operate in response to the inborn annual rhythm alone. When Emlen kept indigo buntings under an unchanging light-and-dark schedule prior to fall migration, the birds molted, put on fat, exhibited *Zugunruhe,* changed bill color, and sang the following spring; but they did not molt into winter plumage the second autumn. He concluded that the circannual rhythm requires a late-summer environmental stimulus (the German term is *Zeitgeber:* "time-giver") to keep the cycle going.

More than one *Zeitgeber* may be at work here, but photoperiod is thought to be most important. Light-and-dark schedules are easy to manipulate in the laboratory, and the effect of photoperiod on the controlling glands is clear. It has been over a half century now since Canadian biologist William Rowan amazed the scientific world by bringing juncos into breeding condition in midwinter Alberta simply by exposing them to artificially increasing day length. The birds' sexual organs became enlarged; the males sang. It seems clear that, under normal circumstances, photoperiod (and perhaps other external stimuli) synchronizes and fine-tunes innate rhythms.*

The seasons turn, and once again the birds' circannual clocks read migration. But a physiologically prepared bird cannot fly on automatic; it must be able to suppress the urge to initiate migration until circumstances are right. Different species apparently respond to different immediate stimuli. Weather birds leave the North when temperatures fall, when food becomes scarce. Flocking migrants seem to require social stimuli of some sort; hand-raised social migrants have refused to migrate on their own. Presumably those great chattering flocks of red-wings and tree swallows are synchronizing — or even stimulating — individual migratory drives ("awaiting the 'signal' to depart" is the popular expression). Typical long-range migrants wait on adequate fat deposition and favorable flying weather.

What ornithologists call the premigratory state is identified by *Zugunruhe,* mi-

---

* *This raises a special question for calendar migrants wintering in the Southern Hemisphere, where day length is decreasing during North American spring. Can the same Zeitgeber — i.e., a diminishing light schedule — stimulate post-breeding physiological development and southward migration at one time of the year, and prebreeding physiological development and northward migration at another? And what about those birds wintering on the equator, where photoperiod is constant? We simply don't know.*

gratory restlessness. The bird wakes at night, flutters from perch to perch. It has been noticed in the laboratory that *Zugunruhe,* at least for long-distance migrants, seems to persist throughout the migratory period. Migrants trapped halfway along their fall migratory route, then transported to the normal wintering grounds and released, have proceeded to fly the second half of their normal migratory flight to winter in new, sometimes inappropriate, areas. These observations suggest that the migratory drive may be quantitative, may burn itself out over the period of time required to complete a migration appropriate to the species. This would neatly solve the problem of how a bird — especially a solitary, inexperienced bird — knows when to quit migrating: "I don't feel like migrating any more; this must be Nicaragua."

If we do not perfectly understand what triggers and controls migration, how autonomous rhythms interrelate with environmental stimuli, it is not for lack of trying. Birds have been castrated. Pineal glands have been excised. Birds have been injected with hormones, thyroid extract, adrenaline. But the problems, like those concerning navigation, remain obdurate. Progress is made — but the frontiers recede. We earlier condescended to J. A. Thomson on the matter of navigation, but the good Scottish don's analysis of migration control was right on. He wrote that "the constitution of the creature has been, as it were, wound up to become restless at particular times of the year, but this is linked on to the regular changes of the seasons." Of course, no biologist would be caught dead saying that as the 21st century approaches. He would say that "events in the endogenous circannual cycle are entrained by exogenous stimuli." The latter sounds more impressive, but the two statements mean exactly the same thing.